Post-Traumatic Stress Theory

Post-Traumatic Stress Theory

Research and Application

Edited by

John H. Harvey, Ph.D.
University of Iowa, Iowa City, Iowa

Brian G. Pauwels
University of Iowa, Iowa City, Iowa

BRUNNER/MAZEL
Taylor & Francis Group

USA	Publishing Office:	BRUNNER/MAZEL *A member of the Taylor & Francis Group* 325 Chestnut Street Philadelphia, PA 19106 Tel: (215) 625-8900 Fax: (215) 625-2940
	Distribution Center:	BRUNNER/MAZEL *A member of the Taylor & Francis Group* 7625 Empire Drive Florence, KY 41042 Tel: 1-800-634-7064 Fax: 1-800-248-4724
UK		BRUNNER/MAZEL *A member of the Taylor & Francis Group* 27 Church Road Hove E. Sussex, BN3 2FA Tel: +44 (0) 1273 207411 Fax: +44 (0) 1273 205612

Post-Traumatic Stress Theory: Research and Application

1 2 3 4 5 6 7 8 9 0

Printed by Sheridan Books, Ann Arbor, MI, 2000.
Cover design by Joe Dieter.

A CIP catalog record for this book is available from the British Library.
   The paper in this publication meets the requirements of the ANSI Standard Z39.48-1984 (Permanence of Paper).

Library of Congress Cataloging-in-Publication data is on file with the publisher.

ISBN 1-58391-014X (paper)

TABLE OF CONTENTS

List of Contributors

Nanette C. Auerhahn
Bellefaire/Jewish
Children's Bureau
Cleveland, Ohio

Carrie Barnes
University of Iowa
Iowa City, Iowa

Paul Barreira
Massachusetts Department of
Mental Health
Boston, Massachusetts

Liora Bar-Tur
Tel Aviv University
Ramat-Aviv, Israel

Michael Basso
University of Tulsa
Tulsa, Oklahoma

Heather Carlson
Loyola University Chicago
Chicago, Illinois

Patricia A. Frazier
University of Minneapolis
Minneapolis, Minnesota

John H. Harvey
University of Iowa
Iowa City, Iowa

Alex Johnston
Anchorage, Alaska

Barbara Krahe
University of Potsdam
Potsdam, Germany

Rachel Levi-Shiff
Bar-Ilan University
Ramat Gan, Israel

Aurora Liiceanu
Institute of Psychology
Bucharest, Romania

Cathaleene Macias
Fountain House
New York, New York

Ruth Malkinson
Tel Aviv University
Ramat-Aviv, Israel

Elana Newman
University of Tulsa
Tulsa, Oklahoma

Marc Orlitzky
Australian Graduate School of
Management
Sydney, Australia

Harvey Peskin
San Francisco State
University
Berkeley, California

Charles Rodican
Fountain House
New York, New York

Cristina Vintila
University of Iowa
Iowa City, Iowa

Robert Young
Fountain House
New York, New York

PREFACE

BRIAN G. PAUWELS and JOHN H. HARVEY

Few phenomena are as widely experienced across different individuals, cultures, and contexts as that of traumatic stress. Whether as victims, perpetrators, supporters, or simply observers, most if not all people can identify to some extent with the psychological and physical consequences produced by traumatic events. Such incidents are as varied as the individuals who must deal with them: The grief produced by the sudden death of a loved one, the self-doubt present in a victim's response to rape, the loss of autonomy following a debilitating injury, and the absence of social identity in the wake of genocidal terror are just a few of the experiences that make up the subject matter of traumatic stress. The consequences of such events also reach beyond the individuals who directly suffer these ordeals. Those who interact with the victims as they attempt to overcome the traumas often endure their own costs. The child who survives the death of a sibling does so in the difficult context of the parents' grief. Individuals close to a victim of severe physical injury frequently must take on new responsibilities as they deal with a friend whose capabilities and limitations have been forever altered. The family of a man who has lost his beloved wife must attempt to find solace for themselves while still offering comfort to the one who was closest to her. The consequences of traumatic events, while certainly devastating for the most immediate victims, are therefore also experienced by the people in the social network that surrounds those victims.

Despite the widespread and often personal relevance it has for most people, the issue of traumatic stress has only recently emerged as a cohesive, identifiable area of interest for theorists, researchers, and practitioners. Although its historical roots can be traced back to physicians' observations of stress-related reactions in ancient

Egypt, the process by which various trauma-related topics joined into a unitary field of study and application has been a gradual one. Certainly, different theoretical perspectives, different methodologies, and even the practical difficulties of studying trauma have all played a role in slowing the evolution of what is now commonly called "traumatology" (see Figley, 1993, for a brief synopsis of this history).

Fortunately, the last two decades have seen a number of important developments that have enabled scholars who share curiosities and concerns about traumatic phenomena to discuss their theories, methods, findings, and interventions. Such events include the founding of the *Journal of Traumatic Stress* in 1988 and the publication of the impressive *International Handbook of Traumatic Stress Syndromes* (1993), edited by John P. Wilson and Beverly Raphael. By fostering communication between scholars, these and similar forums have contributed greatly to the establishment and growth of traumatology as a more formal area of endeavor for both basic and applied scholars.

In the present volume, we offer another contribution that we hope will add to the progress of this young field. In reviewing the chapters, two main themes emerged. First, the sheer diversity of contexts in which traumatic stress occurs was readily apparent. Indeed, the general definition of *traumatology* offered by Figley (1993), "investigation and application of knowledge about the immediate and long-term psychosocial consequences of highly stressful events and the factors which affect those consequences" (p. xvii), hints at a potentially broad area of investigation. The contributions of the authors to this work certainly fulfill that potential. Therefore, we intend for the first section, Post-traumatic Stress: Contexts and Consequences, to provide a brief sampling of the circumstances in which traumatic stress can occur and the unique issues that each raises for both victims and scholars. The two opening chapters address the difficulties of diagnosing and treating post-traumatic stress disorder (PTSD) when it coexists with other disorders or dysfunction. Cathaleene Macias and her associates take a clinical perspective in addressing the comorbidity of PTSD and severe mental illnesses such as schizophrenia-related disorders, major depression, and bipolar disorder. The frequency with which PTSD coexists with mental illness, the specific nature of this relationship, and the resulting implications for assessment and treatment are examined. Michael Basso and Elana Newman also focus on PTSD diagnosis, this time in the context of closed head injuries. In a very practical and instructive manner, they outline the nature of head injuries and the cognitive, somatic, and affective symptoms that frequently follow such trauma. Next, the similarities and differences between these symptoms and those of PTSD are described, and the potential difficulties of accurately delineating the two are highlighted. Finally, some general suggestions are offered to ensure the accurate discrimination of head injury and PTSD during assessment and to address the particular needs of patients who are recovering from both syndromes.

Barbara Krahé's contribution describes how the traumatic stress from childhood sexual abuse results in a number of severe long-term consequences for this group of victims. At a general level, the manner in which childhood sexual trauma may affect the subsequent development of sexual behavior and sexual relationships in adulthood is addressed. In addition, particular attention is given to the mechanisms by which such victimization in childhood may put individuals at greater risk for revictimization later in life. As Krahé notes, although this link between early trauma and later victimization has been documented a number of times, we are still trying to understand the mechanisms and pathways that account for this relationship. Krahé offers some valuable insight for addressing that very issue.

The horror of war is a central topic of interest for many traumatic stress scholars. The costs of war for both soldiers and civilians have been studied extensively, owing in part to technological advances in the media that have made the traumas associated with battle relevant even to those not physically engaged in combat. However, as time passes and more veterans die each year, the opportunities to document the experiences and personal traumas of war diminish. Carrie Barnes and John Harvey make a valuable contribution to this literature by using an account-making perspective to collect the reflections, memories, and losses of veterans from World War II and the United States involvement in Vietnam. Although the physical traumas and dangers of war were in many ways similar for veterans of both conflicts, it becomes clear from their own stories that the vastly different political and social contexts in which the two wars occurred shaped the long-term consequences with which the veterans had to cope. In addition, the narratives reveal that the opinions the veterans developed about themselves, their country, and even other veterans were influenced in part by experiences unique to the particular war in which they fought.

Stress and trauma are not always generated by single, isolated events that affect a limited number of people and those close to them. In some contexts, Heather Carlson and her associates illustrates, extreme stress may be produced by a formal institution. Carlson et al.'s reports on middle-aged women's accounts in modern Romania illustrate how the economic policies of a government and the enforcement of such policies can generate considerable widespread stress for an entire population. By describing the conditions of life under a communist dictatorship and the difficulties of surviving after its dissolution, these women's accounts place the experience of trauma and stress into a historical, economic, and political context.

The second section of this volume, Responding to and Coping With Traumatic Stress, focuses more directly upon the reactions to trauma and how those reactions themselves may evolve over time. Patricia Frazier's contribution examines the role of victim attributions in response to rape. A wide variety of thoughts and reactions relating to control, distress, blame, and recovery have been described in this literature, with occasionally conflicting results. By integrating recent and current studies with past research on victim attributions, the author helps clarify the nature of attributions that either help or hinder the recovery process and how such attributions are relevant for rape victim counselors.

Marc Orlitzky expands the scope of the traumatic stress field by discussing the role organizations may play when reacting to disasters. Governments, private industries, or help-oriented agencies often respond with some type of assistance when major disaster strikes. However, as Orlitzky contends, the needs of the survivors change as time passes, and well-intentioned assistance efforts are not always wholly appropriate for these needs at the time they are offered. This prescriptive approach specifies how survivor needs change and the manner in which organizations can implement seemingly paradoxical models of assistance in their attempts to help survivors cope with traumatic stress.

The chapter on the loss experienced by parents of Israeli soldiers, by Ruth Malkinson and Liora Bar-Tur, and the chapter on coping with losses and trauma in old age, by Bar-Tur and Rachel Levy-Shiff, provide insight into how the nature of grief continues to evolve even decades after the initial traumatic event. Malkinson and Bar-Tur's work focuses on the tragedy of losing a son to war or terrorism, an all-too-common occurrence during modern Israel's brief existence. They describe the different phases that occur as grief "ages" and the perhaps unique culture of bereavement that has developed in a country where the loss of young life is particularly salient. Bar-Tur and Levy-Shiff's work also shares this emphasis on the dynamic nature of coping and grief while examining the process of separation-individuation throughout the life span and across several different contexts of trauma and loss. They suggest that at least some of the elderly engage in inner adaptive processes that help them compensate for past traumas even though they realize that certain valuable people or opportunities are no longer available to them. However, as the authors demonstrate, the extent to which these adaptive processes actually occur may depend in part upon the nature of the traumatic event or events those individuals endured many years ago.

The final contribution, by Harvey Peskin and Nanette Auerhahn, centers on Holocaust survivors who find themselves struggling with the conflicting costs and benefits of sharing their traumatic experience with those closest to them. Peskin and Auerhahn articulate the numerous imposing dilemmas that can characterize these particular victims' worlds. For example, sharing with a loved one the experience of genocide may provide the survivor with a valuable witness, but the survivor does so at the potential cost of recalling horrors that he or she has often attempted to eradicate from memory. In addition, Holocaust survivors must decide whether sharing their experiences with the next generation provides those descendants with a valuable family history and context or instead conveys the message that evil can occasionally and inexplicably dominate in the world. For the survivors, the consequences of such decisions are great as they try to function normally in a world so different from that which they witnessed more than 50 years ago. These issues become more important as the number of living survivors diminishes and the burden of transmission becomes heavier upon the few who are left.

At the end of this volume, we present some closing remarks regarding the nature of traumatic stress as a field of inquiry and the contributions of these particular works. We believe the following chapters reflect the growing breadth of the area, as well as the varied theoretical perspectives and methods by which we have come to understand in greater depth the nature of traumatic stress and its consequences. Ultimately, we hope that the accumulated body of knowledge produced by scholars will better enable individuals to interpret, cope with, and overcome the traumatic events in their own lives.

References

Figley, C. R. (1993). Foreword. In J. P. Wilson & B. Raphael (Eds.), *International handbook of traumatic stress syndromes*. New York: Plenum.

Wilson, J. P., & Raphael, B. (Eds.). (1993). *International handbook of traumatic stress syndromes*. New York: Plenum.

PART I
POST-TRAUMATIC STRESS: CONTEXTS AND CONSEQUENCES

As mentioned in the introduction to this volume, the contexts in which traumatic events occur and can be studied are numerous. The specific nature of a given traumatic event can raise unique challenges for the victims who endure the event, the scholars who attempt to understand the event, and the practitioners who assist in the event's aftermath. Traumatic events vary on dimensions beyond the physical stressors that initially produce discomfort or disability. For example, they also differ in the extent to which cultural contexts contribute to that initial stressor. They vary in terms of the immediate and long-term consequences of the event, both for the victims and for those close to them. Finally, the nature of the trauma often dictates both the opportunities and obstacles faced by researchers and practitioners who seek to understand or intervene after the event occurs. The following chapters illustrate this diversity by describing a number of different contexts in which trauma can occur and the particular consequences that follow from those contexts.

CHAPTER ONE

LOSS OF TRUST: CORRELATES OF THE COMORBIDITY OF PTSD AND SEVERE MENTAL ILLNESS

CATHALEENE MACIAS and ROBERT YOUNG

Research Unit, Fountain House, Inc., New York, New York, USA

PAUL BARREIRA

Massachusetts Department of Mental Health, Boston, Massachusetts, USA

The prevalence of post-traumatic stress disorder (PTSD) in the general population of the United States is a topic of speculation, with estimates ranging from 0.4% to 9% (Breslau, Davis, Andreski, & Peterson, 1991; Helzer, Robins, & McEvoy, 1987; Kessler, Sonnega, Bromet, Hughes, & Nelson, 1995). Likewise, estimates of the prevalence of PTSD within the population of persons with serious mental illness have varied widely, depending on how PTSD has been measured. While record verification of PTSD within mental health outpatient samples has routinely been very low (0%–3%), research assessments of PTSD have resulted in estimated rates of co-occurrence of 29% to 43% (Cascardi, Mueser, DeGirolomo, & Murrin, 1996; Craine, Henson, Colliver, & MacLean, 1998; Mueser et al., 1998). A lack of documentation of PTSD in clinical records and inattention to PTSD in clinical diagnoses are thought to greatly underestimate the extent of PTSD within mental health treatment populations. The general consensus among researchers has been that the occurrence of PTSD is much higher within the population of persons with diagnoses of mental illness than in the general population, particularly among those who have major depression (Friedman & Rosenheck, 1996).

For the most part, the prevalence of PTSD co-occurrence with mental illness is still a matter of speculation (Friedman & Rosenheck, 1996). There are few published rates of documented PTSD diagnoses within large representative samples of people with serious mental illness. A confirmed diagnosis of PTSD requires a clinician assessment using specific criteria of the *Diagnostic and Statistical Manual of Mental Disorders* (4th edition; *DSM-IV*; American Psychiatric Association, 1994; Biere, 1997; Blake et al., 1995), a costly undertaking for any research study. Moreover, the debate as to whether general PTSD has distinct comorbid syndromes specific to particular experiences of trauma further complicates the measurement of prevalence (Ford, 1999). To avoid these diagnostic debates and to estimate the prevalence of PTSD in a more pragmatic and general way, researchers have resorted to a variety of research assessment instruments (Blanchard, Jones-Alexander, Buckley, & Forneris, 1996; Foa, Riggs, Dancu, & Rothbaum, 1993; Zilberg, Weiss, & Horowitz, 1982) and structured interviews designed to solicit memories of traumatic experience (Goodman, Rosenberg, Mueser, & Drake, 1997; Mueser et al., 1998; Weathers, Litz, Herman, Huska, & Keane, 1993). However, identification of PTSD through self-reports and symptom checklists has not yet been standardized, and, while promising instrumentation exists (e.g., Foa, Cashman, Jaycox, & Perry, 1999), the validity and reliability of this instrumentation for the study of co-occurring mental disorders have not been explored. It may well be that disclosing traumatic memories during retrospective research assessments is problematic for people with serious mental illness, triggering the expression of more immediate affect and pain than what the person normally experiences. If so, then existing research estimates of PTSD using self-report methodologies may be overestimates of occurrence.

The present study provides another opportunity to observe the extent of PTSD documentation within the clinical records of a general sample of persons with mental illness, as well as an opportunity to test assumptions regarding the relationship of PTSD to mental illness. Correlates of PTSD and mental illness co-occurrence have generated clinical hypotheses regarding both symptom formation and recovery. Persons diagnosed as having PTSD have been found to have more current or past substance abuse, a more chronic history of hospitalizations, and an earlier onset of major depression (Brown & Wolfe, 1994; Zlotnick, Warshaw, Shea, & Keller, 1997) or psychotic symptoms (Greenfield, Strakowski, Tohen, Batson, & Kolbrener, 1994; Paykel, 1978). PTSD has also been associated with poor interpersonal skills, generally low self-esteem, and a pervasive feeling of shame, all of which contribute to isolation and social conflicts (Cresswell, Kuipers, & Power, 1992; Zlotnick et al., 1996). However, the most sophisticated studies of PTSD suggest that the relationship between PTSD and mental illness is reciprocal, with trauma both precipitating and intensifying the symptoms of mental illness, and the symptoms of mental illness in turn increasing the chances that an individual will have a traumatic experience (Horowitz, 1993). For instance, a woman who has suffered repeated physical abuse may want to withdraw from close relationships, but the apathy of depression may not allow her to sever even the one relationship that is abusive. This type of reciprocal cause-effect relationship probably also exists between correlates of PTSD, such as alcoholism and depression (Schutte, Hearst, & Moos, 1997). In this case, the interaction becomes three way, with both drinking and depression inviting the reoccurrence of trauma at the same time as they escalate one another (Kilpatrick, Acierno, Resnick, Saunders, & Best, 1997).

This complex cause-effect relationship between PTSD and related variables also suggests that if an individual is able to cope with either the symptoms of mental illness or the impact of trauma, he or she may develop psychological resources that generalize to other life difficulties and actually improve the chances of recovery. Such a possibility is fully realized in the folklore concept of the "wounded healer" and the social work roles assumed by many recovering mental health consumers (Dixon, Hackman, & Lehman, 1997; Mowbray & Moxley, 1997; Solomon & Draine, 1997). What is unique about a pattern of recovery from patient to mental health worker is the return from person-inflicted trauma to fulfilling personal relationships. This readily observable phenomenon suggests that interpersonal vulnerability is both a cause of extreme pain for PTSD victims and a catalyst for growth and emotional maturity.

The present study was designed to explore the complex relationship of PTSD to mental illness and to test the assumption that PTSD typically goes undocumented in a representative sample of persons with serious mental illness. The study compared a group of persons with both mental illness and chart-diagnosed PTSD and a comparison group of persons with serious mental illness but no formal chart diagnosis of PTSD. To the extent that there is a similarity between these two groups in regard to variables theoretically related to PTSD, we assume that there is substantial undiagnosed PTSD within the comparison sample. On the other hand, statistically significant differences between PTSD and no-PTSD groups would suggest that PTSD manifests unique symptoms over and above the depressive symptomatology that characterizes most people with serious mental illness. Meaningful group differences theoretically linked to PTSD would also confirm the general reliability of chart records and suggest that there are not high rates of undetected PTSD within the wider population of persons with serious mental illness.

Method

The present study was conducted as part of the ongoing Employment Intervention Demonstration Program (EIDP) of the federal Substance Abuse and Mental Health Services Administration (SAMHSA). The eight-project EIDP is funded for a period of 5 years (1995–2000) and is distinctive in its inclusion of a coordinating center as well as a common data collection protocol. The present research study was conducted with baseline data from only the Massachusetts EIDP project.

Characteristics of the EIDP Participants

Admission criteria for the EIDP project were (a) 18 years of age or older, (b) a *DSM-IV* diagnosis of serious mental illness, and (c) absence of severe mental retardation ($IQ > 65$). The EIDP sample was recruited from within and around the city of Worcester, Massachusetts. The recruitment plan was designed by the project's Advisory Council, composed primarily of representatives from local National Alliance for the Mentally Ill (NAMI) chapters and consumer advocacy groups. A strong effort was made to recruit participants from diverse locations in order to obtain a heterogeneous and representative sample of people with serious mental illness. Referral sources included advocacy organizations, mental health programs, the regional department of mental health, treatment and correctional facilities, and homeless shelters. Applicants who did not have a diagnosis of serious mental illness at the time of referral, but who reported related symptoms, were provided a diagnostic assessment before admission to the project.

The subsample of persons with a diagnosis of PTSD and the comparison subsample of all persons with a diagnosis of major depression without PTSD used in the present analysis were drawn from the total sample of 177 persons recruited for the Massachusetts EIDP. The total EIDP sample was representative of the Worcester-area Department of Mental Health (DMH) population of persons with serious mental illness in regard to all demographic and diagnostic characteristics. About one half (51.8%) of the participants were diagnosed as having a schizophrenia spectrum disorder, 30.7% as having major depression, 16.9% as having bipolar disorder, and 0.6% as having another type of psychotic disorder. Nearly all participants (98%) were on psychiatric medication, averaging 2.75 concurrent medications. The participants generally had a long history of mental illness, with an average of seven hospitalizations beginning at an average age of 25 years. The majority (61%) also had a documented history of serious substance abuse. Two thirds (69%) of the participants received Social Security benefits, with 43% receiving only supplemental security income (SSI). In spite of the chronicity of their illnesses, a large percentage (43%) of study participants were parents, and 20% of the total sample had minor children living with them.

The residential status of participants at the time of enrollment in the project reflects the diversity of recruitment, with 56% ($n = 93$) living independently, 7.8% ($n = 13$) in supported or assisted living housing, 16% ($n = 27$) living as a dependent with their family, and 15% ($n = 24$) in the hospital. A few participants were in jail ($n = 5$; 3%) or homeless ($n = 4$; 3%) at the time of intake.

The work history of participants reflects the debilitating effects of serious mental illness on employment. About half of the sample (55%) had been unemployed for 30 months or longer at the time of enrollment, and 39.4% had not worked at all during the 5 years preceding enrollment in the project. None of the participants held a paying job at the time of entry into the project.

Research Instruments

The data for the present study included (a) clinical information received from referring agencies, the current treating physician, or diagnostic tests conducted by the project and (b) baseline interviews with all project participants. Data collection for the entire SAMHSA EIDP is overseen by a coordinating center jointly administered by the National Research and Training Center of the University of Illinois at Chicago (Judith Cook, director) and the Human Services Research Institute in Boston (Steve Leff, director). All eight research projects send their clinical, interview, employment, and services data to the coordinating center on a quarterly basis for quality review and verification that data have been collected in keeping with EIDP mandates.

Clinical Data

Diagnosis

Clinical records from both referring agencies and previous hospitalizations were requested for all project applicants. If the formal diagnosis contained in these records fit the eligibility requirements and was not ambiguous, the participant's record diagnosis was accepted as valid for the project. If two or more contradictory diagnoses were obtained, if the applicant described symptoms that clearly conflicted with the record diagnosis, or if an applicant had no formal diagnosis, the Structured Clinical Interview for the DSM-IV (First, Spitzer, Gibbon, & Williams, 1996) was administered by medical faculty of the Department of Psychiatry, University of Massachusetts at Worcester, to verify eligibility for the project and provide a reliable diagnosis for research purposes. Diagnoses of PTSD were retrieved from clinical records ordered by the project for the purpose of documenting participant eligibility and from information forms routinely received from referring clinicians.

Substance Abuse

History of substance abuse was also documented through clinical records and clinician responses to a referral form that requested information on current alcohol and drug use. Any participant whose records showed residential treatment or a *DSM-IV* Axis II diagnosis of substance abuse, or whose referring clinician indicated that he or she had a current serious problem, was coded as having a history of substance abuse.

Interview Data

The participant interview was designed by the steering committee of the EIDP, which consisted of representatives from the eight EIDP projects and the coordinating center, the SAMHSA project monitor, and a SAMHSA consumer representative. The baseline interview package required approximately 1 hour to administer. The research and demographic variables from the interview package included in the present study were those that were deemed relevant to the study of PTSD and mental illness.

Quality of Life Scale (*QOL; Lehman, 1988*)

The self-report QOL used in the present study was the brief version of Lehman's original scale (Lehman, Kernan, & Postrado, 1997). Domains of measurement include such diverse areas of experience as living situation, family relations, nonfamily social relations, daily activities, finances, safety and legal problems, work, school, and physical health. For purposes of the present study, the Personal Safety subscale (Items 15a, 15b, 15c) was used to measure variations in participants' perceptions of the safety of their living situations and/or residential neighborhoods that might contribute to anxiety and stress. The three QOL items composing this subscale addressed perceived safety on the streets, safety when at home, and protection against being robbed or attacked.

Self-Esteem Scale (*Rosenberg, 1979*)

The Rosenberg Self-Esteem Scale is a 10-item questionnaire designed to assess levels of positive and negative self-regard. Large-scale administrations of the instrument have reported internal validities (alphas) of .72 to .88 and test-retest reliabilities of .50 to

.82 for periods of 1 year and 1 week, respectively (Gray-Little, Williams, & Hancock, 1997).

Positive and Negative Syndrome Scale (PANSS: Kay, Fiszbein, & Opler, 1987)

The PANSS is a structured clinical interview composed of the 18-item Brief Psychiatric Rating Scale (BPRS; Overall & Gorham, 1962) together with 12 additional items from the Psychopathology Rating Scale (Singh & Kay, 1975), designed to assess negative and general symptoms not addressed by the BPRS. The PANSS provides standard probe questions and descriptive rating anchors for each single-item symptom measurement, as well as thresholds for identifying clinical significance. The total PANSS requires approximately 45 minutes to administer. The reliability and validity of the PANSS are well established (Bell, Milstein, Beam-Goulet, Lysaker, & Cicchetti, 1992), and it has been used extensively in clinical research. The 30 items have a factor structure that reflects three basic dimensions: positive, negative, and general symptoms.

Interviewers for the present study were trained by Lewis Opler of Columbia-Presbyterian Medical Center in New York City, a close collaborator on the development of the PANSS. Assessments conducted by researchers from Dartmouth University confirm that the Worcester EIDP interviewers ($n = 2$) evidenced high rates of inerrater reliability for the positive ($r = .95$), negative ($r = .89$), and general ($r = .94$) subscales of the PANSS. The Worcester site 2-week test-retest reliability was also acceptably high, with coefficients of .93, .95, and .87 for the positive, negative, and general subscales, respectively (Trumbetta, McHugo, & Drake, 1997).

For purposes of the present study, specific items of the PANSS (1–7 Likert ratings) were paired with participant responses to corresponding terms on an adjective checklist (1–5 Likert ratings) to create several two-item composite measures of symptomatology. A sum of self-assessments and clinician assessments recorded at the same point in time was considered to be more reflective of an individual's emotional level of functioning than either self-report or clinician report used alone. Self-report adjectives (listed first) and corresponding PANSS items (listed second) all had moderate to high biserial correlations statistically significant at $p < .01$: (a) *Depression*: depressed and depression ($r = .69$); (b) *Loneliness*: lonely and social avoidance $(r = .31)$; (c) *Anxiety*: edgy and anxiety $(r = .53)$; (d) *Anger*: enraged and hostility $(r = .28)$; (e) *Hallucinations*: hearing voices and hallucinations $(r = .66)$; and (f) *Trust*: trusting and suspiciousness (reversed) $(r = .23)$. The mean biserial correlation (r) between PANSS scores and adjective self-ratings was .40 $(p < .001)$. In addition, one PANSS variable, somatization, was paired with a reversed 4-point self-rating of participants' physical health $(r = .25, p < .001)$ to create a seventh symptom variable, *Somatization*.

Level of Functioning Self-Report

Participants were also asked to rate their overall level of daily functioning on a 4-point scale ranging from *excellent* to *very poor*.

Report on Current Medications

The name and dosage of all psychotropic medications prescribed for the participant were requested during the research interview. Newer antipsychotic medications (i.e., clozapine, risperidone, olanzapine) that have demonstrated effectiveness for improving daily functioning were identified and coded as "atypical" medications for inclusion in the present analyses.

Financial Status Report

Two income variables were included in the present analyses: (a) total personal income for the month preceding enrollment and (b) whether or not the participant was a recipient of SSI. The latter was a dummy variable identifying recipients of SSI who did not also receive Social Security disability insurance. Because receipt of SSI requires documentation of extreme disability and the inability to be self-supportive, this variable was considered a proxy for level of functioning. Monthly personal income was considered a proxy measure for socioeconomic status.

Star Social Network Scale

The social network instrument used by the Massachusetts EIDP was originally designed by Courtenay Harding, John Strauss, and colleagues for the Yale University longitudinal study of schizophrenia. Harding and Macias modified the original scale for purposes of the present study and for ease of data recording and entry. The Star Social Network Scale measures density of (ego) social networks, types of relationships, and frequency of contact, in addition to a variety of other measures reflective of the quality of interpersonal relationships (e.g., reciprocity, negativity, and level of confidential disclosure). Three social network variables were used in the present study of PTSD: (a) number of strong family relationships, (b) number of important friendships, and (c) level of confidential disclosure. (i.e., number of confidants available and frequency of disclosure).

Work History

A work history questionnaire designed by the National Research and Training Center at the University of Illinois at Chicago requested information about participants' previous employment. Two work history variables were used in the present study: (a) length of time on longest job ever held and (b) whether the participant had worked at all during the 5 years preceding project enrollment. Participant responses to the latter question were corroborated through a calculation of length of unemployment from end date of most recent job to date of enrollment in the project.

Results

The research samples for the present study consisted of all project participants with a record diagnosis of PTSD ($n = 21$) and all project participants with a *DSM-IV* Axis I diagnosis of major depression without a documented diagnosis of PTSD ($n = 38$). The subsample of 21 persons with PTSD represents a 12% rate of clinically documented PTSD within the total sample ($N = 177$) of persons with serious mental illness taken from the Worcester community. The majority of persons with PTSD (71.4%) had a primary *DSM-IV* Axis I diagnosis of major depression; the remainder (28.6%) had a primary diagnosis of schizophrenia with co-occurring depressive symptomatology.

Characteristics of the Samples

Table 1 presents percentages and average scores on the research measures for both samples. The two groups were similar in regard to all demographic and socioeconomic characteristics except gender (i.e., age, education, ethnic minority status, residential autonomy, monthly personal income, and receipt of SSI). As would be expected, the PTSD and no-PTSD groups were also similar to one another in regard to those variables theoretically related to their shared depressive symptomatology: (a) current symptoms (i.e, depression, anxiety, and social avoidance) and

TABLE 1 Scores on Study Variables for PTSD and No-PTSD Groups ($N = 59$)

Variable	n	PTSD: M (SD) or %	n	Major depression: M (SD) or %
Demographics				
Age (years)	21	37.20 (8.21)	38	39.24 (10.34)
Gender (male)	21	29	38	55
Ethnic minority status	21	33	38	21
Living independently	21	71	38	71
At least high school	21	57	37	76
Monthly personal income ($)	21	515 (287)	38	692 (693)
Social Security income	21	29	38	37
Chronicity/severity				
Age at first hospitalization	18	20.69 (8.27)	33	28.55 (9.71)
Number of hospitalizations	20	7.95 (11.72)	38	3.68 (3.16)
History of substance abuse	21	57	38	63
Depression symptoms[a]	21	8.81 (2.36)	38	9.08 (1.91)
Anxiety symptoms[a]	21	8.29 (1.82)	38	8.11 (2.26)
Hallucinations[a]	21	5.57 (3.19)	38	4.71 (2.46)
Atypical medications	21	19	38	24
Worked in past 5 years	21	48	38	71
Months on longest job	21	40.33 (47.57)	38	69.60 (83.34)
Emotions/relations				
Loneliness[a]	21	7.86 (2.06)	38	7.92 (2.01)
Size of family network	21	3.48 (2.58)	38	4.68 (3.25)
Size of friendship network	21	1.33 (1.24)	38	1.76 (2.10)
Confidant friendships[a]	20	52.05 (11.77)	38	43.65 (9.48)
Perceived physical safety[a]	21	11.10 (6.05)	38	13.71 (4.28)
Interpersonal trust[a]	21	5.48 (2.21)	38	7.29 (1.81)
Anger[a]	21	4.76 (1.73)	38	4.53 (2.05)
Somatization/physical health[a]	21	5.14 (1.39)	38	6.29 (1.99)
Global self-esteem[a]	20	24.80 (6.20)	37	23.19 (4.75)

[a] Rating scale total scores.

TABLE 2 Logistic Regression Analysis Predicting PTSD Group Membership

Predictor variable	PTSD vs. no PTSD	β	Exp(B)	SE	Wald	p
Control						
Gender (male) (%)	28 vs. 54	.920	2.510	.937	0.965	.326
Depression[a]	8.61 vs. 9.24	−.287	0.751	.265	1.176	.278
Anxiety[a]	8.17 vs. 8.24	.335	1.398	.335	1.000	.317
Anger[a]	4.56 vs. 4.56	−.049	0.952	.258	0.036	.850
Hallucinations[a]	5.44 vs. 4.73	.175	1.191	.164	1.133	.287
PTSD						
Somatization[a]	5.11 vs. 6.35	−.667	0.513	.308	4.688	.030
Loneliness[a]	7.61 vs. 8.05	−.158	0.854	.295	0.286	.854
Self-esteem	25.44 vs. 23.19	.079	1.083	.087	0.828	.363
Interpersonal trust[a]	5.44 vs. 7.30	−.846	0.429	.306	7.658	.006

Note. Full model $\chi^2 = 26.74$, $df = 9$, $p < .01$.
[a] 12-point composite score: 5-point self-rating plus 7-point interviewer PANSS rating.

(b) behavioral correlates of depression (i.e., substance abuse, small social networks). Interestingly, one symptom known to correlate with both depression and PTSD, somatization, showed more functional mean scores for the PTSD sample. There were no group differences in regard to psychotic symptomatology (i.e., hallucinations).

By contrast, the PTSD group had significantly lower functional scores than the no-PTSD group on three variables theoretically related to PTSD in previous research studies: age of first hospitalization, number of hospitalizations, and the composite measure (self-report adjective plus PANSS rating) of interpersonal trust. Mean differences for these variables reached the $p < .05$ level of statistical significance in univariate analyses of variance. Two other study variables had mean differences that were marginally significant: whether the person had worked at all in the past 5 years ($p = .08$) and perceived physical safety ($p = .06$). One demographic variable, gender—which is closely associated with victimization from childhood sexual abuse and spouse abuse, and hence with PTSD—also had a chi-square value that was statistically significant ($p < .05$). The conceptual similarity within this set of statistically significant (or near-significant) variables reflects a greater level of disability and stronger perceptions of interpersonal vulnerability within the PTSD sample.

Distinctiveness of PTSD Chart Diagnoses

The PTSD and no-PTSD research samples were compared in a logistic regression analysis (Table 2). The purpose of this analysis was to identify a minimum set of conceptually distinct variables related to PTSD while controlling for consumer demographic characteristics and the general psychiatric symptoms of serious mental illness. A model that included 16 distinctly different variables from Table 1 was first fit, followed by a reduced model that included 9 of the 16 variables that had either large beta coefficients or significant p values.

The nine variables shown in Table 2 were grouped into two blocks. The first block consisted of gender together with symptoms generally reflective of either major depression or schizophrenia: depression, anxiety, anger, and hallucinations. The second block consisted of the interpersonal trust, loneliness, somatization, and self-esteem variables. The first variable is a self-report measure of interpersonal vulnerability; the last three variables are measures of emotionality that are known to correlate with PTSD but are distinct from depression or schizophrenia per se.

The variables in the first block were not significantly related to group membership ($\chi^2 = 8.14$, $df = 5$, $p = .149$). This indicates that the PTSD and no-PTSD groups did not differ with respect to gender or the basic symptoms of serious mental illness. Adding the second block of variables led to a reduction in -2 log-likelihood of 18.61 ($df = 4$, $p < .001$), indicating that these four variables together significantly predicted group membership. The full model, with all nine variables, correctly predicted group membership for 85.5% of the 55 cases ($\chi^2 = 26.74$, $df = 9$, $p < .01$). The significance of the full regression model, which controlled for the symptoms of depression and schizophrenia, demonstrates that chart records of PTSD do identify a psychiatric disorder distinct from the recognized symptoms of serious mental illness.

Tests of individual variables show that only one variable, interpersonal trust, was related to PTSD group membership at a level of statistical significance appropriate for this small sample ($p < .01$). Participants with formal diagnoses of PTSD reported less trust of other people than participants with comparable symptoms of mental illness who did not have a formal diagnosis of PTSD.

Discussion

The fact that persons with documented PTSD typically report less trust in other people than persons without a diagnosis of PTSD suggests that PTSD inflicts an emotional isolation unrelated to size of social network, level of intimacy, or frequency of social interaction. Persons diagnosed with PTSD have family and friend networks that are comparable in size, proximity, and contact to those of other people with mental illness (i.e., an average of seven total ties to people considered important in their lives), and they report comparable levels of loneliness, in spite of a general lack of trust. Apparently, the distinguishing characteristic of PTSD is a pervasive feeling of interpersonal distrust even in the face of existing family and friend relationships.

The lack of other significant differences between the PTSD and no-PTSD samples in the logistic regression analysis indicates that people with PTSD apparently have the same generally low self-esteem and physical health problems that are associated with major depression. Likewise, the consistently high rate of documented substance abuse (60%) for both PTSD and non-PTSD participants within the study sample suggests that the widely observed co-occurrence of PTSD and substance abuse may simply reflect a strong correlation between co-occurring depression and substance abuse. The overall pattern of similarities between major depression and PTSD suggests a model of PTSD that is composed of separate, but highly correlated, sets of symptoms (i.e., distrust, depression, substance abuse) that interact to escalate one another. If this is true, then we might endorse clinical interventions specific to each of these three symptoms, assuming that a decrease in any one symptom would have a corresponding positive impact on related symptoms. On the other hand, it may well be that depression is so essential an element in PTSD that even the seemingly distinct characteristic of distrust is always accompanied by depressive symptomatology, with co-occurring high rates of alcoholism and drug abuse. If so, it may be impossible to treat any separate component of PTSD effectively without simultaneously providing treatment for depression. If *PTSD depression* is itself a unique entity, characterized by interpersonal distrust and, at times, paranoia, then there is a very great need to reconsider the value of existing mental health interventions for persons with PTSD and mental illness comorbidity.

The complex symptomatology observed in our small study presents intriguing hypotheses for the development of competing theoretical models of PTSD that might one day be tested with larger research samples. The study findings also suggest that sufficiently large consumer samples with documented PTSD–mental illness comorbidity may be readily available. In fact, the discrepancy between the 12% rate of documented co-occurring PTSD and mental illness in the current EIDP study and the very low rates (e.g., 0%–3%) observed in other studies is puzzling. It may be that the current study sample, drawn from a wide variety of sources within a natural community, is more representative of the general population of persons with mental illness than previously studied samples (e.g., Craine et al., 1988; Museser et al., 1998). It may also be that the presence of a teaching hospital in Worcester at the University of Massachusetts ensured more thorough psychiatric evaluations throughout the medical community. The extent to which the currently observed 12% rate is a valid estimate of the overall prevalence of co-occurring PTSD and severe mental illness at a national or international level must await confirmation by future research studies. Regardless of the actual prevalence of PTSD within the general population of persons with serious mental illness, the identification of a unique correlate of documented PTSD within our logistic regression analysis suggests that chart records of PTSD are generally reliable and that PTSD does not usually go undetected within the wider population of persons with serious mental illness, at least within localities similar to Worcester, Massachusetts.

Conclusion

The statistical relationship of PTSD to trust and vulnerability is perhaps better understood through personal experience. The second author, a researcher on this current SAMHSA Massachusetts project and a social worker at Fountain House, has recorded a history of his own long recovery from PTSD. This account provides a perspective on both the individual experience of PTSD and the therapeutic milieu of the clubhouse (Propst, 1992) mental health intervention. The value of a supportive intentional community for building interpersonal trust is without a doubt a viable topic for future research on the effectiveness of mental health services for PTSD.

A Personal Story

I don't often look back into my childhood; there are only flashes of brutal chaos. But as a child the nightmare never leaves you. There is no peace. At the bus stop, you hear the echo of that morning's horror show. Your heart races. You hope you won't be sore all day. The other kids sense how lost you are, and they come down on you with that relentless, merciless cruelty found only in children. Your teachers are either too burnt or too busy to care. All you do is fall further and further behind in school. Then you go back home. To the place where things happened that are only spoken of now with downcast eyes in barely audible whispers in the confines of a therapist's office.

As far back as I can remember, it would be 5 or 6 years old, I would do things in hope that I would become unconscious. I would play with electrical outlets or take whatever pills I could find to see if I could escape into oblivion. When I entered the hormonal tempest known as adolescence, things went from ugly to worse in a hurry. I would eventually be hospitalized when I reached 16. I was sent to a series of foster homes and bounced around to this therapist or that day program. I floundered around the mental health community for 5 or 6 years. It seemed a dead end. So, at the age of 21, I set out on my own.

For the next 10 years, I survived. I marginally scratched, muddled, and screwed up my way through life. Life was like reading a stack of unbound papers in a stiff ocean breeze. It can be done, but it gets a little complicated. When I turned 30, that ocean breeze became a hurricane. My world came crashing down once too often. In the span of 6 months, I would leave an abusive marriage, but in the process I would also lose my daughter, my job, and my home. In a short period of time, I went from being a moderately successful employee and father to become a lonely and homeless drifter. After being picked up again by the mental health community, I found myself in the very same system of therapists and day programs I had left so many years ago. I was thirty-something. I was grim as death and seething in cynicism. I wore my apathy like armor and I was untouchable. I truly felt that this would be the rest of my life. Until, one day, someone at the mental health clinic decided that a clubhouse would be beneficial to my recovery. They liked the idea so much that they made attending the clubhouse a requirement for my leaving the clinic's day program.

So, with as little enthusiasm as I could muster, I showed up at Baybridge Clubhouse. I sat and I watched. The people working there continually approached me. They spoke to me as if I was an adult with a brain. It was a unique experience. They started giving me things to do. At this point I had very little experience on computers, but I learned very quickly. And the more I did, the more responsibility they gave me. All the time they were treating me as an equal. I was slowly starting to allow myself to dream of a better life. I watched other members at the clubhouse who had more profound illnesses than I did also work and heal and dream. It was indeed a remarkable experience.

I would like to say this. Individual counseling and group therapy are essential ingredients in the recovery of any victim of PTSD. It was in these settings that I would discover that what had happened to me was not a normal upbringing. It was in these sessions that I learned to accept that I really did not do anything to deserve the pain I endured. Therapy was also a place where I discovered I was not alone. Individual counseling has always had a positive influence on my life. That is, of course, when I bothered with it. On the other hand, to put a finger on what makes a clubhouse work is not all that easy. Obviously, it is about work. You build an ability to work, and the work grows with you. But I guess most of all, clubhouses are about friendships, real friendships, not doctor and patient relationships.

Today, I am still thirty-something. I work in the oldest and largest clubhouse in the world, Fountain House. And I live in New York City (the center of the known universe). Quite a change from the little town in Massachusetts I came from. I've taken that stack of papers indoors to read where the wind can't blow, but I still find a window open every now and then. That's when it's good to have a friend.

Acknowledgments

We would like to express appreciation to the members and staff of the Research Unit at Fountain House, New York, especially Charles Rodican (research administration), Andrew Schonebaum (unit leader), and Qi Wang (senior researcher), for their competent data management of the Massachusetts EIDP project over the past 4 years. Appreciation is also extended to Kenneth Hetzler of Community Healthlink, Inc., Kevin Bradley of Genesis Club, Inc., Gerald Kokernak of the Worcester Area Department of Mental Health, and the entire EIDP Project Advisory Council for their help in sample recruitment. Thanks go also to the research interviewers, Julia Vera and Kathy Smith, and to the faculty and students of the University of Massachusetts Medical School, who ensured that the project data and diagnostic information were reliable.

This study is part of the Employment Intervention Demonstration Program (EIDP), a multisite collaboration among eight research demonstration projects, a coordinating center, and the Center for Mental Health Services, Substance Abuse and Mental Health Services Administration, U.S. Department of Health and Human Services, which funds the Massachusetts research project described in this study as well as the larger eight-project initiative. Substantial support for staffing and project activities was also provided by the van Ameringen Foundation, New York City.

References

American Psychiatric Association (1994). *Diagnostic and statistical manual of mental disorders* (4th ed.) Washington, DC: Author.

Bell, M., Milstein, R., Beam-Goulet, J., Lysaker, P., & Cicchetti, D. (1992). The Positive and Negative Syndrome Scale and the Brief Psychiatric Rating Scale: Reliability, comparability, and predictive validity. *Journal of Nervous and Mental Disease, 180,* 723–728.

Biere, J. (1997). *Psychological assessment of adult posttraumatic states.* Washington, DC: American Psychological Association.

Blake, D. D., Weathers, F. W., Nagy, L. M., Kaloupek, D. B., Charney, D. S., & Keane, T. M. (1995). *Clinician-Administered PTSD Scale for DSM-IV*. Boston: National Center for Posttraumatic Stress Disorder.

Blanchard, E. B., Jones-Alexander, J., Buckley, T. C., & Forneris, C. A. (1996). Psychometric properties of the PTSD Checklist. *Behavior Research and Therapy*, *234*, 669–673.

Breslau, N., Davis, G. C. Andreski, P., Peterson, E. (1991). Traumatic events and post-traumatic stress disorder in an urban population of young adults. *Archives of General Psychiatry*, *48*, 216–220.

Brown, G. W., & Wolfe, J. (1994). Substance abuse and post-traumatic stress disorder comorbidity. *Drug and Alcohol Dependence*, *35*, 51–59.

Cascardi, M., Mueser, K. T., DeGirolomo, J., & Murrin, M. (1996). Physical aggression against psychiatric inpatients by family members and partners: A descriptive study. *Psychiatric Services*, *47*, 531–533.

Craine, L. S., Henson, C. E., Colliver, J. A., & MacLean, D. G. (1988). Prevalence of a history of sexual abuse among female psychiatric patients in a state hospital system. *Hospital and Community Psychiatry*, *39*, 300–304.

Cresswell, C. M., Kuipers, L., & Power, M. J. (1992). Social networks and support in long-term psychiatric patients. *Psychological Medicine*, *22*, 1019–1026.

Dixon, L., Hackman, A., & Lehman, A. (1997). Consumers as staff in assertive community treatment programs. *Administration and Policy in Mental Health*, *25*, 199–208.

First, M. B., Spitzer, R. L., Gibbon, M., & Williams, J. B. W. (1996). *Structured Clinical Interview for Axes I and II DSM-IV Disorders (SCID-I/P)*. New York: Biometrics Research Department, New York State Psychiatric Institute.

Foa, E. B., Cashman, L., Jaycox, L., & Perry, K. (1999). The validation of a self-report measure of posttraumatic stress disorder. The Posttraumatic Diagnostic Scale. *Psychological Assessment 9*, 445–451.

Foa, E. B., Riggs, D. S., Dancu, C. B., & Rothbaum, B. O. (1993). Reliability and validity of a brief instrument for assessing post-traumatic stress disorder. *Journal of Traumatic Stress*, *6*, 459–474.

Ford, J. D. (199). Disorders of extreme stress following war-zone military trauma: Associated features of posttraumatic stress disorder or comorbid but distinct syndromes? *Journal of Consulting and Clinical Psychology*, *67*, 3–12.

Friedman, M. J., & Rosenheck, R. (1996). PTSD as a chronic disorder. In S. Soreff (Ed.), *Handbook for the treatment of the seriously mentally ill*. Seattle, WA: Hogrefe & Huber.

Goodman, L., Rosenberg, S. D., Mueser, K. T., & Drake, R. (1997). Physical and sexual assault history in woman with serious mental illness: Prevalence, impact, treatment, and future directions. *Schizophrenia Bulletin*, *23*, 685–696.

Gray-Little, B., Williams, V. S., & Hancock, T. D. (1997). An item response theory analysis of the Rosenberg Self-Esteem Scale. *Personality and Social Psychology Bulletin*, *23*, 443–451.

Greenfield, S. F., Strakowski, S. M., Tohen, M., Batson, S. C., & Kolbrener, M. L. (1994). Childhood abuse in first-episode psychosis. *British Journal of Psychiatry*, *164*, 831–834.

Helzer, J. E., Robins, L. E., & McEvoy, L. (1987). Post-traumatic stress disorder in the general population. *New England Journal of Medicine, 317*, 1630–1634.

Horowitz, M. J. (1993). Stress-response syndromes: A review of posttraumatic stress and adjustment disorders. In J. P. Wilson & B. Raphael (Eds.), *International handbook of traumatic stress syndromes*. New York: Plenum.

Kay, S. R., Fiszbein, A., & Opler, L. A. (1987). The Positive and Negative Syndrome Scale (PANSS) for Schizophrenia. *Schizophrenia Bulletin, 13*, 261–276.

Kessler, R. C., Sonnega, A., Bromet, E., Hughes, M., & Nelson, C. B. (1995). Posttraumatic stress disorder in the National Comorbidity Survey. *Archives of General Psychiatry, 52*, 1048–1060.

Kilpatrick, D. G., Acierno, R., Resnick, H. S., Saunders, B. E., & Best, C. L. (1997). A 2-year longitudinal analysis of the relationships between violent assault and substance use in women. *Journal of Consulting and Clinical Psychology, 65*, 834–837.

Lehman, A. F. (1988). A quality of life interview for the chronically mentally ill. *Evaluation and Program Planning, 11*, 51–62.

Lehman, A. F., Kernan, E., & Postrado, L. (1997). *Toolkit for evaluating quality of life for persons with severe mental illness*. Cambridge, MA: HSRI.

Mowbray, C. T., & Moxley, D. (1997). A framework for organizing consumer roles as providers for psychiatric rehabilitation. In C. Mowbray, D. Moxley, C. Jasper, & L. Howell (Eds.), *Consumers as providers in psychiatric rehabilitation*. Columbia, MD: International Association of Psychosocial Rehabilitation Services.

Mueser, K. T., Goodman, L. B., Trumbetta, S. L., Rosenberg, S. D., Osher, F. C., Vidaver, R., & Auciello, P. (1998). Trauma and posttraumatic stress disorder in severe mental illness. *Journal of Consulting and Clinical Psychology, 66*, 493–499.

Overall, J. E., & Gorham, D. R. (1962). Brief Psychiatric Rating Scale. *Psychological Reports, 10*, 799–812.

Paykel, E. (1978). Contribution of life events to causation of psychiatric illness. *Psychological Medicine, 8*, 245–254.

Rosenberg, M. (1979). *Conceiving the self*. New York: Basic Books.

Schutte, K. K., Hearst, J., & Moos, R. H. (1997). Gender differences in the relations between depressive symptoms and drinking behavior among problem drinkers: A three-wave study. *Journal of Consulting and Clinical Psychology, 65*, 392–404.

Singh, M. M., & Kay, S. R. (1975). A comparative study of haloperidol and chlorapromazine in terms of clinical effects and therapeutic reversal with benztropine in schizophrenia: Theoretical implications for potency differences among neuroleptics. *Psychopharmacologia, 43*, 103–113.

Solomon, P., & Draine, J. (1997). Consumers as providers in psychiatric rehabilitation. In P. Corrigan & D. Giffort (Eds.), *Building teams and programs for effective psychiatric rehabilitation*. San Francisco: Jossey-Bass.

Trumbetta, S., McHugo, G. J., & Drake, R. E. (1997). *EIDP study interview reliability report*. Concord, NH: Dartmouth University.

Weathers, F. W., Litz, B. T., Herman, D. C., Huska, J. A., & Keane, T. M. (1993, October). *The PTSD checklist: Reliability, validity, and diagnostic utility.* Paper presented at the annual meeting of the International Society for Traumatic Stress Studies, San Antonio, TX.

Zilberg, N., Weiss, D., & Horowitz, M. J. (1982). Impact of Event Scale: A cross-validation study and some empirical evidence. *Journal of Consulting and Clinical Psychology, 50,* 407–414.

Zlotnick, C., Warshaw, M., Shea, M. T., & Keller, M. B. (1997). Trauma and chronic depression among patients with anxiety disorders. *Journal of Consulting and Clinical Psychology, 65,* 333–336.

Zlotnick, C., Zakriski, A., Shea, M. T., Costello, E., Begin, A., Pearlstein, T., & Simpson, E. (1996). Long-term sequelae of childhood sexual abuse: Support for a complex PTSD. *Journal of Traumatic Stress 9,* 195–205.

CHAPTER TWO

A PRIMER OF CLOSED HEAD INJURY SEQUELAE IN POST-TRAUMATIC STRESS DISORDER

MICHAEL R. BASSO and **ELANA NEWMAN**

Department of Psychology, University of Tulsa, Tulsa, Oklahoma, USA

By definition, an individual diagnosed with post-traumatic stress disorder (PTSD) has been exposed to a serious threat of physical harm that engenders concomitant feelings of fear, helplessness, or horror (American Psychiatric Asociation, 1994). According to the current diagnostic taxonomy, PTSD may develop when the person witnesses harm against someone else or learns of harm occurring to an intimate other. Yet, all too often, PTSD is associated with the direct experience of physical injury through assault, accident, or other violence. As such, individuals with PTSD are at increased risk of having sustained a head injury, particularly during the traumatic events that elicited the PTSD symptoms (Knight, 1996). Consistent with this assertion, there are indications that individuals who sustain a head injury are increasingly likely to develop subsequent PTSD (Bryant & Harvey, 1998; Chemtob et al., 1998), with the prevalence of PTSD in this population estimated to be as high as 30% (Bryant & Harvey, 1996). Moreover, among people with PTSD, those who have sustained head injuries are apt to have more severe symptoms than those who have not (Chemtob et al., 1998).

Granted, these findings neither indicate that all patients with PTSD have sustained a head injury nor do they suggest that all individuals who sustain a head injury will display PTSD symptoms (cf. Sbordone & Liter, 1995). Nonetheless, it seems likely that some individuals who sustain a head injury will subsequently develop

PTSD. Because investigators have only recently elaborated upon this possibility, the apparent comorbid presentation of PTSD and head injury may not be recognized. Owing to their similar presentations, head injury symptoms may be mistakenly attributed to PTSD, and vice versa. To clarify these issues, the present chapter serves as a primer regarding the neurobehavioral effects of head injury in adults and highlights the similarities and differences in the presentation and treatment of PTSD and head injury.

Head Injury

Epidemiology

In the United States, it is estimated that one-half million people sustain head injuries each year (Kraus, et al., 1984). Approximately 90% of these injuries are classified as mild, with the individual losing consciousness for less than 30–60 minutes (Kraus, Fife, & Conroy, 1987). Men are twice as likely as women to sustain such injuries, with overall peak ages of these injuries ranging from 10–34 years. Most head injuries occur during motor vehicle accidents, followed in frequency of occurrence by falls and assaults (Kraus & Nourjah, 1988). Because the majority of head injuries are mild, relatively few individuals require hospitalization for more than 1 to 2 days.

Pathophysiology of Head Injuries

When a head injury occurs, either of two events generally take place. The person's head may serve to stop the motion of a rapidly decelerating object (e.g., being struck with an object during an assault), or the person's head may rapidly decelerate as it impacts a static object (e.g., striking against the dashboard of a car during an accident). As a result of these rapid acceleration-deceleration forces, several mechanisms of brain damage tend to take place. Contusions, or bruises to brain tissue, occur as the brain decelerates against the rough interior surfaces of the cranium, particularly over the frontal and temporal lobes. Other processes that may injure the outer surface, or cortex, of the brain include depressed skull fractures and hematomas (collections of blood and fluid over the brain surface). These lesions are apt to yield circumscribed areas of brain dysfunction, which in turn may result in a corresponding circumscribed area of cognitive deficit.

More common than contusions, fractures, or hematomas, however, is diffuse axonal damage. Axons are a component of nerve cell anatomy and serve as the "wiring" of the brain. Neurons communicate with one another through their axonal connections. During a head injury, the rapid deceleration or impact of the head against an object may strain axons to the point that they shear and sever. This microscopic damage to axons is not restricted to the location of impact against the head (Povlishock, 1986), with damage to cells in the cortex, lower brainstem, or upper brainstem possible (Gennarelli, 1986). As a result of axonal shearing, the wiring of the brain is disrupted, thereby decreasing an individual's capacity to process information in an efficient manner. With each of the mechanisms outlined here, as more force is exerted against the head, more damage occurs. Contusions, fractures, and hematomas tend to occur with more severe injuries, whereas axonal damage tends to occur with nearly all injuries. Notably, axonal shearing may even occur in the absence of a loss of consciousness, wherein the individual may be only dazed from an injury (Povlishock & Coburn, 1989).

Classifying Severity of Injury

Severity of head injury is classified in a number of ways. One index of severity is length of unconsciousness secondary to head injury. The longer an individual is unconscious and unresponsive to stimulation, the more severe the injury. Although somewhat varied, mild head injury tends to be defined as a period of unconsciousness not exceeding 20–60 minutes. In comparison, moderate head injury often is defined as a period of unconsciousness greater than an hour and not exceeding 1 day, with severe injury being greater than 1 day. Alternatively, injury severity is sometimes measured by depth of coma. For example, the Glasgow Coma Scale (Teasdale & Jennett, 1974) assesses the individual's capacity to respond to commands, express coherent speech, and open his or her eyes in response to stimulation. As the person is able to perform these activities, more points are assigned. Mild head injuries tend to be given scores of 13–15, moderate injuries are assigned scores of 9–12, and scores falling below 9 indicate a severe injury.

Cognitive Sequelae

Memory

Perhaps the most common cognitive symptom resulting from head injury is forgetfulness. In some instances, the individual may have difficulty recalling events leading up to the injury, and this is described as retrograde amnesia (RA). The time period forgotten prior to the injury tends to increase with severity of injury. RA may remain after the initial period of acute recovery is concluded, but the time frame of forgotten material tends to shrink as the person recovers.

Other forms of forgetfulness will tend to be seen primarily during the acute recovery from injury. In particular, post-traumatic amnesia (PTA) refers to an inability to form continuous memories, such that the individual appears confused and disoriented. PTA tends to encompass events during the injury and immediately following it.

Because of the combination of RA and PTA, many individuals who have sustained even mild injuries may have little or no recollection of the events leading up to, during, and after the injury. When the patient is no longer confused and is reliably orientated to time and place, the PTA is assumed to be concluded. Yet, despite the cessation of PTA, memory disturbance can continue to occur. For instance, patients may report an inability to recall names of people, or they might forget to meet obligations. If a student, the patient may have increased difficulty learning and recalling facts and other materials from classes. Such forgetfulness in which the individual has difficulty maintaining new memories is referred to as anterograde amnesia, and it may remain chronic long after the injury has been sustained.

Attention

Another common cognitive complaint of head injured patients is difficulty with attention. In particular, divided attention, or the capacity to simultaneously pay attention to multiple information sources, may be diminished. For instance, the individual may be unable to converse with one person in a group setting, because the multiple conversations are too distracting. Span of attention also tends to be affected, and, as such, the amount of information that an individual may concentrate upon at any given time is reduced. Furthermore, sustained attention is often diminished, such that the individual may have difficulty maintaining attention over any extended length of time. In some instances, focusing on even a situation comedy for the entire program may be too taxing for the individual.

Speed of Information Processing

In addition to attention problems, patients sustaining a head injury have a slowed speed of information processing (Hugenholtz et al., 1988). Accordingly, they may have difficulty keeping up with lectures, conversations, or television or radio broadcasts. Such slowing probably diminishes a patient's ability to reason through problems, pay attention, or learn new information.

Problem Solving

Individuals sustaining head injuries also tend to have difficulties with problem solving. In particular, they may have a reduced capacity to identify and set appropriate goals, plan how to achieve them, carry out goal-oriented behaviors, and monitor progress toward achieving the goals (Lezak, 1983). Continuing to engage in inappropriate or unsuccessful behaviors is especially salient in this population, and such a problem is called perseveration. Impulsivity and disinhibition may also occur, with the individual acting in a socially inappropriate manner or acting without adequate forethought and planning.

Occurrence of Cognitive Symptoms

As may be expected, the occurrence of these cognitive symptoms varies across patients, with more severely injured patients showing more cognitive impairment. For instance, a patient with a mild injury may demonstrate only mild attention and memory problems, whereas an individual who has sustained a severe injury may display severe neurobehavioral impairment across nearly all areas of cognitive function.

The chronicity of cognitive symptoms also seems to vary as a function of injury severity. Accordingly, cognitive difficulties associated with severe injuries take longer to remit than those associated with mild injuries. Indeed, individuals who have sustained a severe head injury are more likely to have unremitting cognitive symptoms than those with mild symptoms. In contrast, individuals with the mildest head injuries (sustaining no loss of consciousness) are likely to recover fully within several days (Barth et al., 1989). With loss of consciousness, individuals with mild injuries may take several months to completely recover (Levin et al., 1987) but are apt to demonstrate no residual cognitive deficits 1 year after their injury (Dikmen, McLean, & Temkin, 1986). Yet, as many as 10%–15% of mild head injury patients have persistent cognitive difficulties (Alexander, 1995). Persisting symptoms are more likely attributable to psychological factors than to brain dysfunction associated with the injury (cf. Bohnen, Twijnstra, & Jolles, 1992). Nonetheless, individuals more than 40 years of age are also at increased risk of having unremitting residual deficits from their injuries (Binder, 1986). Because the brains of older patients are thought to have less resilience to injury, some residual symptoms in older patients may be attributable to unremitting brain dysfunction.

Somatic Symptoms

As may be expected of anyone who has sustained physical trauma, individuals sustaining head injuries tend to have somatic complaints. Generally, these symptoms are experienced soon after consciousness returns, and they occur in the majority of patients (Rutherford, 1989). In particular, somatic complaints tend to occur regardless of injury severity, with even mildly injured individuals experiencing them. Physical symptoms also seem to have a long duration, with some data showing that somatic complaints remain present in approximately 45% of patients for as long as 5 years after injury (Rutherford, 1989).

One of the most common problems is fatigue. While recovering from an injury, patients may not be able to resume their normal activity levels because of decreased energy levels and rapid onset of exhaustion. Perhaps contributing to this problem is insomnia, which is also experienced by a large proportion of patients with head injuries. Early during the course of recovery, headache, hypersensitivity to noises, increased sensitivity to light, blurred or double vision, nausea, vomiting, and dizziness are especially apt to occur, but nausea and vomiting become less common after the acute recovery period (Rutherford, 1989). Similarly, headaches and dizziness tend to be experienced less frequently, but some patients will continue to experience these symptoms for months afterward.

Affective Sequelae

In addition to cognitive and somatic symptoms, head injuries tend to yield symptoms of affective disturbance. As the individual emerges from unconsciousness, irritability, agitation, combativeness, and emotional lability are apt to be present. For instance, the individual may be far more short tempered than prior to the injury, and sudden and uncontrollable outbursts of laughing or crying may occur. As confusion and disorientation diminish, the intensity of these symptoms is likely to decrease, but some symptoms of lability and short temper may tend to remain chronic for months after injury. Family members of injured patients may report that they are more aggressive, angry, and irritable than prior to the injury.

Depression

Some patients may display apathy, behavioral inertia, social withdrawal, loss of interests, emotional numbness, and blunted affect, which may be taken as symptoms of depression. Indeed, depressive symptoms are likely in the aftermath of a head injury, and as many as 25% of head-injured patients may actually enter a major depressive episode within 12 months of injury (Robinson & Jorge, 1994). Apparently, the presenting symptoms of depression are apt to change as the individual recovers from the head injury. Early during the course of recovery, decreased appetite, insomnia, weight loss, and diurnal variation are significantly more common in depressed patients. However, after 6–12 months, depressed individuals are no more likely to display these symptoms than nondepressed head-injured patients. Rather, depressed patients are more likely to show poor concentration, diminished libido, and early morning awakening in addition to negative self-perceptions (Robinson & Jorge, 1994).

Secondary Mania

In contrast to depressive symptoms, elevated and expansive mood may result from head injury, and, in some cases, patients may exhibit secondary mania. Robinson and Jorge (1994) estimate that 9% of patients sustaining a head injury will develop a manic episode within a year of being injured. These episodes tended to last approximately 2 months regardless of whether the patient received treatment for the disorder. Similar to patients with major depression after head injury, Robinson and Jorge suggested that secondary mania is associated with localized brain lesions involving the temporal lobes and orbital regions of the frontal lobes.

Anxiety Disorders

Estimated prevalence rates of anxiety disorders in head-injured patients range from 30%–65%, with symptoms being present as early as 3 months (Epstein & Ursano, 1994) and as late as 7 years postinjury (Brooks, McKinlay, Symington, Beattie, & Campsie, 1987). These rates are higher than reported in the general population, and, similar to the general population, anxiety disorders tend to coincide with depression in many patients (Robinson & Jorge, 1994). It is uncertain whether anxiety symptoms are chronic or only associated with acute symptoms of head injury. Some studies suggest that anxiety symptoms are short lived, with most anxiety symptoms supposedly remitting within 6 months of the head injury (Robinson & Jorge, 1994). In contrast, other studies imply that anxiety symptoms remain chronic (Brooks et al., 1987). These data demonstrate significant inconsistencies among empirical studies, and reflect a relative paucity of research in this area.

Regarding diagnoses of specific anxiety disorders, reliable prevalence estimates are generally lacking. Lezak (1978) reported that 76% of head-injured patients display persistent tension, worry, fearfulness, perplexity, distractibility, and fatigue, symptoms that are highly consistent with a presentation of generalized anxiety disorder (GAD). Yet, there is little systematic research examining whether such patients actually meet diagnostic criteria for GAD. Consequently, prevalence rates of GAD in patients with a head injury remain uncertain. Similarly, to our knowledge, there are few, if any, controlled studies of panic or phobic disorders in this population, thereby providing no clear understanding of how commonly these disorders occur secondary to head injury.

Post-Traumatic Stress Disorder

Exposure to a qualifying traumatic event is a necessary but insufficient condition for the presence of PTSD. According to the *Diagnostic and Statistical Manual of Mental Disorders (4th edition; DSM-IV;* American Psychiatric Association, 1994), PTSD requires exposure to a stressor (Criterion A), as explained earlier, and three other groups of symptoms, Criterion B (reexperiencing symptoms), Criterion C (avoidance and numbing symptoms), and Criterion D (hyperarousal symptoms). Criterion B refers to symptoms indicative of reexperiencing the trauma, such as intrusive recollections, psychological or physiological distress when exposed to events, flashbacks, and distressing dreams of the events. Criterion C refers to avoidant and numbing symptomatology, such as efforts to avoid trauma-related thoughts, feelings, or situations; psychogenic amnesia for salient aspects of the experience; diminished interest in activities; detachment; restricted range of affect; and a sense of a foreshortened future. Criterion D refers to symptoms of increased arousal such as sleep difficulty, irritability, concentration impairment, hypervigilance, and exaggerated startle response. To reach criterion for PTSD, the person must have one intrusive symptom (Criterion B), three avoidance/numbing symptoms (Criterion C), and two arousal symptoms (Criterion D) for at least 1 month. In addition, these symptoms must be associated with symptomatic distress or impairment in functioning.

Like other anxiety disorders, the prevalence of PTSD among head-injured patients is uncertain. Some researchers assert that PTSD is a common outcome of head trauma, whereas others hold that it is a rare or nonexistent outcome (Boake, 1996; Sbordone &

Liter, 1995).[1] Contributing to this controversy is the relative paucity of controlled research concerning the occurrence of PTSD in this population. Some case studies and small empirical studies have demonstrated that PTSD is possible, if not likely, following head injury (Bryant, 1996; King, 1997). For example, Wright and Telford (1996) found that PTSD symptoms are common after head injury. At both 6 months and 3 years subsequent to injury, 40%–55% of patients reported intrusive images of the trauma, reliving the events of their injury, avoidance of thoughts concerning their injury, diminished interests, sleep difficulties, irritability, poor concentration, exaggerated startle response, and increased physiological reactivity.

Apart from symptoms, formal diagnoses of PTSD also appear common after head injury. Using a self-report measure to diagnose PTSD, Rattok and Ross (1993) examined 35 head injury patients and found that 20% could be characterized as having PTSD. Using a structured clinical interview to diagnose patients, Bryant and Harvey (1998) found that 24% of 79 mild head injury patients met diagnostic criteria for PTSD 1 month postinjury. Similarly, Ohry et al. (1996) found that 33% of their sample of 24 head-injured patients met criteria for PTSD. These rates are similar to the rates of PTSD found among trauma-exposed civilians (Breslau, Davis, Andreski, & Peterson, 1991).

In contrast to these findings, other studies have found little support for the assertion that PTSD occurs in association with head injury. Warden et al. (1997) examined 47 service personnel who had sustained moderate closed head injuries and who had amnesia for the events surrounding their injury. PTSD was assessed with a semistructured interview multiple times over the 24-month duration of the study. None of the patients met full criteria for PTSD. Although they were at increased risk to report some symptoms (e.g., diminished interests, hyperarousal), none reported intrusive thoughts or reexperiencing their traumatic injuries. Similarly, in a sample of mildly injured patients, Sbordone and Liter (1995) found that no patient met diagnostic criteria for PTSD.

---

[1] For the purposes of this chapter, we have confined our discussion to examining events in which both PTSD or head injury symptoms are probable. It should be noted that a person with preexisting PTSD could sustain a head injury, and a person with head injury sequelae could develop PTSD from another event (in the absence of further head injury).

Their findings led Sbordone and Liter to assert that brain injury and PTSD are mutually exclusive disorders.

In addition to contradictory evidence regarding prevalence, details concerning the natural course of PTSD (i.e., onset, duration, etc.) subsequent to head injury are uncertain. PTSD symptoms can theoretically emerge at any point 1 month postinjury for an individual to qualify for the diagnosis, and there are case studies supporting both early and delayed onset of symptoms (Bryant, 1966; Bryant & Harvey, 1998). Although some authors believe that it is extremely rare for PTSD symptoms to be dormant for long periods of time and subsequently exacerbated in cases of head injury (e.g., Sbordone & Liter, 1995), knowledge of head injury would suggest otherwise. As the acute effects of head injury subside, the period of amnesia for events preceding and following the trauma tends to shrink. Thus, it becomes more likely that the patient will begin remembering frightening events concerning trauma, thereby eliciting traumatic stress symptoms. With respect to duration of symptoms among head-injured patients, PTSD has been documented as lasting from a few weeks to 8 years postinjury (Hibbard et al., 1998); this wide range of duration is consistent with that found in trauma survivors who have not been assessed for head injury (e.g., Foa & Meadows, 1997).

Although there is little consensus, the data reviewed here suggest that PTSD does occur after head injury. In fact, there is some evidence that head injury increases the risk of developing PTSD. Hibbard et al. (1998) examined 100 head-injured patients approximately 8 years subsequent to their injury. Regardless of injury severity, 44% of their sample demonstrated depression and anxiety disorders (including PTSD) on structured clinical interviews. These disorders developed subsequent to their head injuries, leading Hibbard et al. to hypothesize that head injury is a risk factor for mood disorders. Among combat veterans, Chemtob et al. (1998) found that those with a history of head trauma were more likely to have PTSD than those who never had sustained such an injury. Moreover, their PTSD was more severe than individuals with PTSD who had no history of head injury. Thus, there is some evidence that head injury increases the risk of developing PTSD.

Collectively, the research concerning the prevalence and course of PTSD subsequent to head injury is inconclusive. In some respects, this situation may be attributable, at least in part, to inconsistencies between studies in assessing PTSD. In some investigations, PTSD was defined by scores on self-report questionnaires, whereas other investigations assessed PTSD with structured diagnostic interviews. Given that each assessment will have varying sensitivity and specificity in detecting PTSD (Newman, Kaloupek, & Keane, 1996), it is unsurprising that PTSD may have been overdiagnosed in some studies and underdiagnosed in others. Consequently, the existing research gives indefinite estimates of PTSD prevalence in head injury. Furthermore, given that memory lapses may subside in those with head injuries, the inconsistent findings regarding PTSD prevalence and onset among the head injured may result from measurement variability in the timing of the PTSD assessments post–head injury.

Another potential contributor to this unsettled area of research is the complex relationship between head injury and PTSD. In particular, many head injury sequelae parallel PTSD symptoms. Specifically, among Criterion C symptoms of PTSD, inability to recall events of the trauma, diminished interest in pleasurable activities, and interpersonal detachment coincide with head injury sequelae. Similarly, under Criterion D, sleep disturbance, irritability, anger, poor concentration, and exaggerated response to noises may follow head injuries. Consequently, it may be especially difficult or even impossible to determine whether these symptom types are indicative of PTSD or solely reflective of head injury.

The one set of PTSD criterion symptoms in which there is no overlap with head injury symptoms are those falling within the group of Criterion B symptoms: reexperiencing the traumatic event. The reexperiencing symptoms involve recurrent distressing recollections of the event(s), nightmares, and physiological or psychological distress in response to trauma-related cues such as thoughts, body sensations, emotions, events, or locations. Among head-injured patients, trauma-related cues could include the symptoms of head injury itself (e.g., headaches, concentration difficulties, problem-solving difficulties). Alternatively, hospital personnel, who remind the head-injured client of the injury, might serve as a traumatic cue.

Notably, it is argued whether Criterion B PTSD symptoms are even possible in head-injured patients. In particular, recurrent and intrusive memories and flashbacks regarding the onset of injuries may be nonexistent because of retrograde and anterograde amnesia. In support of this assertion, Warden et al. (1997) found that none of their patients with moderate head injuries displayed any Criterion B symptoms, although many of the patients did demonstrate numerous symptoms under Criteria C and D. The authors hypothesized that patients could not re-experience the traumatic events because of amnesia secondary to brain injury. Nonetheless, according to current diagnostic criteria, it is unnecessary for an individual to directly witness a traumatic event for PTSD to develop. Rather, as head-injured patients emerge from post-traumatic amnesia, they tend to ask family and medical staff what has happened to them. As a result, they may learn about the traumatic event, thereby providing for subsequent recurrent thoughts and recollections concerning trauma.

In addition, as head-injured patients emerge from post-traumatic amnesia, they may begin to recall isolated events associated with their head injury (e.g., ambulance crews arriving on the scene, arrival at the emergency room). These circumscribed pockets of explicit traumatic memory have been reported by head-injured patients who subsequently displayed PTSD symptoms associated with these memories (King, 1996). Some authors have speculated that explicit recall of trauma-related events is unnecessary for PTSD to occur (Layton & Wardi-Zonna, 1995). Rather, implicit recollections of trauma events may yield PTSD. For instance, a patient may not have explicit recall of trauma, but implicit recall (memory without explicit knowledge of how or when information was learned) of trauma may yield emotional distress upon hearing an ambulance siren. Furthermore, certain psychological and physiological responses may be conditioned at the time of the injury, without conscious awareness. Collectively, these data and theories suggest that head-injured patients may remember events associated with their trauma. Consequently, if they report distress when recalling what they know about their injury, they may be at risk of displaying PTSD symptoms.

Assessment

These findings imply that head-injured patients will probably present with a complex array of cognitive, somatic, and affective symptoms. Because comorbid PTSD may increase the likelihood that the patient will have a complicated recovery from injury, and given that neuropsychological sequelae of head injury may complicate recovery from PTSD, it is necessary to conduct a careful evaluation and assessment of both symptom profiles. Essentially, in order to provide necessary and optimal care to the patient, a thorough assessment of symptoms is required. In this section, we detail general principles of assessment of each syndrome and highlight important distinctions and procedures for discriminating the two.

Head Injury

Although a detailed discussion concerning neuropsychological assessment of head-injured patients is beyond the scope of this paper (the interested reader may consult a thorough review of neuropsychological assessment by Lezak, 1995), we make several general comments in this regard. In planning the scope of assessment, several aspects of function should be considered, including intelligence, executive function, language, memory, attention, speed of information processing, perceptual acuity (including visual-spatial perception), and motor function. Affective symptoms, somatic complaints, and self-reports of cognitive problems should also be assessed, and this can be done with standardized measures as well as informal interviews. With the latter method of assessment, the clinician should pay careful attention to the nature, severity, and chronology of the patient's complaints, since this information will be relevant to interpreting the psychometric data. Accordingly, information regarding loss of consciousness, presence of retrograde and anterograde amnesia, and nature of head injury (i.e., contusions, hemorrhages, depressed skull fractures, radiological studies, etc.) should be obtained, and it is helpful to gain corroborating information concerning these details from medical records or family members. In order to obtain a meaningful and relatively stable estimate of the patient's acute postinjury level of cognitive function, an assessment should probably not be conducted at least until posttraumatic amnesia has cleared.

PTSD

When conducting an assessment of PTSD, the clinician should first establish that the person has indeed experienced an event or events that meet both Criterion A requirements. Specifically, the clinician should ascertain that events involved both actual or threatened injury to oneself or others and concomitant feelings of fear or helplessness. Toward this end, several novel instruments for assessing Criterion A requirements have been developed (see Norris & Riad, 1996, or Newman, Kaloupek, & Keane, 1996, for reviews). Apart from such measures, it is important to assess exactly what the patient recalls and what the patient (not the clinician) believes were the worst aspects of the traumatic event. After open-ended questioning, direct and behaviorally specific factual questions regarding the trauma can enhance accurate disclosure. For example, rather than asking whether one was battered, it is more effective to ask whether one was "attacked, beaten, pinched, or hit by another." Next, the clinician should systematically inquire as to whether fear, horror, or helplessness were present at the time of the event or thereafter.

If the head-injured patient has been exposed to a life-threatening event but fails to describe intense fear, horror, or helplessness in response to the trauma, the systematic assessment of the requisite number of B, C, and D PTSD criterion symptoms still may be warranted. Given the likelihood that a head-injured person's memory trauma may increase as the acute post–head injury symptoms subside, these symptoms may inform diagnostic formulation and treatment planning in the event that memory lapses do indeed remit. Furthermore, because head-injured patients may begin remembering upsetting aspects concerning their trauma and thereby elicit new symptoms, it may be useful to periodically reassess for PTSD symptoms, regardless of whether an initial diagnosis of PTSD is merited. Despite such careful assessment, individuals with PTSD still may have difficulty recalling their trauma experiences because of denial, amnesia, avoidance, minimization, and/or cognitive impairment. Thus, the use of police or other collateral reports may provide details of the injury and the patient's initial reaction to the trauma events to allow a Criterion A assessment.

Upon verifying that Criterion A is satisfied or partially satisfied, Criteria B, C, and D symptoms of PTSD should be assessed. A multimodal assessment strategy is recommended, because no existing single measure can function as a definitive indicator of PTSD

(Keane, Wolfe, & Taylor, 1987; Malloy, Fairbank, & Keane, 1983). Although a comprehensive description of psychometrically validated instruments is beyond the scope of this paper, there are many assessment methods available that are probably valid for use with head-injured patients (see Briere, 1997; Newman et al., 1996; and Wilson & Keane, 1997, for reviews). When time and resources are unlimited and detailed information is needed, we advocate the use of a semi-structured interview for PTSD, such as the Clinician Administered PTSD Scale (Weathers & Litz, 1994), validated PTSD rating scales, and general symptom measures, supplemented with collateral information from family and others.

In conducting a multimodal assessment of the head-injured person, specific clinical guidelines may be useful. When assessing Criterion B symptoms, the clinician should establish which, if any, aspects of the injury are involuntarily reexperienced as intrusions, flashbacks, or nightmares. Specification of such details can help determine what should be the focus of PTSD exposure treatment. Similarly, it is important to determine which specific trauma-related cues evoke distress or physiological arousal. Otherwise, if anxiety or somatic distress occur on a generalized basis, the symptom pattern may reflect head injury sequelae instead of PTSD.

Regarding Criteria C and D symptoms, there are no definite means of distinguishing certain symptoms of PTSD from postconcussive symptoms. Although some symptoms are solely associated with PTSD (e.g., avoidance of trauma-related cues, feelings of detachment, emotional numbness, a foreshortened future, and hypervigilance for threat-related cues), other symptoms may be confused with lingering effects of head injury. For example, under most circumstances, insomnia, irritability, and inattention are difficult to differentiate as PTSD symptoms or head injury sequelae. However, the subtle phenomenology of some symptoms may distinguish etiology. In PTSD, hypervigilance and exaggerated startle response reflect a client's increased physiological arousal and vigilance for danger in the environment. By comparison, in head injury, hypersensitivity to noise may be more reflective of pain and other somatic responses rather than hyperarousal. Similarly, in PTSD, psychogenic amnesia for acute events is typically restricted to salient trauma-related aspects of the event, whereas retrograde and posttraumatic amnesia may be more diffuse and less specific. In head injury diminished interest in pleasurable activities may reflect overwhelming fatigue, whereas in PTSD lack of interest is a symptom in and of itself. Although research needs to investigate and elaborate upon these proposed distinctions, these suggestions may be useful to the clinician in generating hypotheses concerning particular patients.

Differential Diagnosis of PTSD and Head Injury Sequelae

Granted, these suggested approaches and rules of thumb may not be applicable with each patient, so differentiating symptoms of PTSD from head trauma sequelae may be nearly impossible in some instances. In such cases, the purpose of the assessment will dictate how best to make diagnostic decisions. If assessment is being performed to assist in treatment planning, a liberal approach to assessment may be acceptable. Specifically, when considering symptoms that may reflect PTSD or post-concussive syndrome, it probably would not harm the patient to initially assume that symptoms are attributable to both PTSD and head trauma. As symptoms remit or a clearer diagnostic picture emerges, treatment plans may be refined. Alternatively, if the differential diagnosis is the key aim of the evaluation, a conservative approach to assessment may be warranted. In this case, we suggest that only unambiguous symptoms be linked to the respective syndromes. In particular, symptoms that may be attributed to either traumatic stress or head injury sequelae might be omitted from the pool of symptoms necessary to reach PTSD diagnostic criteria. For example, for Criterion C of PTSD, the presence of general amnesia might not be considered as counting toward the three required symptoms. Similarly, for head injury sequelae, shared symptoms with PTSD should be disregarded, and the clinician should look for unique memory, attention, problem-solving, somatic, and affective symptoms that do not overlap for PTSD as evidence of head injury symptoms. Although these decision rules are arbitrary and require empirical verification, they may serve as useful guides to the clinician. Insofar as a patient is thoroughly assessed, the probability of PTSD symptoms or head injury symptoms going undetected will be diminished, thereby increasing the likelihood of a better treatment outcome.

Treatment of Head Injury Symptoms

It should be recognized that individuals with head injuries frequently require complex and intensive medical interventions that are beyond the scope of this brief review. In particular, in the acute postinjury period, disruptions of consciousness, cerebral edema, and hemorrhages tend to be treated medically. In the post-acute phase of recovery, especially after post-traumatic amnesia has cleared, subsequent pain, mood disorders, and post-traumatic seizures are often targets of medical treatment.

Apart from medical management, a critical aspect of treatment is education. Perhaps because health care providers often fail to recognize that head injury symptoms may linger for weeks or months after injury, patients are often ignorant of their expected course of recovery (Mittenberg & Burton, 1994). Patients may feel that they are "going crazy" or "losing their mind" when, several weeks after even a mild injury, they continue to have difficulty concentrating, remembering, or maintaining control over their temper. Family members may similarly become frustrated with patients owing to a lack of knowledge concerning head injury recovery. Thus, patients and family should be informed of the various cognitive, affective, and somatic complaints that are apt to occur after injury and should be aware that these symptoms are apt to gradually remit (at least partially) over the course of several weeks or months (cf. Mittenberg & Burton, 1994). Patients may also benefit from receiving specific advice. For instance, they may be advised to "take it easy" and not overextend themselves as they begin to feel fatigued. Use of mnemonic cues (e.g., task list, daily planner) may be recommended, and tips on eliminating distractions (e.g., shut off the TV while concentrating, focus only on one activity at a time) may be helpful to the patient. Essentially, patients should expect and recognize that they may not return to their normal level of function for several weeks or months after the injury, but there are ways in which they may compensate or adapt to symptoms in the meantime.

PTSD Treatment

Several psychotherapeutic interventions have demonstrated great efficacy in treatment of symptoms of PTSD, with most treatments involving exposure (Foa & Meadows, 1997; Solomon, Gerrity, & Muff, 1992). With these interventions, traumatic experiences are repeatedly recalled, eventually eliminating conditioned emotional responses to trauma. In addition, cognitive therapy has been effective with some PTSD patients. Such treatment involves reinterpreting the cognitive-affective meaning of traumatic events, and it addresses trauma-related issues such as grief, loss, betrayal, justice, and evil (Newman, Riggs, & Roth, 1997). Antidepressant medication can also be beneficial in reducing the frequency or intensity of (a) intrusive symptoms, (b) avoidance symptoms, (c) hyperarousal, (d) impulse dysregulation, (e) sleep difficulties, and (f) acute dissociative episodes (Davidson & van der Kolk, 1996). Notably, many PTSD experts recommend the use of multiple-drug therapy to tailor medication regimens to comorbid problems (possibly those associated with head injury) and to adjust for changes in the course of PTSD over time.

The patient's subjective sense of safety is a central therapeutic concern because PTSD treatment requires that an individual identify and describe traumatic memories, feelings, and symptoms. Of great importance is the patient's trust in the clinician, since this influences the capacity to communicate overwhelming feelings and reactions. The interviewer's sensitivity in the form and pacing of treatment can foster this safe atmosphere, especially given head-injured patients' tendency toward irritability and dysphoria.

Merging the psychosocial treatment of head injury and the psychological treatment of PTSD can be difficult at times. In particular, psychosocial treatment of head injury symptoms may be difficult to implement among patients, because discussion of pain management or memory aids may cue recall of trauma in patients with PTSD. It may be helpful to alert patients to this possibility through psychoeducation, and address trauma-specific symptoms with the patient, prior to focusing on psychosocial treatment. In fact, exposure treatment targeting the symptoms of head injury might be effective. Furthermore, while head-injured patients may need limited choices to prevent them from feeling overtaxed, it is important for a client who feels helpless from the impact of PTSD symptoms to perceive a sense of agency in the therapeutic relationship. Hence, clinicians need to allow the client to have as many choices and opportunities as possible to feel in control of the process, without overwhelming the client's cognitive or emotional capacity.

Finally, if clients have experienced a head injury as a result of human-induced trauma exposure (e.g., rape, domestic violence), trust of others, especially those in authority, can be difficult (Herman, 1992). It is important to approach clients in a non-authoritarian manner and carefully focus on building rapport and trust. Explicit discussion of potential changes in trust may facilitate a more productive therapeutic alliance.

Summary

Individuals who experience head injuries may in fact be suffering from (a) symptoms attributable to head injury, (b) symptoms attributable to PTSD, or (c) symptoms attributable to both. We have reviewed the current research in the field, the similarities and differences between the two, and made some clinical suggestions based on the current evidence. It is clear from this review that PTSD researchers need to systematically examine and quantify head injury in their studies so that we can begin to determine what is caused by the psychological and physical trauma distinct from head injury. Similarly, individuals who study head injury need to systematically assess PTSD in their samples to determine the role of PTSD symptomatology after head injury. Only by combining these perspectives can the field advance and assist patient care. In the meantime, clinicians should entertain both possibilities when conducting clinical assessments.

References

Alexander, M. P. (1995). Mild traumatic brain injury: Pathophysiology, natural history, and clinical management. *Neurology, 45,* 1253–1260.

American Psychiatric Association. (1980). *Diagnostic and statistical manual of mental disorders* (3rd ed.). Washington, DC: Author.

American Psychiatric Association. (1994). *Diagnostic and statistical manual of mental disorders* (4th ed.). Washington, DC: Author.

Barth, J. T., Alves, W. M., Ryan, T. V., Macciocchi, S. N., Rimel, R. W., Jane, J. A., & Nelson, W. E. (1989). Mild head injury in sports: Neuropsychological sequelae and recovery of function. In H. S. Levin, H. M. Eisenberg, & A. L. Benton (Eds.), *Mild head injury* (pp. 257–275). New York: Oxford University Press.

Binder, L. M. (1986). Persisting symptoms after mild head injury: A review of the postconcussive syndrome. *Journal of Clinical and Experimental Neuropsychology, 8,* 323–346.

Boake, C. (1996). Do patients with mild brain injuries have posttraumatic stress disorder too? *Journal of Head Trauma Rehabilitation, 11,* 98–100.

Bohnen, N., Twijnstra, A., & Jolles, J. (1992). Post-traumatic and emotional symptoms in different subgroups of patients with mild head injury. *Brain Injury, 6,* 481–487.

Breslau, N., Davis, G. C., Andreski, P., & Peterson, E. (1991). Traumatic events and posttraumatic stress disorder in an urban population of young adults. *Archives of General Psychiatry, 48,* 216–222.

Briere, J. (1997). *Psychological assessment of adult posttraumatic states.* Washington, DC: American Psychological Association.

Brooks, N., McKinlay, W., Symington, C., Beattie, A., & Campsie, L. (1987). Return to work within the first seven years of severe head injury. *Brain Injury, 1,* 5–19.

Bryant, R. A. (1996). Post-traumatic stress disorder, flashbacks, and pseudo-memories in closed head injury. *Journal of Traumatic Stress, 9,* 621–629.

Bryant, R. A., & Harvey, A. G. (1996). Initial post-traumatic stress responses following motor vehicle accidents. *Journal of Traumatic Stress, 9,* 223–234.

Bryant, R. A., & Harvey, A. G. (1998). Relationship between acute stress disorder and post-traumatic stress disorder following mild traumatic brain injury. *American Journal of Psychiatry, 155,* 625–629.

Chemtob, C. M., Muraoka, M. Y., Wu-Holt, P., Fairbank, J. A., Hamada, R. S., & Keane, T. M. (1998). Head injury and combat-related post-traumatic stress disorder. *Journal of Nervous and Mental Disease, 186,* 701–708.

Davidson, J. R. T., & van der Kolk, B. A. (1996). The pharmacological treatment of post-traumatic stress disorder. In B. van der Kolk, A. C. McFarlane, & L. Weisaeth (Eds.), *Traumatic stress: The effects of overwhelming experience on mind, body, and the society* (pp. 510–523). New York: Guilford Press.

Dikmen, S., McLean, A., & Temkin, N. (1986). Neuropsychological and psychosocial consequences of minor head injury. *Journal of Neurology, Neurosurgery, and Psychiatry, 49,* 1227–1232.

Epstein, R. S., & Ursano, R. J. (1994). Anxiety disorders. In J. M. Silver, S. C. Yudofsky, & R. E. Hales (Eds.), *Neuropsychiatry of traumatic brain injury* (pp. 285–312). Washington, DC: American Psychiatric Press.

Foa, E. B., & Meadows, E. A. (1997). Psychosocial treatments for post-trauamtic stress disorder: A critical review. *Annual Review of Psychology, 48,* 449–480.

Genarelli, T. (1986). Mechanisms and pathophysiology of cerebral concussion. *Journal of Head Trauma Rehabilitation, 1,* 23–29.

Herman, J. L. (1992). *Trauma and recovery.* New York: BasicBooks.

Hibbard, M. R., Uysal, S., Kepler, K., Bogdany, J., & Silver, J. (1998). Axis I psychopathology in individuals with traumatic brain injury. *Journal of Head Trauma Rehabilitation, 13,* 24–39.

Hugenholtz, H., Stuss, D. T., Stethem, L. L., & Richard, M. T. (1988). How long does it take to recover from a mild concussion? *Neurosurgery, 22,* 853–858.

Keane, T. M., Wolfe, J., & Taylor, K. L. (1987) Post-traumatic stress disorder: Evidence for diagnostic validity and methods of psychological assessment. *Journal of Clinical Psychology, 43,* 32–43.

King, N. S. (1997). Post-traumatic stress disorder and head injury as a dual diagnosis: "Islands" of memory as a mechanism. *Journal of Neurology, Neurosurgery, and Psychiatry, 62,* 82–84.

Knight, J. A. (1996) Neuropsychological Assessment in post-traumatic stress disorder. In J. P. Wilson & T. M. Keane (Eds.), *Assessing psychological trauma and PTSD: A handbook for practitioners* (pp. 448–492). New York: Guilford Press.

Kraus, J. F., Black, M. A., Hessol, N., Ley, P., Rokaw, W., Sullivan, C., Bowers, S., Knowlton, S., & Marshall, L. (1984). The incidence of acute brain injury and serious impairment in a defined population. *American Journal of Epidemiology, 119,* 186–201.

Kraus, J. F., Fife, D., & Conroy, C. (1987). Incidence, severity, and outcomes of brain injuries involving bicycles. *American Journal of Public Health, 77,* 76–78.

Kraus, J. F., & Nourjah, P. (1988). The epidemiology of mild, uncomplicated brain injury. *Journal of Trauma, 28,* 1637–1643.

Levin, H., Mattis, S., Ruff, R., Eisenberg, H., Marshall, L., Tabaddor, K., High, W., & Frankowski, R. (1987). Neurobehavioral outcome following minor head injury: A three center study. *Journal of Neurosurgery, 66,* 234–243.

Lezak, M. (1978). Subtle sequelae of brain damage: Perplexity, distractibility and fatigue. *American Journal of Physical Medicine, 57,* 9–15.

Lezak, M. (1983). *Neuropsychological assessment* (2nd ed.). New York: Oxford University Press.

Lezak, M. (1995). *Neuropsychological assessment* (3rd ed.). New York: Oxford University Press.

Malloy, P. F., Fairbank, J. A., & Keane, T. M. (1983). Validation of a multimethod assessment of post-traumatic stress disorders in Vietnam veterans. *Journal of Consulting and Clinical Psychology, 83,* 488–494.

Mittenberg, W., & Burton, D. B. (1994). A survey of treatments for postconcussion syndrome. *Brain Injury, 8,* 429–437.

Newman, E., Kaloupek, D. G., & Keane, T. M. (1996). Assessment of PTSD in clinical and research settings. In B. van der Kolk, A. C. McFarlane, & L. Weisaeth (Eds.), *Traumatic stress: The effects of overwhelming experience on mind, body, and the society* (pp. 242–275). New York: Guilford Press.

Newman, E., Riggs, D., & Roth, S. (1997). Thematic resolution, PTSD, and complex PTSD: The relationship between meaning and trauma-related diagnoses. *Journal of Traumatic Stress, 10*, 197–213.

Norris, F. H., & Riad, J. K. (1996). Standardized self-report measures of civilian trauma and post-traumatic stress disorder. In J. P. Wilson & T. M. Keane (Eds.), *Assessing psychological trauma and PTSD: A handbook for practitioners* (pp. 7–42). New York: Guilford Press.

Ohry, A., Rattok, J., & Solomon, Z. (1996). Post-traumatic stress disorder in brain injury patients. *Brain Injury, 10*, 687–695.

Povlishock, J. T. (1986). Traumatically induced axonal damage without concomitant change in focally related neuronal somata and dendrites. *Acta Neuropathologica, 70*, 53–59.

Povlishock, J. T., & Coburn, T. H. (1989). Morphopathological change associated with mild head injury. In H. S. Levin, H. M. Eisenberg, & A. L. Benton (Eds.), *Mild head injury* (pp. 37–53). New York: Oxford University Press.

Rattok, J., & Ross, B. (1993). Post-traumatic stress disorder in the traumatically head injured. *Journal of Clinical and Experimental Neuropsychology, 6*, 243.

Robinson, R. G., & Jorge, R. (1994). Mood disorders. In J. M. Silver, S. C. Yudofsky, & R. E. Hales (Eds.), *Neuropsychiatry of traumatic brain injury* (pp. 219–250). Washington, DC: American Psychiatric Press.

Rutherford, W. H. (1989). Concussion symptoms: Relationship to acute neurological indices, individual differences, and circumstances of injury. In H. S. Levin, H. M. Eisenberg, & A. L. Benton (Eds.), *Mild head injury* (pp. 217–228). New York: Oxford University Press.

Sbordone, R. J., & Liter, J. C. (1995). Mild traumatic brain injury does not produce post-traumatic stress disorder. *Brain Injury, 9*, 405–412.

Solomon, S. D., Gerrity, E. T., & Muff, A. M. (1992). Efficacy of treatments for post-traumatic stress disorder. *Journal of the American Medical Association, 268*, 633–638.

Teasdale, G., & Jennett, B. (1974). Assessment of coma and impaired consciousness. *Lancet, 2*, 81–84.

Warden, D. L., Labbate, L. A., Salazar, A. M., Nelson, R., Sheley, E., Staudenmeier, J., & Martin, E. (1997). Post-traumatic stress disorder in patients with traumatic brain injury and amnesia for the event? *Journal of Neuropsychiatry and Clinical Neurosciences, 9*, 18–22.

Wilson, J. T., & Keane, T. M. (1996). *Assessing psychological trauma and PTSD: A handbook for practitioners.* New York: Guilford Press.

Wright, J. C., & Telford, R. (1996). Psychological problems following minor head injury: A prospective study. *British Journal of Clinical Psychology, 35*, 399–412.

Weathers, Frank W., & Litz, Brett T. (1994). Psychometric properties of the Clinician-Administered PTSD Scale, CAPS-1. *PTSD Research Quarterly, 5*(2), 2–6.

CHAPTER THREE

CHILDHOOD SEXUAL ABUSE AND REVICTIMIZATION IN ADOLESCENCE AND ADULTHOOD

BARBARA KRAHÉ

Department of Psychology, University of Potsdam, Potsdam, Germany

Childhood sexual abuse must be seen as a pervasive risk factor in children's lives: No demographic or family characteristics have as yet been identified to rule out the possibility that a child will be or has been sexually abused (Finkelhor, 1993). The adverse consequences of sexual abuse, both immediate and long term, have been documented by a large body of research. After a summary of the main findings from this research, the main objective of the present chapter is to examine the impact of childhood sexual abuse on a particular aspect of psychological functioning: the development of sexual behavior and sexual relationships. In this analysis, special consideration is given to the question of whether individuals who were sexually abused as children are at greater risk of experiencing sexual victimization in later life than individuals without experience of abuse. This question has generated a substantial body of evidence (see Messman & Long, 1996, for a review), and researchers are beginning to understand pathways from the experience of abuse in childhood to revictimization in adolescence and adulthood.

Psychological Consequences of Childhood Sexual Abuse

Sexual abuse is a traumatizing experience that leads to both immediate and long-term consequences in many, if not most, victims. A wide range of problems have been identified that were found with notable consistency to be more prevalent among victims of childhood sexual abuse than among nonabused samples (see reviews by Beitchman, Zucker, Hood, daCosta, & Akman, 1991; Beitchman et al., 1992; Cahill, Llewlyn, & Pearson, 1991; Jumper, 1995; Wiehe, 1998). An integrative overview of the current state of knowledge concerning the behavioral, emotional, cognitive, and physical effects of sexual abuse in childhood is presented by Barnett, Miller-Perrin, and Perrin (1997). The present section highlights some domains of psychological functioning adversely affected by the experience of sexual abuse, excluding sexuality-related problems, which are discussed in more detail in the following sections. No justice can be done here to the impressive body of evidence on potential moderators of the link between childhood sexual abuse and the magnitude of negative effects (e.g., nature of the abusive act, duration and frequency of the abuse, age of victim and offender). This evidence is well covered in the reviews just cited.

Among the initial effects of sexual abuse (i.e., effects occurring within the first 2 years following the abuse; Browne & Finkelhor, 1986), higher rates of depression, loneliness, and suicidal ideation have been identified in victim samples. Many victims show the symptomatology of post-traumatic stress disorder (PTSD) as an immediate reaction and/or as a long-term consequence of the abuse. Indeed, Kendall-Tackett, Williams, and Finkelhor (1993) conclude that PTSD is one of two core symptoms that seem to be more common in victims of abuse than in other clinical groups and carry particular diagnostic relevance (the second core symptom being sexualized behavior, described subsequently). Behavioral problems, such as sleep disturbances, hyperactivity, and aggression, are also common as initial responses to the trauma of sexual abuse. Victims often attempt to dissociate themselves from the experience of abuse and deny feelings of shame and anger, a coping strategy that makes them susceptible to the development of dissociative personality disorders. Furthermore, lowered self-esteem and feelings of worthlessness seem to be common reactions to the experience of sexual abuse.

Evidence from a multitude of sources suggests that the adverse effects of childhood sexual abuse frequently extend into adolescence and adulthood (see Barnett et al., 1997, p. 88). In a sample of more than 1,000 female adolescents, Chandy, Blum, and Resnick (1996) found that those with a history of childhood sexual abuse had significantly higher prevalence rates on 21 of their 22 negative outcome variables. As noted earlier, high rates of PTSD have been found in survivors long after the abuse itself. The same is true for higher rates of depression, anxiety, and poor self-esteem among adults abused as children. Other long-term sequelae include health problems, substance abuse, and eating disorders, all found to be more prevalent in survivors of sexual abuse. One reason why victims of sexual abuse are vulnerable to substance abuse is that alcohol or drugs enable them to blot out painful memories of the abuse. Eating disorders, such as bulimia or anorexia, are seen as responses to the reduction in self-esteem caused by the abuse experience. At the interpersonal level, victims of child sexual abuse have been found to have problems in establishing and maintaining satisfying relationships, not only with sexual partners (see next section) but also with their children (Banyard, 1997). Thus, sexual abuse predisposes victims to develop a wide range of emotional and behavioral problems that persist well beyond childhood and severely impair their psychological well-being and social functioning.

Childhood Sexual Abuse and Later Sexual Development

Given that sexual abuse involves an infringement on the victim's sexual integrity and self-determination, sexual development is particularly likely to be affected in a negative way by the experience of abuse. In Finkelhor and Browne's (1985) "traumagenic dynamics model" of sex abuse traumatization, "traumatic sexualization" is identified as a key mechanism leading from sexual abuse to specific sexuality-related symptoms and adjustment problems. While many of the symptoms found in relation to sexual abuse can also be observed as a result of other forms of childhood traumatization, sexualized behavior seems to be a specific consequence of sexual abuse. Its prevalence is significantly higher among survivors of sexual abuse than among other clinical groups (see Kendall-Tackett et al., 1993).

Sexuality-related problems manifest themselves in different ways depending on the victim's stage of development. In childhood, evidence of inappropriate sexual behavior has consistently been found at a higher rate among abuse victims than among both nonabused children and children affected by other types of clinically relevant experiences. Indeed, the majority of behavioral symptoms listed by Barnett et al. (1997, p. 86) for school-aged survivors of sexual abuse are sexuality related. Their list includes sexualized behavior, sexual preoccupation, precocious sexual knowledge, seductive behavior, excessive masturbation, sex play with others, sexual language, genital exposure, and the sexual victimization of others.

In adolescence, preoccupation with sexuality remains characteristic of abuse survivors. Several sources suggest that childhood sexual abuse is associated with early sexualization, manifested in an earlier age at first sexual intercourse and a greater number of sexual partners (e.g., Chandy et al., 1996; Miller, Monson, & Norton, 1995). Kendall-Tackett et al. (1993) summarize findings from two studies in which 38% of adolescents abused as children were classified as promiscuous.

In late adolescence and adulthood, problems in initiating and maintaining intimate relationships are consistently reported in the literature. These problems are also reflected in higher divorce rates in abused relative to nonabused samples. Beyond the difficulty of establishing close emotional bonds, many survivors show problems in sexual adjustment. Victims of sexual abuse have been found to be more sexually anxious, to experience more sexual guilt, to have lowered sexual self-esteem, and to be more likely to seek sexual therapy (Browne & Finkelhor, 1986). Furthermore, there is evidence to suggest a link between sexual abuse in childhood and prostitution (Cahill et al., 1991).

The majority of studies have focused on female victims of childhood sexual abuse. Studies including male victims suggest two potential effects of the abuse experience specific to this group. First, the possibility has been examined that childhood experience of abuse is linked to the development of a homosexual orientation, mediated by the victim's uncertainty about his sexual identity. However, evidence to support this link is limited (Beitchman et al., 1992; Browne & Finkelhor, 1986). Second, several sources have identified an increased risk for male abuse victims to become perpetrators of sexual aggression (Bagley, Wood, & Young, 1994; Barnett et al., 1997; Browne, 1994).

Childhood Sexual Abuse and Sexual Revictimization

Rather than being an isolated event, a characteristic feature of sexual abuse is that it often occurs repeatedly and/or over prolonged periods of time. Even after disclosure, a substantial proportion of victims become victimized again. According to studies reviewed by Kendall-Tackett et al. (1993), between 6% and 19% of victims were reabused within 2 years after the first abuse experience had been disclosed.

The present section examines evidence on revictimization beyond the childhood period. This research is guided by the question of whether women with a history of sexual abuse are more vulnerable to sexual victimization in later life than nonabused women. The focus of the discussion is thus on *sexual* revictimization. It should be noted, however, that an increased risk of revictimization in the form of physical assault, such as spouse battering, in subsequent relationships has also been identified as a consequence of sexual abuse (see Beitchman et al., 1992).

Two methodological approaches to addressing the revictimization hypothesis can be identified in the literature. One approach is concerned primarily with the experience of child abuse and looks at revictimization as one potential adverse effect (see Beitchman et al., 1992, for a review based on this approach). The second approach takes sexual victimization in adolescence and adulthood as its point of departure and examines childhood sexual abuse as a potential antecedent or risk factor of later victimization (e.g., Gidycz, Hanson, & Layman, 1995; Koss & Dinero, 1989).

Evidence for the Revictimization Hypothesis

The most comprehensive summary of evidence on sexual revictimization currently available is provided by Messman and Long (1996), who reviewed 18 studies published between 1977 and 1993. Eight of these studies investigated revictimization in college samples. With the exception of one study (Mandoki & Burkhart,

1989), these studies found significant links between childhood experiences of abuse and subsequent sexual victimization. Five studies providing data from clinical samples also lent support to the revictimization hypothesis. The remaining five studies found evidence for the link between sexual abuse and revictimization in unselected community samples.

The high consistency of support for the revictimization hypothesis across the three types of samples is noteworthy because each of these sources of evidence carries particular problems potentially likely to bias both the prevalence and the strength of the link between sexual abuse and revictimization. College samples may lead to an underestimation because they include only those victims of abuse who coped sufficiently well with the abuse experience to function in an achievement-oriented environment. In contrast, revictimized women may be overrepresented in clinical samples because repeated traumatization makes it more likely for victims to develop clinical symptoms. Some of the community studies relied on convenience samples not necessarily representative of the population at large. Thus, it may be concluded from Messman and Long's (1996) review that sexual revictimization in women abused as children is a pervasive phenomenon that may be detected with a considerable degree of consistency across different data sources.

Recent studies not discussed by Messman and Long corroborate this conclusion (e.g., Fleming, Mullen, Sibthorpe, & Bammer, 1999; Sanders & Moore, 1999; Urquiza & Goodlin-Jones, 1994; Wyatt, Newcomb, & Riederle, 1993). In a study with adolescents, Krahé, Scheinberger-Olwig, Waizenhöfer, and Kolpin (1999) found significantly higher rates of victimization for victims of childhood sexual abuse on the majority of items of the Sexual Experiences Survey (Koss, Gidycz, & Wisniewski, 1987; Koss & Oros, 1982). In particular, higher frequencies were found for victims of sexual abuse on sexual aggression involving the threat or use of physical violence. Mayall and Gold (1995) explored the prevalence of revictimization as a function of using inclusive versus restrictive definitions of both sexual abuse and adult victimization. Restrictive definitions of abuse (either genital contact and intercourse only or contact abuse including nongenital contact experiences) were associated with adult victimization using correspondingly restrictive definitions (genital touch or intercourse through use or threat of force and intercourse through the use of force, respectively). However, when noncontact experiences (such as exhibitionism) were included in the definition of abuse and verbal coercion was included in the definition of adult victimization, no significant relationship was found.

The importance of taking the severity of the abuse experience into account is further underlined by Fergusson, Horwood, and Lynskey (1997). They assigned respondents to one of four groups of childhood abuse on the basis of their self-reported experiences before the age of 16: no abuse, noncontact abuse, contact abuse, and abuse involving attempted or completed intercourse. The prevalence of rape and sexual assault between the ages of 16 and 18 years was then examined in each of the four groups. All three abused groups had significantly increased odds of reporting rape or sexual assault relative to the nonabused group, and the increase was a function of the severity of abuse. For the most severe form of abuse (i.e., intercourse), the odds for experiencing rape or attempted rape were 11 times higher than for the nonabused group and more than twice as high as for the contact abuse/no intercourse group.

In addition, there is evidence that childhood sexual abuse, while not directly increasing the likelihood of adult sexual victimization, predicts adolescent or precollege victimization (Himelein, 1995). In one of the few prospective longitudinal studies of sexual victimization, Gidycz et al. (1995) followed an initial sample of 796 college women over a 9-month period. Those respondents who reported a history of childhood or adolescent sexual abuse at the beginning of the study were significantly more likely to experience sexual victimization during the first 3-month interval of the study. As in other studies reviewed earlier, more severe forms of abuse were associated with a particular risk of experiencing severe forms of revictimization.

All of the evidence considered so far refers to female victims of childhood sexual abuse and their risk of subsequent victimization. Little is known about the sexual victimization of men generally and about the link between sexual abuse and revictimization in particular. This issue was addressed in a recent study by Krahé, Scheinberger-Olwig, and Schütze (1999) on sexual aggression among homosexual men, in which childhood sexual abuse was included as a potential risk factor. The findings lend clear support to the revictimization hypotheses: Homosexual men with a childhood history of contact sexual abuse were significantly more likely to report severe sexual victimization in subsequent relationships than nonabused men. (The same study also corroborated the victim-to-perpetrator cycle mentioned earlier in that victims of sexual abuse were found to be more likely to commit sexually aggressive acts than nonvictims.).

Thus, evidence from child sex abuse research and evidence from the literature on sexual victimization in adolescence and adulthood converge on the conclusion that women who were sexually abused as children are more likely to become victims of sexual aggression in later life than women who were not exposed to this negative childhood experience. Furthermore, there is tentative evidence to suggest a similar revictimization pattern for male victims in subsequent homosexual relationships.

Explanations of the Revictimization Cycle

Several explanations have been proposed to account for the increased risk of abuse victims to be sexually victimized in later life (see Messman & Long, 1996). From the perspective of learning theory, it has been argued that abuse victims are unable to develop a sense of self-efficacy in exerting control over their own body and rejecting unwanted sexual advances. They also learn that resistance to sexual advances is likely to entail punishment and may therefore be more likely to succumb to a man's coercive behavior. Moreover, being subjected to sexual abuse can generate a gender stereotype suggesting that the role of women is to satisfy men's sexual desires regardless of their own interests. To the extent that this stereotypical notion of female subordination is carried over into adolescence and adulthood, abused women are less likely to defend or protect themselves against unwanted sexual contacts.

A second explanatory approach concentrates on the emotional effects of the abuse experience. In particular, the corrosive effect of sexual abuse on self-esteem may make abuse victims dependent on social relationships as a source of self-worth. This dependency may explain why abused women tolerate sexual aggression in subsequent relationships. Moreover, it has been noted that this dependency makes them easy targets for sexually exploitative men (Beitchman et al., 1992).

Finally, revictimization has been explained with reference to the construct of learned helplessness. Victims who perceive their attempts at avoiding abuse to be unsuccessful experience noncontingency between their self-protective efforts and the occurrence of the abuse. The experience of learned helplessness is known to give rise to emotional, motivational, and behavioral deficits. While emotional deficits were discussed earlier in terms of increased rates of depression among victims of sexual abuse, motivational deficits refer to victims' reduced efforts at identifying and avoiding high-risk situations and/or partners. Behavioral deficits refer to their impaired ability to perceive options for escaping victimization and to judge the trustworthiness of potential partners.

These explanations represent building blocks of a conceptual framework for understanding *why* victims of abuse are particularly vulnerable to the risk of sexual victimization in later development, but—as Messman and Long (1996) noted—they have not as yet been tested empirically. More empirical evidence is available on the issue of *how* the experience of sexual abuse is connected to renewed sexual victimization in adolescence and adulthood. This issue refers to potential mediators between sexual abuse, that is, variables that are influenced by abuse and in turn affect the probability of subsequent victimization. Moreover, to qualify as mediators, these intervening variables must be shown to strengthen or attenuate the direct link between childhood abuse and subsequent victimization (Baron & Kenny, 1986). One variable shown to meet these criteria is the extent to which victims of abuse are sexually active in adolescence and adulthood.

Sexual Activity as a Mediator Between Sexual Abuse and Subsequent Victimization

To assess the proposition that childhood sexual abuse leads to revictimization through an increased level of sexual activity, two lines of evidence are relevant: (a) studies showing that victims of sexual abuse differ from nonvictims by being more sexually active and (b) studies showing that high levels of sexual activity are associated with an increased risk of sexual victimization.

As far as the first link is concerned, promiscuity and early sexual victimization are reported throughout the literature as common sequelae of childhood sexual abuse in adolescence as well as adulthood (as described earlier). For example, Mayall and Gold (1995) found that women with a childhood history of sexual abuse had significantly more sexual experience (defined by a combination of number of different sexual practices and number of partners) than a nonabused control group. In Chandy et al.'s (1996) teenaged sample, the proportion of respondents with coital experience was significantly higher in the abused than in the nonabused group, and a greater proportion of abused girls had a history of pregnancy. Further support for the link between sexual abuse and high levels of subsequent sexual activity is provided by Fergusson et al. (1997). They found that, among victims of severe sexual abuse (attempted or completed intercourse), 72.4% had their first consensual intercourse before the age of 16 (vs. 28.4% among nonvictimized respondents), and 58.6% reported more than five sexual partners by the age of 18 (vs. 13.3% in the nonvictimized group). Similar findings are reported in other studies with regard to number of sexual partners (e.g., Gidycz et al., 1995; Krahé, Scheinberger-Olwig, Waizenhöfer, & Kolpin, 1999) and onset of dating activity (Vicary, Klingaman, & Harkness, 1995). Thus, there is a consistent body of evidence showing that victims of childhood sexual abuse take up sexual activity at an earlier age and engage in sexual contacts with a greater number of partners than nonvictims.

The second part of the proposed pathway from sexual abuse to revictimization refers to the link between sexual activity and risk of sexual victimization. This link is plausible given that higher numbers of sexual partners increase the likelihood of encountering a sexually aggressive man, and it has been substantiated by a number of studies. Abbey, Ross, McDuffie, and McAuslan (1996) found that both lifetime number of sexual partners and number of times a woman had consensual sex discriminated between victims and nonvictims of sexual coercion as well as attempted or completed rape. In Gidycz et al.'s (1995) prospective study, number of sexual partners at initial assessment was significantly related to victimization in the subsequent 3 months. In another longitudinal study, Himelein (1995) used a combined index of consensual sexual activity that comprised both age at first intercourse and number of partners. She found that high scores on this index were associated with an increased risk of sexual victimization over a period of 32 months. In addition, the link between high levels of sexual activity and sexual victimization has been supported by many other studies (e.g., Gidycz, Coble, Latham, & Layman, 1993; Koss & Dinero, 1989; Mandoki & Burkhart, 1989; Mayall & Gold, 1995; Miller et al., 1995; Mynatt & Allgeier, 1990; Tyler, Hoyt, & Whitbeck, 1998; Wyatt et al., 1993).

Beyond the fact that the statistical probability of encountering an aggressive man increases as the number of partners goes up, victims of childhood abuse may be particularly susceptible to this increased risk because their ability to detect warning signs and identify potentially aggressive men may have been undermined by the abuse experience (Messman & Long, 1996). Moreover, Wyatt et al. (1993) showed that "early sexual experiences, both voluntary and coerced, are linked to greater partner initiation of sexual behavior in adulthood" (p. 120). This finding points at an important aspect of high sexual activity not sufficiently explored in past research: It may be that not a high level of sexual activity as such, but sexual activity that is more frequently initiated by the partner rather than the woman herself, mediates the effect of childhood abuse on later victimization.

Thus, there is convincing evidence to support each of the two proposed elements of the revictimization cycle: (a) the link between sexual abuse in childhood and higher levels of subsequent sexual activity and (b) the link between high levels of sexual activity and sexual victimization. However, few studies have examined both elements within one analytical design. Gidycz et al. (1995) present a path-analytical model showing that adolescent victimization predicted number of sexual partners, which, in turn, predicted victimization in the first 3 months of their 9-month assessment period. Fergusson et al. (1997) reported a decrease in the link between childhood sexual abuse and subsequent sexual victimization after controlling for the effects of age at first intercourse. Finally, Krahé, Scheinberger-Olwig, Waizenhöfer, and Kolpin (1999) showed that the link between childhood sexual abuse became weaker when number of sexual partners was included as a covariate prior to the inclusion of childhood abuse status. Nonetheless, in the last two studies the link between childhood sexual abuse and subsequent victimization, although reduced, remained significant, suggesting that revictimization is not entirely attributable to the mediating role of sexual activity.

Other Childhood Risk Factors for Later Sexual Victimization

Just as sexual activity is an important, but not the only, mediator of revictimization, sexual abuse is not the only adverse childhood experience related to subsequent sexual victimization. Several authors have claimed that other adverse childhood experiences, such as physical abuse and emotional neglect, lead to negative effects similar to those observed as a consequence of sexual abuse. This view represents a broader understanding of the revictimization cycle in that nonsexual forms of childhood victimization are also seen as risk factors for subsequent sexual victimization (e.g., Becker-Lausen, Sanders, & Chinsky, 1995; Moeller, Bachmann, & Moeller, 1993; Mullen, Martin, Anderson, Romans, & Herbison, 1993). For example, in the study by Krahé, Scheinberger-Olwig, Waizenhöfer, and Kolpin (1999), respondents who indicated that they had often felt worthless in their family were more likely to report sexual victimization in adolescence. This finding is consistent with Beitchman et al.'s (1992) conclusion that a sense of worthlessness "may antedate, co-exist or follow CSA [childhood sexual abuse] leading these women to expose themselves to men who revictimize them" (p. 108).

Sanders and Moore (1999) showed that date rape victims had significantly higher scores on a measure of negative home environment and neglect than a nonvictimized control group, even though no corresponding difference was found with respect to sexual abuse in childhood. Furthermore, Schaaf and McCanne (1998) reported that sexual victimization in adults with a history of childhood physical abuse was higher than for adults with a history of sexual abuse.

Several studies suggest that victims of sexual abuse differ from nonvictims in terms of negative home environments (see Beitchman et al., 1992). For example, 53.4% of the sexually abused respondents in Schaaf and McCanne (1998) and 55% in Rowan, Foy,

Rodriguez, and Ryan (1994) had experienced physical abuse as well. Maker, Kemmelmeier, and Peterson (1998) found a significantly higher rate of sexual abuse as well as physical abuse among children who witnessed marital violence in their family than in a comparison group of nonwitnesses. The question, therefore, is how different risk factors relate to each other as antecedents of later sexual victimization. While failing to find an effect of sexual abuse on revictimization, Schaaf and McCanne (1998) report evidence of a joint effect of sexual abuse and physical abuse on both revictimization and trauma. Fergusson et al. (1997) identified parental use of physical punishment as a significant covariate in the relationship between childhood sexual abuse and the experience of rape or attempted rape in late adolescence.

Further support for an additive model of childhood trauma comes from Fox and Gilbert (1994). In their study, respondents with a childhood history of incest, physical abuse, and parent alcoholism had significantly higher prevalence rates of sexual assault in dating relationships than respondents who had experienced only one of these childhood traumas. Similarly, Sanders and Moore (1999) showed that adult sexual victimization, while significantly linked to childhood sexual abuse, was co-determined by physical abuse and emotional neglect: These two adverse childhood experiences remained significantly related to adult sexual victimization after the effects of sexual abuse had been controlled for.

These findings suggest that the search for childhood-based risk factors for sexual victimization in adolescence and adulthood should extend beyond sexual abuse to include physical abuse, emotional neglect, and other indicators of poor family environment.

Summary and Conclusion

The present chapter was concerned with the long-term effects of sexual abuse in childhood with respect to subsequent sexual development and sexual relationships. In particular, the discussion focused on the significance of childhood sexual abuse as a risk factor for subsequent sexual victimization. A large body of research is available on these issues, showing a remarkable degree of consistency. There is ample evidence to show that childhood sexual abuse is related to a wide range of immediate as well as long-term emotional, behavioral, and relationship difficulties. Not surprisingly, sexual development is among the key problem areas affected by the experience of abuse. Sexualized behavior is commonly observed in children who were sexually abused and seems to carry over into adolescence and adulthood, where it appears in the form of promiscuity and indiscriminate partner choices.

As far as the revictimization hypothesis is concerned, there is now compelling evidence to document that women exposed to sexual abuse in childhood face a substantially higher risk of sexual victimization than women without this adverse childhood experience. It has also become clear, though, that sexual abuse is not the only childhood trauma that adversely affects the risk of later sexual victimization. Other negative childhood experiences, such as physical and emotional abuse, may also lead to an increased risk of later sexual victimization and/or compound the negative impact of sexual abuse.

While hypotheses explaining *why* victims of childhood sexual abuse are at greater risk of being sexually victimized as adolescents or adults are still awaiting empirical investigation, the process of *how* childhood sexual abuse is linked to revictimization has been explored by several studies. A significant role as a mediating variable between the experience of sexual abuse in childhood and renewed victimization is assigned to increased levels of sexual activity. Victims of sexual abuse seem to take up consensual sexual activity at an earlier age, engage in a greater variety of sexual acts, and have higher numbers of sexual partners. This pattern of sexual behavior enhances the likelihood that they will encounter sexually aggressive men. Low self-esteem and lack of self-worth, which are characteristic of abuse victims, exacerbate this risk.

The degree of consistency of the studies reviewed in this chapter is all the more remarkable given the variety of designs, measures, and definitions of abuse found in the literature. However, the vast majority of studies also share the problem of relying on retrospective self-reports of childhood sexual abuse, subsequent sexual victimization, or both. Prospective longitudinal studies of adolescent or adult sexual victimization (e.g., Fergusson et al., 1997; Gidycz et al., 1995; Himelein, 1995) represent a major improvement over the cross-sectional assessment of victimization, but they, too, rely on retrospective reports to gather information about childhood sexual abuse. Longitudinal studies following sexually abused children into adolescence and, possibly, adulthood would further clarify the pathway from the experience of abuse to later sexual behavior and revictimization.

Despite these limitations, the evidence reviewed in this chapter clearly highlights the need to recognize the risk of revictimization as a significant adverse consequence of sexual abuse and to address this risk factor in counseling and intervention. This is particularly important in view of the finding (e.g., by Arata, 1999) that coping with the trauma of rape and sexual assault is even more difficult for revictimized women than for victims not burdened with a childhood history of sexual abuse.

References

Abbey, A. A., Ross, L. T., McDuffie, D., & McAuslan, P. (1996). Alcohol and dating risk factors for sexual assault among college women. *Psychology of Women Quarterly, 20,* 147–169.

Arata, C. M. (1999). Coping with rape: The roles of prior sexual abuse and attributions of blame. *Journal of Interpersonal Violence, 14,* 62–78.

Bagley, C., Wood, M., & Young, L. (1994). Victim to abuser: Mental health and behavioral sequels of child sexual abuse in a community survey of young adult males. *Child Abuse and Neglect, 18,* 683–697.

Banyard, V. L. (1997). The impact of childhood sexual abuse and family functioning on four dimensions of women's later parenting. *Child Abuse and Neglect, 21,* 1095–1107.

Barnett, O. W., Miller-Perrin, C. L., & Perrin, R. D. (1997). *Family violence across the lifespan.* Thousand Oaks, CA: Sage.

Baron, R. M., & Kenny, D. A. (1986). The moderator-mediator variable distinction in social psychological research: Conceptual, strategic, and statistical considerations. *Journal of Personality and Social Psychology, 51,* 1173–1182.

Becker-Lausen, E., Sanders, B., & Chinsky, J. M. (1995). The mediation of abusive childhood experiences: Depression, dissociation, and negative life outcomes. *American Journal of Orthopsychiatry, 65,* 560–573.

Beitchman, J. H., Zucker, K. J., Hood, J. E., daCosta, G. A., & Akman, D. (1991). A review of the short-term effects of childhood sexual abuse. *Child Abuse and Neglect, 15,* 537–556.

Beitchman, J. H., Zucker, K. J., Hood, J. E., daCosta, G. A., Akman, D., & Cassivia, E. (1992). A review of the long-term effects of child sexual abuse. *Child Abuse and Neglect, 16,* 101–118.

Browne, A., & Finkelhor, D. (1986). Impact of child sexual abuse: A review of the research. *Psychological Bulletin, 99,* 66–77.

Browne, K. (1994). Child sexual abuse. In J. Archer (Ed.), *Male violence* (pp. 210–230). London: Routledge.

Cahill, C., Llewlyn, S. P., & Pearson, C. (1991). Long-term effects of sexual abuse which occurred in childhood: A review. *British Journal of Clinical Psychology, 30,* 117–130.

Chandy, J. M., Blum, R. W., & Resnick, M. D. (1996). Female adolescents with a history of sexual abuse. *Journal of Interpersonal Violence, 11,* 503–518.

Fergusson, D. M., Horwood, L. J., & Lynskey, M. T. (1997). Childhood sexual abuse, adolescent sexual behaviors and sexual revictimization. *Child Abuse and Neglect, 21,* 789–803.

Finkelhor, D. (1993). Epidemiological factors in the clinical identification of child sexual abuse. *Child Abuse and Neglect, 17,* 67–70.

Finkelhor, D., & Browne, A. (1985). The traumatic impact of child sexual abuse: A conceptualization. *American Journal of Orthopsychiatry, 55,* 530–541.

Fleming, J., Mullen, P. E., Sibthorpe, B., & Bammer, G. (1999). The long-term impact of childhood sexual abuse in Australian women. *Child Abuse and Neglect, 23,* 145–159.

Fox, K. M., & Gilbert, B. O. (1994). The interpersonal and psychological functioning of women who experienced childhood physical abuse, incest, and parental alcoholism. *Child Abuse and Neglect, 18,* 849–858.

Gidycz, C. A., Coble, C. N., Latham, L., & Layman, M. J. (1993). Sexual assault experience in adulthood and prior victimization experiences. *Psychology of Women Quarterly, 17,* 151–168.

Gidycz, C. A., Hanson, K., & Layman, M. J. (1995). A prospective analysis of the relationships among sexual assault experiences. *Psychology of Women Quarterly, 19,* 5–29.

Himelein, M. J. (1995). Risk factors for sexual victimization in dating. *Psychology of Women Quarterly, 19,* 31–48.

Jumper, S. A. (1995). A meta-analysis of the relationship of child sexual abuse to adult psychological adjustment. *Child Abuse and Neglect, 19,* 715–728.

Kendall-Tackett, K. A., Williams, L. M., & Finkelhor, D. (1993). Impact of sexual abuse of children: A review and synthesis of recent empirical studies. *Psychological Bulletin, 113,* 164–180.

Koss, M. P., & Dinero, T. E. (1989). Discriminant analysis of risk factors for sexual victimization among a national sample of college women. *Journal of Consulting and Clinical Psychology, 57,* 242–250.

Koss, M. P., Gidycz, C. A., & Wisniewski, N. (1987). The scope of rape: Incidence and prevalence of sexual aggression and victimization in a national sample of higher education students. *Journal of Consulting and Clinical Psychology, 55,* 162–170.

Koss, M. P., & Oros, C. J. (1982). Sexual Experiences Survey: A research instrument investigating sexual aggression and victimization. *Journal of Consulting and Clinical Psychology, 50,* 455–457.

Krahé, B., Scheinberger-Olwig, R., & Schütze, S. (1999). *Risk factors of sexual aggression and victimization among homosexual men.* Manuscript submitted for publication.

Krahé, B., Scheinberger-Olwig, R., Waizenhöfer, E., & Kolpin, S. (1999). Childhood sexual abuse and revictimization in adolescence. *Child Abuse and Neglect, 23*, 383–394.

Mandoki, C. A., & Burkhart, B. R. (1989). Sexual victimization: Is there a vicious cycle? *Violence and Victims, 4*, 179–190.

Maker, A. H., Kemmelmeier, M., & Peterson, C. (1998). Long-term psychological consequences in women of witnessing parental physical conflict and experiencing abuse in childhood. *Journal of Interpersonal Violence, 13*, 574–589.

Mayall, A., & Gold, S. R. (1995). Definitional issues and mediating variables in the sexual revictimization of women sexually abused as children. *Journal of Interpersonal Violence, 10*, 26–42.

Messman, T. L., & Long, P. J. (1996). Child sexual abuse and its relationship to revictimization in adult women: A review. *Clinical Psychology Review, 16*, 397–420.

Miller, B. C., Monson, B. H., & Norton, M. C. (1995). The effects of forced sexual intercourse on White female adolescents. *Child Abuse and Neglect, 19*, 1289–1301.

Moeller, T., Bachmann, G., & Moeller, J. (1993). The combined effect of physical, sexual, and emotional abuse during childhood: Long-term health consequences for women. *Child Abuse and Neglect, 17*, 623–640.

Mullen, P. E., Martin, J. L., Anderson, J. C., Romans, S. E., & Herbison, G. P. (1993). Childhood sexual abuse and mental health in adult life. *British Journal of Psychiatry, 163*, 721–732.

Mynatt, C. R., & Allgeier, E. R. (1990). Risk factors, self-attributions, and adjustment problems among victims of sexual coercion. *Journal of Applied Social Psychology, 20*, 130–153.

Rowan, A. B., Foy, D. W., Rodriguez, N., & Ryan, S. (1994). Post-traumatic stress disorder in a clinical sample of adults sexually abused as children. *Child Abuse and Neglect, 18*, 51–61.

Sanders, B., & Moore, D. L. (1999). Childhood maltreatment and date rape. *Journal of Interpersonal Violence, 14*, 115–124.

Schaaf, K. K., & McCanne, T. R. (1998). Relationship of childhood sexual, physical, and combined sexual and physical abuse to adult victimization and posttraumatic stress disorder. *Child Abuse and Neglect, 22*, 1119–1133.

Tyler, K. A., Hoyt, D. R., & Whitbeck, L. B. (1998). Coercive sexual strategies. *Violence and Victims, 13*, 47–61.

Urquiza, A., & Goodlin-Jones, B. L. (1994). Child sexual abuse and adult revictimization with women of color. *Violence and Victims, 9*, 223–232.

Vicary, J. R., Klingaman, L. R., & Harkness, W. L. (1995). Risk factors associated with date rape and sexual assault of adolescent girls. *Journal of Adolescence, 18*, 289–306.

Wiehe, V. R. (1998). *Understanding family violence*. Thousand Oaks, CA: Sage.

Wyatt, G. E., Newcomb, M. D., & Riederle, M. H. (1993). *Sexual abuse and consensual sex*. Newbury Park, CA: Sage.

CHAPTER FOUR

COMPARISON OF NARRATIVES OF LOSS EXPERIENCES OF WORLD WAR II AND VIETNAM COMBAT VETERANS

CARRIE BARNES and JOHN H. HARVEY

Department of Psychology, University of Iowa, Iowa City, Iowa, USA

While their continuing grief now is receiving periodic media attention, for years and even decades, American soldiers who fought in World War II (WWII) and who fought in Vietnam have suffered their life-altering experiences of loss in silence. Many of the WWII generation now have died and cannot share their grief with us. We as scholars of loss and trauma have a special obligation to reach out to the living survivors of WWII for information about their experiences. As has been often noted (e.g., Kuenning, 1990), for years after the conclusion of the Vietnam War, the stories of loss and grief of Vietnam veterans were not welcomed. The purpose of this chapter is to report some comparative narrative evidence from veterans of these two wars. Our major question was whether strong differences between groups in perceived long-term impact of combat experience would be reported.

In comparing WWII and Vietnam veterans' experiences, it is noteworthy that the recent release of the film *Saving Private Ryan* (1998) renewed people's general understanding and appreciation of Normandy invasion veterans' sacrifices in WWII. A little more than a decade before that movie, the movie *Platoon* (1986) also contributed to general understanding of some of the horrors faced by troops in the Vietnam War. These films were so popular that they served as cultural markers of public interest in these wars and the people who fought them. Before *Platoon* and the creation of the

Vietnam Memorial in Washington, D.C., in 1981, there was a mixture of silence, disregard, and dismissal about the sacrifices of Vietnam veterans. Writing about the "Vietnam veteran's experience" was replete with stories of loss and dismay by returning veterans (e.g., Baritz, 1985; Scurfield, 1993). But it took U.S. citizens and the media about a decade to process the events of this war such that the veterans were given greater concern, if not appreciation, for their service in a divisive civil war in Vietnam in which so many thought the United States should play no role.

Work on post-traumatic stress disorder (PTSD) among Vietnam veterans was extensive in scope for at least the first decade and a half after the conclusion of that war (Herman, 1992). Scurfield (1993) reports that of the 3.14 million Vietnam theater veterans who served in the war zone in Southeast Asia between 1964 and 1975, it is estimated that 15.2% had complete PTSD as of the late 1980s. Scurfield attributed this extraordinarily high number to the unresolved issues that many Americans, U.S. institutions, and the country as a whole have about the Vietnam War. Such issues, in turn, have been projected onto the people who fought the war. Vietnam was more than just an unpopular war. It was an albatross strangling America. Its legacy of shame was widely recognized. U.S. statesman Joseph Califano said in 1973, "It is truly Kafkaseque thinking for public officials who call themselves liberals to support this six billion dollar investment of scarce public sector resources so the lower class can fight our wars" (Califano, 1973, p. 11).

On the other hand, work on traumatic stress, then called "combat fatigue," has not been as extensively conducted with WWII veterans. In fact, many WWII veterans such as those interviewed in the present study have felt that their long-term experience of trauma has not been widely appreciated. Others, as shown later, felt that the emphasis on PTSD after the Vietnam War was not applicable to them, however traumatic their experiences. They felt that they had not needed the type of support-group help from which so many Vietnam veterans benefited.

Account-Making Perspective

This study was concerned with how combat veterans cope with traumatic experiences over the long run. In posing this question, we adopted what we have referred to as an account-making model of dealing with major loss (Harvey, 1996; Harvey, Weber, & Orbuch, 1990). This model was developed in the context of work with combat veterans, incest survivors, survivors of airline disasters, and family members of persons recently deceased. The basic idea is that people often effectively deal with major loss over time by developing an account, or story, pertaining to the loss. The story explains the loss, as best one can explain it, and provides descriptive information about events surrounding the loss that capture the meaning of the loss for the individual. Presumably, people develop accounts of their major experiences in life as part of an overall master life account, and within this major account are sub-accounts, such as love affairs that ended and why they ended and their effects on the person's life. People probably develop accounts about all matters of moment in their lives, including many positive experiences, but our work focuses mainly on their accounts of negative, stressful experiences.

A final area of analysis in the account-making model pertains to a person's work on a personal story and related confiding about it to the point that a feeling of acceptance and understanding occurs. This stage is accompanied by identity change. The person feels that he or she has changed in fundamental ways as a result of the loss and how he or she processed it in terms of feelings, thoughts, and social interactions. This latter stage is comparable to what Horowitz (1976) and others have referred to as the development of schema change associated with severe stressors.

In the account-making model, it also is argued that parts of one's story need to be confided to close others in order for adaptation to occur. This confiding experience is invaluable to the grieving person if the confidant reacts in an empathic, helpful manner (Harvey, Orbuch, Chwalisz, & Garwood, 1991). One general expectation was that veterans would readily report accounts of loss experiences associated with their combat activities and that Vietnam veterans would report less resolve and understanding of their traumas than would the WWII veterans. We also expected that the veterans who were able to develop and confide parts of their accounts to close, caring others would report that they were able to adapt more readily after their service tenure than would veterans who, for whatever reasons, did not engage in such account making and confiding.

Comparison of WWII and Vietnam Veterans' Experiences

Method

Fifty WWII and 50 Vietnam veterans who indicated that they had experienced traumatic experiences as part of combat activity volunteered to participate in the study. They were recruited from veterans groups and by word of mouth. The average age of WWII veterans participating was 77 years, and the average age of Vietnam veterans participating was 49 years. There were 5 WWII veterans who had participated both in WWII and the Korean War. None of the Vietnam War veterans had participated in other wars.

The method of this study involved development of a questionnaire that invited veterans to describe the following events and experiences: (a) their greatest losses experienced, as well as those experienced by persons close to them; (b) the most positive influence of their service on them; (c) the most vivid memories of traumatic events in their wartime experience; (d) whether and how dreams and idle moments of reflection have been affected by wartime experience; (e) perceived depression associated with their war service; (f) how they have coped with their war experiences; (g) whether they have confided in close others about their war experiences and, if so, the reactions of those others; (h) possible help or hurt by others in reacting to their reported losses and pain; and (i) possible links in their minds between their wartime losses and other losses they have experienced in life. The last three questions were based on the account-making model, with the seventh and eighth questions referring to coping and the ninth question pertaining to cognized relations among loss experiences. The latter refers to the assumption that people contextualize and tie together loss experiences in their overall life stories (Harvey & Miller, 1998).

Questionnaires were answered via mail and, as possible, personal interviews. Several veterans sent accompanying memoirs with their questionnaire answers. Veterans were encouraged to be as thorough as possible in reporting their experiences. Some veterans typed out multipaged responses to the questionnaire.

Results

Self-reported traumatic experiences in the form of witnessing the death of friends or associates, being wounded in action, and observing death on the part of the enemy were comparable across the two groups of veterans. All indicated having experienced at least witnessing death or having close associates die in combat. A few in each group admitted killing enemy soldiers. Self-reported bouts of past and current depression were indicated by only 10% of the WWII veterans ($n = 5$) but by 50% ($n = 25$) of the Vietnam veterans. Similarly, many more Vietnam veterans (65%; $n = 33$) reported instances of PTSD symptoms in the present than did WWII veterans (20%; $n = 10$). Symptoms reported included difficulty in marriage and/or interpersonal relations, hypervigilance, startle response, nightmares, intrusive imagery, substance abuse, and flattened affect about loss issues.

Narrative Evidence of Veterans' Experiences

This report focuses on themes of narratives reported by WWII and Vietnam veterans in addressing the questions of greatest losses, what were the most positive influences from their wartime experience, vivid memories of traumatic experiences, and intrusions of wartime memories into their idle moments and dreams about such experiences.

Excerpts of WWII Veterans' "Greatest Losses" Narratives

Examples of WWII veterans' narratives are as follows.

The lost years, the years between 18 and 21. One can never go back in time and relive that time in your life. I always felt I missed some of the best years of life. I had to go from a boy to a man too soon.

Separation from family and friends and all of us not knowing if and when I would return.

Friends were killed. Others were hurt. (This veteran went on to describe the most vivid memory that has remained with him as "Friends died in my arms. Others were hurt and I couldn't help them.")

Because of the war, several close friends were killed in combat service. Also, because of the bombings in England, several other friends, both male and female, were killed during air raids. Also my mother died in 1944, and I have wondered if it had something to do with the stress she suffered when my brother who was in the Merchant Marine was missing for two years. Also when I was in the combat zones so much it must have worried her.

Anguish, dignity, inconvenience, loss of time to do what I would prefer to do, self-pity, pathos.

I lost 3 years of my youth. . . . My close friends were killed in action.

This veteran answered the question about his most vivid memory by saying, "How much luck in combat—a matter of inches. I was on a chow run through a swamp, when we were hit with artillery shells. There were 15 men—I was the only one not hit, most were killed. . . . Nights were the worst in jungle fighting." And, in one of the longest responses by a WWII veteran:

The greatest losses were of close friends who were killed or wounded in action, which is always traumatic. I had several friends and school mates either KIA [killed in action] or WIA [wounded in action] during the war. The sight of fellow Americans killed or wounded, even though you may not have known them personally, it still affected you. One of my school mates was bayoneted to death on the second day of the Guam campaign. Another was severely wounded and had a leg amputated and a third was wounded by shrapnel from a mortar shell. . . . My brother-in-law was a navigator on a B-29 flying out of Guam. Chuck had married my sister just prior to entering the Army Air Force. Because we both were stationed in Guam, we managed to get together at least twice a week. I became friends with the entire B-29 crew. Ten days after his 21st birthday, Chuck's plane was shot down, but other plane crews saw that the entire crew parachuted out of the plane. I had to write home and tell my father of the loss, so he could tell my sister. After the war ended, my sister was told that Chuck's crew had been tortured, beaten, beheaded, and their bodies cremated. Eventually, five of the Japanese involved in these murders were tried and executed. The atrocities committed by some during the war I shall never forget or forgive.

Excerpts of Vietnam Veterans' "Greatest Losses" Narratives

WWII veterans emphasized the combat deaths of friends and their own lost youth as themes. How do these types of responses for "greatest losses" among WWII veterans differ from those expressed by Vietnam veterans?

I don't get close to anyone!

You learned how fragile life is . . . the first experience with somebody dying . . . having to put up with it, that it happened instantaneously, it just happens. I mean I'd be like, you know, for three months in the country and hadn't seen any action, and all of a sudden one day, you realize that little kid you were talking to last night is dead. It is about eight hours before he was supposed to go home.

Loss of close friends in combat . . . the utter waste in the conducting of this war.

I don't show emotion. I don't cry. I don't get close to anyone and can't tell anyone how I feel.

I lost friends in Vietnam and it hurts so I don't want to get close to anyone in fear that something will happen to them. I showed no emotion when my mother passed away. I can't say how I feel about my wife or loved ones. I can't tell anyone my feelings. I just keep it all inside and I blow up easily.

Loss of innocence and disillusionment with the government. Not fitting in when I returned back home. Possible exposure to agent orange, health problems.

Thus, while Vietnam veterans also stressed that the loss of friends in combat was one of their greatest losses, they tended to emphasize their own long-term PTSD-like symptoms, especially in terms of being unable to get close to loved ones and to express their feelings.

Excerpts of Narratives: Most Vivid Memories

As has been noted, a common theme for WWII veterans was the witnessing of death on a firsthand basis, often death of friends. It was common to experience death of friends close, in one's arms or foxhole. Luck in survival became a common memory in the context of seeing nearby others die suddenly. Bare escape in grave situations was a common thread for several veterans. Another interesting memory reported referred to mass suicides by the enemy:

> Without a doubt, it had to be watching the mass suicides by both Japanese civilians and military during the battle of Saipan. These people were so brainwashed that they jumped off cliffs on northern Saipan to their deaths. We watched them one afternoon as they jumped, and even though loud-speakers were pleading with them not to do so, they killed themselves anyway. Some of the Japanese whom we had taken prisoners earlier also pleaded with them not to do it. They would not listen. Parents would throw or push their little children over the side, or would hold them in their arms as they jumped over 200 feet to their deaths. Some didn't want to jump, but there were Japanese snipers who shot the ones who refused to jump. We were helpless to prevent the mass suicide of the civilians—there was nothing we could do.

Vietnam veterans noted similar memories; however, there were differences, such as the following: "After killing a man, I then cut his head off and put it on a fence post. I cut his ear off and carried it on the end of my rifle tied by a boot lace." This same veteran, who travels as a salesman for a living, also was one of those to note that he could not get close to anyone now. Similarly, another Vietnam veteran noted his lack of closeness and mentioned this vivid memory: "Discovering a friend who had been skinned alive after capture while his survival radio was held to his mouth by Pathet Lao troops in Laos in December 1972."

Continuing with this type of recall of horror and reported difficulty in social interaction, a Vietnam veteran said, in response to the vivid memory question, "A friend had a grenade blow his guts out. I tried but failed to be of help. I still have nightmares of my hands in his guts." He later described the long-term impact of his service as follows: "I am very jumpy around any Vietnamese people. I like to be with my back to the wall so I can see what's coming. . . . The first twenty years I was withdrawn and quick tempered. Now I volunteer for all of the Vets, helping where I can (Guilt?)."

Another Vietnam veteran wrote:

> First was the stench of the dead bodies coming from a nearby morgue and the seeming lack of concern on the part of the military. Second, the rather astounding lack of comradeship among the ranks—it seemed then and now

to be at the apex of our lack of success. Next, there was an instance in which one member of our company used a claymore mine to kill himself and about 16 others—all of whom were American soldiers. . . . Finally, there were many instances during which you could notice, clearly, that many of the soldiers were wearing the ears of dead North Vietnamese or Viet Cong around their necks, using leather lacing.

A Vietnam veteran wrote of guilt associated with his vivid memory of seeing a buddy shot and killed by a sniper and then thinking "Better him than me." He said he carried guilt for years after reacting in that way to his friend's death.

Excerpts of Narratives: Questions About Long-Term Impacts and Positive Gains

A major difference in the narratives was the greater emphasis placed by WWII veterans on how they went on with life and how much pride they gained from wartime service relative to Vietnam veterans' responses to these questions. More than 80% ($n = 40$) of the WWII veterans provided a statement indicative of pride and a good feeling about what they did in their service time, including gaining respect from people back home, becoming a leader, becoming a man, and learning how to make decisions and survive. Patriotism was a core of these narratives, as shown by the following excerpts:

In WWII almost 15 million of us served. Most of us returned to productive lives. I recognize and respect with regret the enormous cost to others. I know that I have contributed not only to our Nation's freedom but also to others' freedom throughout the world, and this knowledge provides personal satisfaction.

The united patriotism of the American people during World War II was so impressive. Everyone, regardless of age, race, political choice, or rich or poor, supported us who served. Far different then than the support given to our troops and government during the Korean and Vietnam Wars. This made a person proud to be an American, and something I shall never forget.

It made me realize how important it is to be free and live in a country as great as ours.

As might be expected, the Vietnam veterans could offer few such positive commentaries on the benefits of their service. Their most common positive reaction (present in the responses of 50% of these veterans) was that they had made friends in the war. As one said, "I still have after 30 years some comradeship with others—vets." Another expressed the common disappointment in the government: "I learned not to rely on our leaders and the government."

As mentioned previously, Vietnam veterans emphasized long-term negative impacts much more frequently than did WWII veterans. They wrote of problems in interpersonal relations (including relations with spouses and children), divorce, difficulties sleeping, nightmares, difficulties in their jobs and careers, difficulties getting on their feet financially, and difficulties in accepting authority figures in daily life.

WWII veterans wrote of dreaming and daily reflecting about the horrors they had experienced but also of how such events did not adversely affect their lives over the years. As one said:

> I think, dream and reflect upon incidents. They were and are a big part of my young adult life. Most Americans do not go to war, as citizen soldiers at age 17 and return home at age 19. . . . Life must go on and while a day seldom passes without modest reflection (now 55 years later!) on some war-related event, I don't feel inordinately preoccupied with these memories.

Excerpts of Narratives: Coping and Confiding Questions

One WWII veteran said simply, "Some people won't let go. I *have.* Another said, "Made up my mind it was the greatest thing to happen in my life, and feel very lucky to have lived through it. But wouldn't give a nickel to do it again." In general, more than 50% of the WWII veterans showed modest support for the account-making and confiding model of coping, in that they reported behavior consistent with this model. As one said:

> The vast majority of us talked with our spouses, close friends, and fellow veterans about our experiences, and it helped. For the most part, I have found that WWII veterans did not start talking about the war until 40 or so years later [or about the time Vietnam veterans began to be more open and vocal about their experiences, in the 1980s], in the twilight years of life. Without a doubt, it helped; but I feel we dealt with our own individual

memories of horror and death, etc. by ourselves, not through any form of therapy. I truly believe that some of the therapies only burn the memories into the mind more, and increase the problem.

Another WWII veteran supported the account-making and confiding model in indicating how writing and discussing his experiences with close others helped him:

Yes, I wrote an article of my experiences and sent it to the *Reader's Digest*. Although it wasn't published, it was good to put these experiences on paper. I also married a spouse who listened well. It also helped during the 1994 D-Day celebration when I had been asked to talk about WWII events. I needed to talk about the war veterans helping win the war. My daughter is a good listener too.

Similarly, about 50% of the Vietnam veterans—most of whom indicated that they no longer experience grave ill effects of their war experience—stressed talking and confiding as ways of coping over the years. Most said they had attended veterans group meetings, and a few indicated they had been in therapy. One said, "I have learned to talk about Vietnam and my experiences. But not to people who blame or glorify the war when they discuss it. I did my job, that's all."

The comments of another Vietnam veteran constitute an eloquent, representative position about coping (it should be noted that this veteran became a physician after the war):

I hate to seem crass, but my experience is that there are few who either care or understand the experience [we had]. I have moved on!! This was an experience that will live forever in my mind—that I cannot dismiss. But, those who do not move on continue to suffer—and the experience loses its perspective. It was a very critical experience, but nonetheless only one experience in a life full of experiences. It was Soren Kierkegaard who once noted that there are two types of people—those who live their lives and those who simply observe life. I selected the former.

Comments by WWII Veterans About Group Differences

While Vietnam veterans did not make overarching comments about the differences between them and other veterans groups, 10 WWII veterans spontaneously made comments denouncing the emphasis on support groups and recovery from PTSD associated with the Vietnam veteran. It is not clear why the WWII veterans were so relatively outspoken, while Vietnam veterans were silent about such differences.

The WWII veterans expressed a toughness about their endurance and moving on with life without an extensive amount of psychological assistance. It was as if they represented a proud generation that served, sacrificed, and got on with life's tasks, without languishing for years wondering about the meaning of what had occurred in their wartime service. One veteran summarized this feeling without qualms in reacting to the question about mentally linking losses in the war with other losses in one's life:

> Get real. Self-pity must stop somewhere. My generation did what we had to do and came home and got on with life—a life that gave me 51 years and 15 days with a lady who blessed me with 2 sons and 4 daughters before she went to heaven. The best memory I have of WWII is that I met the lady I went to war for.

Another WWII veteran blamed Vietnam veterans' negative effects on the psychologists who created the PTSD category of disorder:

> I don't think we veterans of World War II were affected nearly as much as were the Vietnam veterans. This is not their fault. It is the fault of the psychologists who swooped down on those veterans, trying to convince them that they were suffering from mental delusions, only making things worse. Throughout history people have faced many traumatic events, and they have worked their way through them. We all had memories from our childhood of losing parents, grandparents, brothers, sisters, or close friends. We were not forced to see psychologists to work through the problems. In the long run, I feel that we worked it out of our system much faster because we did not see the "head shrinks."

Conclusions

What did we learn about the similarities and differences in losses, coping, and related experiences of WWII and Vietnam veterans from this study? As has been documented in previous work, the stories of WWII veterans reveal less continuing psychological turmoil than do the stories of Vietnam veterans. This conclusion is supported in part by the reports of greater war-related depression among Vietnam veterans than among WWII veterans. WWII veterans' comments uniformly suggest an embracing of the view that WWII was a patriotic war, possibly the last "good war." Some eschew the PTSD logic of the Vietnam War aftermath and hold the belief that it is unfortunate to view many Vietnam veterans as handicapped by PTSD.

Time magazine (Bruce Nelan column, March 9, 1998) labeled WWII "the last good war." It was a war that had to be fought and won and an unambiguous struggle between good and evil. It was not just about national interests but also about values and the belief that Hitler and Tojo had to be defeated. On the other hand, the Vietnam War was a distinctly bad war. It was even bloodier than the similarly ambiguous Korean War fought a decade earlier. As the Vietnam War wore on, it filled America's streets with demonstrators, tore up university campuses, split society and families, and dragged down one president and made another one much less believable. The Vietnam veterans came home not to frequent references to "our boys," as was true after World War II. Rather, they came home to be stigmatized as baby killers and to be reviled all too often. Aspects of these sociopolitical differences seeped through in the psychological feelings revealed in the narratives of our two samples.

Vietnam veterans' stress on interpersonal difficulties is noteworthy and also consistent with previous reports, especially for veterans who experienced PTSD (Herman, 1992). It should be emphasized that all of the veterans sampled reported some degree of continued grief and memory activity associated with their combat experience. Across the two groups, many men indicated that they still actively work on their memories of loss and the effects of such loss in their lives.

The WWII veteran's comment that veterans began to talk more of their war experiences decades after the fact is consistent with narrative evidence collected by Harvey, Stein, and Scott (1995) in interviews with Normandy invasion veterans. Despite reporting strong psychological health over the years, Normandy invasion veterans reported much more willingness and interest in telling their stories around the time of the 50-year anniversary and celebration in Normandy, France. They also reported long-term grief about the loss of friends during the invasion. Thus, the present data provide modest support for the idea that older veterans are feeling and expressing the pain of their wartime losses to a high degree now, many years after the fact (see Sleek, 1998). Another WWII veteran said that since he had retired, he was able to think more about the war and was more affected now than ever before by his combat experience. Such evidence and speculation suggest that older veterans may now be a particularly good source of information about traumatic events and memory of such events. As these veterans begin to die in greater numbers each year, many of them may be eager to find an audience for their war stories—a valuable repository of knowledge for loss and trauma researchers.

The data in the present study also provide general support for the value of the account-making and confiding model as a way of adapting to the losses experienced both by WWII and Vietnam veterans. Simply by participating in this study, these men implicitly were endorsing the value of telling parts of their stories. It is valuable, in fact, to see the number of veterans in both groups who have spent and continue to spend great amounts of time telling or writing about aspects of their wartime stories. These events were powerfully important in their lives as moments that defined in part who they were and would become. The memories of these events will not go away in the lifetime of these veterans. We owe it to them to share these memories. They help us better understand loss and trauma and alleviate and prevent some of the attendant pain that ripples through veterans' and their families' lives.

References

Baritz, L. (1985). *Backfire*. New York: Ballentine.

Califano, C. (1973, March). Doubts about an all-voluntary army. *New Republic*, p. 11.

Harvey, J. H. (1996). *Embracing their memory: Loss and the social psychology of storytelling*. Needham Heights, MA: Allyn & Bacon.

Harvey, J. H., & Miller, E. D. (1998). Toward a psychology of loss. *Psychological Science, 9*, 429–434.

Harvey, J. H., Orbuch, T. L., Chwalisz, K., & Garwood, G. (1991). Coping with sexual assault: The roles of account-making and confiding. *Journal of Traumatic Stress, 4*, 515–531.

Harvey, J. H., Stein, S. K., & Scott, P. K. (1995). Fifty years of grief: Accounts and reported psychological reactions of Normandy invasion veterans. *Journal of Narrative and Life History, 5,* 315–332.

Harvey, J. H., Weber, A. L., & Orbuch, T. L. (1990). *Interpersonal accounts: A social psychological approach.* Oxford, England: Basil Blackwell.

Herman, J. L. (1992). *Trauma and recovery: The aftermath of violence.* New York: Basic Books.

Horowitz, M. J. (1976). *Stress response syndromes* (2nd ed.). Northvale, NJ: Jason Aronson.

Kuenning, D. E. (1990). *Life after Vietnam.* New York: Paragon Press.

Nelan, B. (1998). The last good war. *Time,* March 9, p. 10.

Scurfield, R. M. (1993). Posttraumatic stress disorder in Vietnam veterans. In J. P. Wilson & B. Raphael (Eds.), *International handbook of traumatic stress syndromes* (pp. 285–295). New York: Plenum.

Sleek, S. (1998, May). Older vets just now feeling pain of war. *APA Monitor,* pp. 1, 29.

CHAPTER FIVE

LESSONS IN THE PSYCHOLOGY OF LOSS: ACCOUNTS OF MIDDLE-AGED ROMANIAN WOMEN

HEATHER R. CARLSON

Department of Counseling Psychology, Loyola University Chicago, Chicago, Illinois, USA

ALEX JOHNSTON

Anchorage, Alaska, USA

AURORA LIICEANU

Institute of Psychology, Bucharest, Romania

CRISTINA VINTILA and JOHN H. HARVEY

Department of Psychology, University of Iowa, Iowa City, Iowa, USA

In studying loss, it is important to develop a cross-cultural, inter-disciplinary approach that is concerned with the historical, cultural, and social contexts in which loss occurs. However, the Western field of psychology is less well informed about the experiences and perspectives of loss across various cultures. Many countries in the contemporary world are seeking greater participation in the international community and control over their destinies. The related cultural, political, and social developments are commanding a need for heightened awareness and understanding of ethnic variations in dealing with the social change phenomenon and the psychology of loss.

Romania is one such country whose political history and dynamics continue to threaten its reintegration into the European community. An exasperating loss issue for Romanian psychology in the late 1990s is that research is becoming nearly extinct because of the financial deprivations in the universities and the pressure on researchers to work other jobs in order to survive. However, part of the value in studying Romania now is that there is a growing number of Romanian psychologists who are amenable to collaboration (Harvey, 1998).

The ideas and research findings presented in this chapter resulted from a Fulbright Fellowship awarded to the fifth author, who spent 4 months living in Romania surveying and interviewing more than 100 women in midlife and beyond about the major losses that they have experienced. This special population was chosen not only because women tend to be more open in discussing loss events (Harvey, Weber, & Orbuch, 1990) but also because they are more likely to have experienced a wider variety of naturally occurring losses owing to their age. Unique to this population are the losses experienced and associated with the country's domination by an oppressive communist government between 1945 and 1989 and the particular impacts of this oppression on Romanian families and women.

While the Revolution of Romania in 1989 was no doubt a victory for the country of Romania, there continues to be a story of unceasing victimization. The debilitating economy, standards of living, and international isolation, all hallmarks of the communist autocracy Romania experienced under the rule of the Ceausescu family for nearly three decades, continue to threaten the country's reintegration into the European economic, political, and cultural space.

The accounts of loss shared by the Romanian women in our study are embedded within a historical, political, and developmental context. The stories told by these women represent losses incurred as a result of historical and political events (i.e., oppression, loss of employment, loss of socioeconomic status), as well as those losses that may occur naturally throughout the course of one's life (i.e., death, illness, divorce). Our hope is to facilitate a greater understanding and appreciation of the losses experienced by middle-aged Romanian women within a unique historical, political, economic, social, and cultural context.

Historical Overview

As its name suggests, Romania traces its cultural and linguistic roots to Imperial Rome. It has been the target of conquests by the Ottoman Empire, Czarist Russia, the Hapsburg Empire, and the German Nazis in the period 1939–1945 and the Soviet Union from 1945 to 1989. Located in central Eastern Europe, Romania has a population of nearly 23 million people. The country's largest ethnic minorites are Hungarian and German. Romania is the only country with a Romance language that does not have a Roman Catholic background, with 70% of the population being Romanian Orthodox (Stanley, 1991).

Throughout the communist period, Romania was unique in central Eastern Europe for its independent foreign policy, which was based on disarmament, détente, and peaceful coexistence with all countries. Starting in 1945 and continuing to varying degrees throughout President Nicolae Ceausescu's reign, approximately 300,000 Romanians were imprisoned or sent to mental institutions for various "crimes" against communism. Unlike other communist bloc countries that had begun degrees of democratic and market reforms prior to 1990, Romania suffered in brutal isolation under Ceausescu's regime. Ceausescu's efforts to chart an independent course for Romania came at great expense to the Romanian people. In order to pay off Romania's $10 billion foreign debt, Ceausescu exported Romania's food, which created massive food shortages throughout Romania. Ceausescu also wanted to transform Romania from an agriculturally based economy to an industrially based one. He wanted the population to increase despite inadequate resources among most of the population to care for additional children in their families. In 1966, Ceausescu restricted legal abortion to women who were more than 45 years of age or who already supported four or more children (a possibility that was eliminated in a further ruling in 1985). In addition, the importation of contraceptives was prohibited, divorce was severely restricted, and illegal abortion became a punishable offense for women and their service providers (David & Baban, 1996). Couples were forced into situations in which they would register the birth of a child to satisfy the authorities and then abandon the child at one of the many state orphanages. These policies contributed to thousands of illegal and sometimes botched abortions. Many deformed children were born, and thousands more deformed children were placed in orphanages.

Throughout the 1980s, the population continued to suffer from prolonged scarcities of almost everything. Yet, despite the dramatic decline in the population's living standard, Ceausescu initiated several grandiose projects in the country's capital of Bucharest that came at huge costs in resources to the Romanian people. To mark his achievements, Ceausescu built imposing buildings and grand boulevards in Bucharest, a program that led to the destruction of thousands of old homes and forced many Romanians to relocate to housing structures that were unfinished or poorly built. These Romanian families incurred a devastating loss in their standard of living. By 1989, there was no money remaining to finish many of Ceausescu's elaborate and functionless projects. Some of these unfinished buildings and half-built streets still lie dormant in central Bucharest today (Harvey, 1998).

By the late 1980s, with the Soviet bloc quickly disintegrating, it seemed only a matter of time before Romania's citizens would challenge the communist regime. In December of 1989, the Romanian people spoke out and denounced Ceausescu's rule. After a week of revolutionary activities in which more than 1,000 people were killed, Ceausescu and his wife Elena were captured, tried, and executed.

While the victory of the revolution opened the way for a reestablishment of democracy, Romania faced a long road to social, political, and economic recovery. The afflictions of Ceausescu's regime continue to live on and threaten the country's postcommunist democracy. Romania continues to have one of the most inflated and harshest economies in central Eastern Europe. As a result of Ceausescu's decision in the 1980s to ban abortion in order to increase the population, as well as the unrelenting financial hardships faced by a great majority of the Romanian population, it has been estimated that nearly 100,000 abandoned children less than 18 years of age were living in orphanages in the late 1990s (Romanian Adoption Committee data). It has even been suggested that, given the socioeconomic difficulties that have endured so long in the country, the population eventually will suffer genetically over the long run from malnutrition experienced by millions of Romanian citizens (personal communication, A. Paduraru). Since 1990, Romania's leaders have shown little effectiveness in turning the country's economy around. At the turn of the 21st century, Romania continues to struggle to overcome its political, economic, and social difficulties and heal the wounds from a long history of isolation and oppression.

Accounts of Loss

It has been proposed that people often conceive their losses in terms of the stories or accounts that contextualize the major events of their lives (Harvey et al., 1990). Thus, we chose to integrate the stories told by middle-aged Romanian women of their loss experiences into our research. Through personal interviews and questionnaire surveys with the fourth author, there were common reports of the struggle to find meaning in their losses and to redirect their lives toward opportunities for growth. A 56-year-old Romanian scientific researcher explained her own ideologies about loss and lessons learned.

> I have learned that a loss or a win can't only be considered such. It is something relative, with positive elements in loss and negative elements in win. That is why a loss must be considered in positive terms because it brings something positive through identity modifications that arise as a result of the loss. You learn from losses, therefore you change. I have reconsidered my relationships and I've become more available to people.

Loss and suffering were not topics that were discussed directly or often. It was typical for these Romanian women to engage in downward social comparison (Wills, 1981) in which they would compare themselves with others less fortunate or living under more difficult conditions. It has been suggested that the use of downward social comparison is a strategy associated with the nation's ideal of fatalism. For example, an accomplished Romanian psychologist shared her story of loss and concluded that her suffering was relative to that of countless Romanians who were locked away in communist prisons.

> In 1985, 10 years after I received my PhD, I was told by the Romanian Communist Party officials that I would be demoted. I gave an interview in Paris in which I discussed transcendental meditation; a topic that I was studying then. They [Romanian Communist Party] said my interview betrayed state secrets. I was taken out of my university teaching job and given first a factory job, and then I was made a janitor in the plant. These jobs lasted about a year and one-half. Then I was allowed to resume my teaching, but I had to start over as if I had just begun.

While the revolution of 1989 opened the way for a democratic government, it has not been an easy transition for the Romanian people. The economic, social, and emotional repercussions are still prevalent nearly a decade after the revolution. For some, there is a sense of loss of community, affliction, and lost identities. For others, there is a sense of victory and optimism:

> One of the most positive experiences for the Romanian people was the Revolution from December 1989. We have more freedom now, but the material (financial) restraints are more acute and serve as a major obstacle for people to enjoy life.

In the face of significant socioeconomic losses over many years, respondents often reported amazing accounts of hope and perseverance. A university professor shared this story:

> There was an accident at a public institution where there was material gathered over a period longer than 20 years for a scientific paper by a 14-person team that I led and worked with for 10 years. Everything was burned down and when the entire staff requested to start it all over, we were not granted permission. Although I suffered much, I never gave up. After 65 years, I wrote and published 2 books.

One woman told of multiple loss experiences that included the death of her 14-year-old daughter in a car accident; divorce; the gang rape of her 17-year-old daughter; having her father imprisoned in a communist jail and her home destroyed, leaving her family homeless; and caring for her handicapped father. Yet, despite all of these losses, which could have left a void in terms of compassion and understanding, this woman shared the lessons learned from her losses: "The losses present in my life have made me better understand other people experiencing loss. I reach out and help people whenever I can."

A university researcher told of her family's experience with the communist regime and how postrevolution economic conditions have negatively affected quality of life and compromised the country's sense of community.

> Before 1989 during the communist regime, my parents, both professors, were periodically harassed for political reasons. Close relatives were imprisoned for political reasons for long periods of time. Some of them died after they were released as a result of the physical and psychological tortures they suffered . . . . My researcher wage after 1990 has become entirely insufficient. I am submitted to unimaginable humiliation of material matters in a country that doesn't feel the need for culture and willingly destroys it.

A 57-year-old journalist wrote in great detail about her losses relevant to the historical events in Romania and subsequent social "freedom" that she experienced.

> The actions of the communist powers had ill-fated consequences on my family. My father lost his job at the ministry as a punishment because he belonged to the [Social Democratic Party]. As a direct result, my family has been deprived of many rights . . . I experienced total dissatisfaction as a journalist. I lived the dramatic experience of being required to avoid the truth, which for a journalist meant total alienation. After the Revolution of 1989, I have been able to work at a decision-making level, to make my publications represent truth and incorporate my own beliefs.

A story was shared by a 56-year-old German woman from Transylvania with Romanian citizenship and the cross-cultural difficulties experienced during a long history of political upheaval that encompassed World War II and the Romanian Revolution of 1989. Her story signifies a loss of identity of nearly three generations, in essence a loss of one's life history.

> Being of German ethnicity, my family was dispossessed of our house, land, vineyard. . . . When my mother tried to get our estates back, she discovered that in the local official archives, the evidence of our estates and the personal information of my grandparents, their 10 children, and their descendants were completely erased from the current register.

Despite the oppressive history that Romania has endured, the poor economic and social conditions that continue to persist, and the personal losses that characterize the lives of these Romanian women, we found much evidence in the accounts of the common themes of strength, courage, hope, and graciousness. The following are illustrative:

> My brother's disease determined me to contribute my time to a humanitarian foundation aimed at people with disabilities.

> I hope from the bottom of my heart that my suffering and losses have made me more understanding, tolerant, and generous. I believe that a person who has suffered has gained greater wisdom.

> I regard my losses as integral parts of life. My philosophy of life is that everything must be balanced. Evil is followed by good, and good by evil. We shouldn't despair when things get hard, nor should we ever take things for granted when things get better. I have compassion for others in sorrow and I get involved in their problems by encouraging them.

> I could never understand why a toddler or infant dies, why a very young friend of mine was exiled a few months ago, why the parents are the ones who have to deal with all of these things. But each loss has made me think about the greatness of some of our actions. Life is our greatest present that must be lived all the way, meaning that each of us has to give him/herself completely to one or more activities, and to improve the relationship among people. Each "little" thing one does in life in good faith means a lot and with willpower, we can all move on in life.

> I have learned with great difficulty, to become more independent, to accept loneliness, to have more self-esteem, to better understand differences and to accept them. I have become more receptive to other people's problems and to support them. I have revised some rigid and categorical opinions of mine and I have come to accept my losses and overcome my desperation by getting involved in different activities of political and social order.

The stories of loss that were shared with us were inextricably tied to the political events and subsequent social and moral degradation suffered by the Romanian people. Their stories are marked by lost opportunities, lost possessions, lost homes, exposure to violence and trauma, and separation from loved ones. Yet, intertwined within these accounts of loss one can find evidence of hope and resiliency. Despite the experience of a violently repressive communist regime and insurmountable social and economic conditions, there is evidence that many of the Romanian women in our study have reconstructed their experiences and found new meaning and purpose in their lives (Harvey, Carlson, Huff, & Green, in press).

Quantitative Findings

In addition to the qualitative analysis of the interviews and surveys in which the participants shared their personal stories of loss, we also conducted a quantitative analysis. Our preliminary research findings are based on information collected via interviews and surveys from 40 Romanian female volunteers who were 35 years of age and older.

Demographic Information

Table 1 provides a demographic profile of the participants. The sample consisted of 40 Romanian women who ranged in age from 35 to 68 years ($M = 52$).

Loss Experience Information

Table 2 provides a profile of the frequency of losses experienced by these Romanian women, including loss by death of a close other, loss of health, loss of employment, loss by divorce, loss as a result of violence, and loss by oppression. It was surprising to note that while all of these women survived oppressive political and economic conditions throughout a major portion of their lives, only 30% of the sample indicated having experienced loss as a result of oppression. Perhaps what Westerners identify as "oppression" is, in fact, a way of life that is accepted by the Romanian people. It is also significant to note that half of our sample has experienced loss of employment.

When affirmative responses were made regarding specific loss experiences, participants were asked to rate how much that particular event(s) made their life more difficult over the years (not at all more difficult to a great deal more difficult). The means, standard deviations, and range of responses are indicated in Table 3. Of those respondents who experienced a loss due to the death of a

TABLE 1 Descriptive Profile for the
Overall Sample

Characteristic	Sample (%)
Age (years)	
35–45	20.0
46–55	62.5
56–65	10.0
66+	5.0
Marital status	
Single	2.5
Married	50.0
Divorced	22.5
Widowed	25.5
Occupation	
Educational field	27.5
Clerical/administrative	17.5
Business and industry	12.5
Custodial work	10.0
Health care	2.5
Retired	17.5
Unemployed	5.0

close other, loss of health or employment, or loss by divorce, violence, or oppression, the extent to which they reported experiencing great difficulty over the years was prominent.

The account-making model (Harvey et al., 1990) posits that our losses are constructed and reconstructed through storylike accounts that become part of who we are. Therefore, we were interested in examining how these Romanian women may have changed as a result of their losses (from their own subjective point of view). Thus, participants were asked to indicate what their history of losses had taught them about life and how these losses had affected their philosophy of living and their relationships with others. Five categories of responses emerged that were indicative of a positive impact from one's losses: (a) increased sensitivity and/or compassion for death, dying, and loss in general (37.5%); increased focus on living (12.5); commitment to loved ones and close others (12.5%); increased service to one's community (7.5%); and commitment to a cause (5%). The one negative effect that was reported was difficulty in interpersonal relationships (i.e., difficulties

TABLE 2 Profile of Loss Experiences for the Overall Sample

Loss experience	Sample (%)
Loss by death of close other	
Yes	82.5
No	15.0
Loss of health	
Yes	67.5
No	32.5
Loss of employment	
Yes	50.0
No	50.0
Loss by divorce	
Yes	27.5
No	70.0
Loss by violence	
Yes	27.5
No	72.5
Loss by oppression	
Yes	30.0
No	70.0

related to trust, compassion, or closeness to others), but this was indicated by only 25% of the sample. Remarkably, 75% of the sample reported positive changes in their philosophy of living and derived meaning from their losses and relationships with others.

Central to the account-making model is the premise that the confiding experience is crucial to the person's assimilation of and

TABLE 3 Difficulty Associated With Loss

Loss experience	M	SD
Death of close other(s)	6.06	2.38
Loss of health	6.58	1.74
Loss of employment	6.33	2.28
Loss by divorce	5.17	2.98
Loss by violence	6.10	2.56
Loss by oppression	7.33	0.98

Note. Scale for all items: 0 (no difficulty at all) to 8 (a great amount of difficulty).

adaptation to the loss. This confiding experience involves social interaction in which a person imparts part of his or her story to close others over time.

Our results were consistent with the premise that confiding is a key step in adaptation to major losses. When asked how helpful it was to confide in others by telling them about their loss, 65% of the sample indicated that it was helpful, while only 15% indicated that it was not at all helpful. This result was further clarified in the accounts obtained. Family, friends, and spirituality were commonly reported sources of support relied upon by these Romanian women as they coped with the variety of losses throughout their lives. In fact, 92.5% of our sample reported that they relied on religion or spirituality to cope with the loss experiences in their life. This points to the important place that religion (especially the Orthodox church) and spirituality has in Romanian culture. Finally, when asked to rate how happy they were with their current life, 75% of the sample indicated that they were happy with their current life.

Correlational Analysis

Pearson product-moment correlations were calculated in order to identify relationships between variables of interest. Table 4 presents this correlational evidence. Several significant findings can be observed in this table. The relationship between difficulty associated with loss of employment and reported helpfulness of spirituality ($r = .61$, $p < .01$) indicates that the more difficulty experienced with the loss of employment, the greater spirituality was found to be helpful. This finding suggests a strong reliance on spirituality as a coping mechanism in facing loss. An underlying belief of the Orthodox religion is that dealing with tragedy, loss, and hard times are considered to be God's challenges and thus are to be accepted and faced with heroism.

A strong positive correlation emerged between the extent to which subjects found confiding their loss experiences to others to be helpful and the extent to which the growth experience from loss had an effect on their life ($r = .70$, $p < .01$). This finding indicates that the greater the perceived helpfulness of confiding in others about their loss experiences, the greater the impact the losses repor-

TABLE 4 Correlation Matrix for Variables Studied

Variable	1	2	3	4	5	6	7	8	9	10	11
1. Loss of employment	—										
2. Employment loss difficulty	.06	—									
3. Loss due to violence	.12	-.24	—								
4. Loss due to divorce	.44**	-.01	.47**	—							
5. Loss due to oppression	.13	.27	-.04	.04	—						
6. Religious service attendance	.00	-.11	-.08	-.07	-.09	—					
7. Religion/spirituality helpful	-.03	.61**	-.35*	-.10	.16	-.41*	—				
8. Confiding helpful	-.13	-.33	.22	.30	-.19	-.47*	.18	—			
9. Growth experience	.05	-.21	-.10	.06	.07	-.11	.08	.11	—		
10. Effect of growth experience	-.21	.44	-.06	.25	.52*	-.46	.21	.70**	.38	—	
11. Happiness	-.21	-.23	-.02	.18	-.13	-.26	.27	.54**	.47**	.32	—

Note. Loss of employment = Have you or members of your immediate family experienced loss of employment or some work-related hardship? (yes/no); Employment loss difficulty = If you or members of your family experienced such employment difficulties, please rate below how much that event made your life more difficult over the years (scaled 0–8); Loss due to violence = Have you or your immediate family been the target of violent acts by others? (yes/no); Loss due to divorce = Have you experienced loss as a result of a divorce? (yes/no); Loss due to oppression = Have you or members of your immediate family experienced loss as a result of oppression (i.e., socioeconomic status, race/ethnicity, gender, government, powerful people, disability)? (yes/no); Religious service attendance = How often do you attend religious services? (every week, 2–3 times per month, once per month, less than one time per month); Religion/spirituality helpful = If religion or spirituality were relied on to cope with loss experiences, how helpful was that approach? (scaled 0–8); Confiding helpful = Please rate how helpful it was to confide in others by telling them about your loss (scaled 0–8); Growth experience = Please indicate if you have had a major growth experience in the last 10 years that resulted because of a loss experience (yes/no); Effect of growth experience = If you have had such a growth experience, please rate below how much that event has affected your life (scaled 0–8); Happiness = Please rate how happy you are with your current life (scaled 0–8).

* $p < .05$; ** $p < .01$.

tedly had on their lives. This correlation coheres with the findings of Barnes, Harvey, Carlson, and Haig (1996). Barnes et al. showed that the sharing of stories of personal loss with others facilitates the meaning reconstruction process in which one begins to adapt to the loss, assimilate the loss experience into one's identity, and recognize the contributions of the loss experience itself to one's life. Barnes et al. also found that confiding in others about loss was significantly related to the extent to which people reported experiencing a significant positive impact from their losses. The relation between confiding and growth-related experience can be witnessed in the account of a retired architect and university lecturer:

> I tell my confidants about my problems, worries, fears, and difficulties. After I talk with them, I feel more optimistic and peaceful and thanks to them, I have more confidence in my ability to get through difficult times. . . . I have learned that loss is a change and from each loss one gains something, too. One learns something, one changes in his/her relationships, one becomes more careful with people, more tolerant, and values their worth.

A significant relationship was found between the extent to which participants reported confiding their loss experiences to others to be helpful and their overall rating of their happiness ($r = .54$, $p < .01$), indicating that those who reported that confiding was helpful to them in coping with loss also reported greater happiness in their current life. A significant positive correlation was found for the relationship between perceived growth experience as a result of loss and reported level of happiness ($r = .47$, $p < .01$). Barnes et al. (1996) suggested that the greater the extent to which account-making and confiding activities have occurred for major loss experiences, the healthier and happier the individual should feel in the long run.

A positive correlation emerged for loss due to divorce and loss due to violence ($r = .47$, $p < .01$). This finding has relevance for respondents' accounts of loss by divorce, which often cited spousal abuse as a reason for separation and divorce. In Romania, the divorce rates for the past two decades have been between 0.7 and 1.7 in 1000 persons, with signs of some increase in the divorce rate toward the late 1990s. Yet, despite this relatively small population, nearly 23% of our particular sample reported being divorced. While divorce in Romania is preferable to never being married, it is considered a social failure that transcends the entire family. With more than one quarter of our sample in the education field, this sample of Romanian women at midlife and beyond may be unusual in the extent to which divorce is represented.

A positive correlation was found between perceived oppression and loss of employment ($r = .44$, $p < .01$). This result was surprising given the history of communist oppression that led to job replacement and job loss for many Romanian people. A negative correlation was found between whether respondents found confiding about their losses to be helpful and how often they attended religious services ($r = -.42$, $p < .05$). This finding suggests that the less respondents found confiding to be helpful, the more often they attended religious services. Once again, such evidence attests to the reliance on religion as a coping mechanism.

A significant relationship was found between loss due to oppression and the extent to which respondents' growth experience from loss had an effect on their life ($r = .52$, $p < .05$), indicating perhaps that the experience of oppression serves as a catalyst for personal growth to occur. Many of the accounts that were shared with us were characterized by elements of extraordinary strength, resilience, and hope. Snyder (1996) posits that it is hope that gets us through our lowest moments and enables us to move ahead from our loss-filled present to an imagined brighter future that is better. For many hopeful Romanians, they are determined to address the country's problems and create a better place for future generations. A university researcher shared this account:

> The events from 1989 along with the loss of those closest to me have changed my relations with others. I now have more patience and I understand better people who suffer. I place a great deal of weight on moral values, responsibility for others, involvement in community life, and the solidarity for a high goal regarding the destiny of our country and of our children.

Discussion

In studying the loss experiences of Romanian women at midlife and beyond, we are reminded of the universal existence of loss in human life. Yet, the experience of loss cannot be separated from our individual uniqueness and the cultures that surround us. Concepts such as "death" and "grief" have culture-specific meanings. Thus, it is misleading to assume that our understanding of these concepts and experiences from a Western perspective applies generally from culture to culture and from person to person. People from other cultures understand and classify their experiences and perceptions differently and place them in the context of their own beliefs about the origin of events, the nature of the person, the proper way to behave, and the meaning of losses (Irish, Lundquist, & Nelsen, 1993). Thus, in studying loss from a multicultural perspective, we are able to gain insight into the unique historical and social influences that contribute to the conceptualization and experience of loss from both an individual and a cultural perspective.

There are several limitations to our research. Most of the interview and questionnaire data were gathered in Bucharest and in a few other large Romanian cities. Thus, the experiences of people living in the outlying villages and rural areas are not represented. However, Bucharest, in its size and complexity, probably represents Romania's woes and its promise better than any other place in the country. Although our questionnaires were translated into the Romanian language, it is uncertain whether our English-language concepts and terminology had the intended meanings for the respondents, thus making it difficult to extract the precise meaning from the response.

While there are certainly instances of greater suffering and more daunting loss and coping circumstances throughout the world that might be studied, scientific research in Romania is becoming quite limited because of financial deprivations in the universities. There is a need to study these phenomena in Romania and countries facing imposing stressful situations to better understand cross-cultural differences in how people cope with major losses.

Harvey (1996) argues that the key to transforming losses into something positive lies in our efforts to give our losses meaning, to learn and gain insights from them, and to impart to others something positive based on the loss experience. Thus, in coping with loss, the process of finding meaning in one's losses is crucial. Meaning reconstruction can be accomplished through a variety of social, psychological, or spiritual processes. One of the most universal approaches to dealing with and finding meaning in loss is story telling (Coles, 1989), or what Harvey et al. (1990) refer to as account making. As people share their stories with others, they give meaning to their unique life experiences. Yet, sharing one's story of loss has the power to have profound effects not only on the teller but also on the listener. In listening to and reading the narratives of the Romanian women in our study, we find validation in the important roles of telling one's stories, confiding in others, and finding meaning as vital ideas in our understanding of human life. Most important in this research, story telling and confiding were associated with participants' loss-related growth, identity transformation, and giving back to others and to their community. The lessons learned from loss that were shared by our respondents should serve as a reminder of the resiliency of the human spirit.

In the face of major loss, we can observe the immense capability of the human spirit to renew and be generative. As a fragile country continually challenged by adversity, Romania represents a place where we can learn invaluable lessons about the interdependent relationships among loss, courage, resiliency, and renewal. We hope that these findings and stories of loss will provide insight into the rich psychological phenomena that are present in the unique loss experiences of these Romanian women.

References

Barnes, M. K., Harvey, J. H., Carlson, H. R., & Haig, J. (1996). The relativity of grief: Differential adaptation reactions of younger and older persons. *Journal of Personal and Interpersonal Loss, 1*, 375–392.

Coles, R. (1989). *The call of stories.* Boston: Houghton Mifflin.

David, H. P., & Baban, A. (1996). Women's health and reproductive rights: Romanian experience. *Patient Education and Counseling, 28*, 235–245.

Harvey, J. H. (1996). *Embracing their memory: Loss and the social psychology of storytelling.* Needham Heights, MA: Allyn & Bacon.

Harvey, J. H. (1998). *Lessons in the psychology of loss: Romania in the late 1990s.* Unpublished manuscript.

Harvey, J. H., Carlson, H. R., Huff, T. M., & Green, M. A. (in press). Embracing their memory: The construction of accounts of loss and hope. In R. A. Neimeyer (Ed.), *Meaning reconstruction and the experience of loss.* Washington, DC: American Psychological Association.

Harvey, J. H., Weber, A. L., & Orbuch, T. L. (1990). *Interpersonal accounts: A social psychological approach.* Oxford, England: Basil Blackwell.

Irish, D. P., Lundquist, K. F., & Nelsen, V. L. (Eds.). (1993). *Ethnic variations in dying, death, and grief.* Washington, DC: Taylor & Francis.

Snyder, C. R. (1996). To hope, to lose, and to hope again. *Journal of Personal and Interpersonal Loss, 1,* 1–16.

Stanley, D. (1991). *Eastern Europe on a shoestring* (2nd ed.). Oakland, CA: Lonely Planet Publications.

Wills, T. A. (1981). Downward comparison principles in social psychology. *Psychological Bulletin, 90,* 245–271.

PART II
RESPONDING TO AND COPING WITH
POST-TRAUMATIC STRESS

In the second part of this volume, the focus switches from the contexts and relatively immediate consequences of trauma to the
active responses and long-term reactions to such events. As a
whole, the chapters highlight a couple of key notions. First, the
eventual success of an individual's effort to respond to a traumatic
event in an adaptive manner can depend on individual, organization, and cultural factors. The resources and strategies available
to a victim coping with trauma may therefore be provided by the
victim himself or herself or by other individuals and institutions in
contact with that victim. A second theme of this section is that the
coping process is frequently dynamic, with victims (and those close
to them) often experiencing an "evolution" of their grief. Issues
regarding the most appropriate way to remember their losses and
to communicate the importance of those losses become salient to
trauma survivors as the passage of time provides them at least with
additional perspective, if not always comfort.

CHAPTER SIX

THE ROLE OF ATTRIBUTIONS AND PERCEIVED CONTROL IN RECOVERY FROM RAPE

PATRICIA A. FRAZIER

Department of Psychology, University of Minnesota,
Minneapolis, Minnesota, USA

It is fitting that a volume on post-traumatic stress includes chapters on sexual assault given both the prevalence of sexual assault and its effects. Specifically, in terms of prevalence, approximately one woman in five in the United States will be raped in her lifetime (Koss, 1993).[1] In terms of the effects of sexual assault, victims experience heightened fear, anxiety, and depression for several months, and sometimes years, following an assault (see Frazier & Borgida, 1997, and Resick, 1993, for reviews). Sexual victimization affects physical health as well and is a more powerful predictor of physician visits and outpatient medical costs than other factors (e.g., age, smoking, alcohol use) known to be related to health problems (Koss, Koss, & Woodruff, 1991). Finally, sexual assault is one of the traumatic events that is most likely to lead to post-traumatic stress disorder (PTSD) (Breslau, Davis, Andreski, & Peterson, 1991; Norris, 1992; Ullman & Siegel, 1994). In a recent national study of trauma exposure and PTSD by Kessler and his colleagues (Kessler, Sonnega, Bromet, Hughes, & Nelson, 1995), almost half of the women who said that a rape was their worst trauma met lifetime criteria for PTSD. This is in comparison, for example, with a PTSD prevalence rate of 5% for those whose worst event was a natural disaster.

---

[1] Because the majority of victims are women, this chapter focuses on female victims of sexual assault.

Although sexual assault can have devastating effects, there also is tremendous variability in the extent to which women are affected. Researchers have examined various factors that might explain these individual differences in levels of postrape trauma (see Koss et al., 1994, for a review). For example, victims who have experienced prior psychological problems and prior victimization tend to experience more distress postrape, as do victims of more severe assaults. Information on victim and assault characteristics associated with greater postrape distress can be used to identify victims who may be at risk of developing more severe mental health problems. However, because these factors (e.g., assault severity) generally cannot be changed after the assault, they do not suggest ways to intervene to improve recovery. Efforts need to be directed at identifying factors associated with recovery that are modifiable and that can be targeted in treatment approaches.

The victim's attributions about why the rape occurred and perceptions of control over the past and future are modifiable factors with important implications for postrape recovery. For example, many studies have shown that causal attributions and control beliefs are associated with recovery from a variety of negative life events (see Joseph, Williams, & Yule, 1995, and Taylor & Armor, 1996, for reviews). Answering questions such as "Why did this happen to me?" and "Will this happen again?" seems particularly important for victims of sudden and unexpected traumatic events like rape. As a result, these questions are central issues in counseling victims of rape, and, in order to facilitate recovery, counselors need to know which kinds of attributions and control beliefs are most adaptive for victims. Finally, the attribution made by the victim about the cause of the rape has important implications for how others respond to her. For example, victims who blame themselves are perceived by others as less adjusted and as more responsible for the rape (Thornton et al., 1988). This, in turn, can affect how the victim feels about herself and, consequently, her recovery.

This chapter presents the results of an ongoing program of research on the role of causal attributions and perceived control in the postrape recovery process. Data from two published studies (Frazier, 1990; Frazier & Schauben, 1994) first are described briefly. The results of a recently conducted study then are presented in more detail, followed by a description of two current studies. These studies all address the role of attributions and perceived control in the recovery process but differ in terms of the nature of the samples; the measurement of attributions, perceived control, and postrape distress; the amount of time elapsed since the assault occurred (i.e., short-term vs. long-term recovery); and the number of postrape assessments (i.e., cross-sectional vs. longitudinal designs). The results of these studies are summarized and integrated with those of other research on attributions/control and postrape symptoms. Finally, implications of the data for counseling rape victims are discussed.

Study 1: Attributions, Control, and Initial Depression

The first study (Frazier, 1990) was designed to test the theory that certain types of self-blame can be adaptive for victims of rape (Janoff-Bulman, 1979). Specifically, Janoff-Bulman proposed that behavioral self-blame is related to better adjustment because it is associated with a sense of future control. That is, victims may feel that, by changing their behaviors, they can avoid being victimized in the future. Alternatively, characterological self-blame, which involves attributions to stable and uncontrollable aspects of the self, is seen as unhelpful because it does not provide the same sense of control. Similarly, blaming an external factor such as chance is not helpful because it may leave victims feeling as if bad things just happen and there is nothing they can do to prevent them.

It is important to note that Janoff-Bulman's (1979) model, although very widely cited in the research literature, is counter to most treatment approaches, which actively discourage self-blame (see, e.g., Foa & Rothbaum, 1998). If, however, behavioral self-blame is associated with greater control and better adjustment, discouraging self-blame actually could be harmful to victims. If, on the other hand, all kinds of self-blame are associated with more distress, it is important that new models of the relations between causal attributions and postrape recovery be developed.

At the time our first study was conducted, only one previous study had examined the relations between behavioral and characterological self-blame and symptoms among rape victims (Meyer &

Taylor, 1986). In this study, both behavioral and characterological self-blame were associated with higher symptom levels. Measures of behavioral and characterological self-blame were highly correlated, suggesting that victims may not make the distinctions between behavior and character that are implied in Janoff-Bulman's (1979) model. Meyer and Taylor did not, however, assess whether behavioral self-blame is, in fact, related to the belief that future rapes can be avoided or whether beliefs about future control are themselves associated with better adjustment.

Thus, our first study (Frazier, 1990) was designed to assess the relations among behavioral and characterological self-blame and postrape distress and to test whether behavioral self-blame is indeed related to perceptions of future control. Data were collected within 1 week postrape from clients seen at the Sexual Assault Resource Service (SARS), a hospital-based rape crisis program in Minneapolis, Minnesota. The primary attribution measures were scores on 15 attributional statements developed by Meyer and Taylor (1986). Scores on these items were factor analyzed, revealing three factors that assessed behavioral self-blame (Poor Judgment), characterological self-blame (Victim Type), and societal blame (Societal Factors). Participants also completed one-item measures of behavioral self-blame, characterological self-blame, the extent to which the past rape could have been avoided, and the extent to which future rapes could be avoided. The Beck Depression Inventory (BDI) was used to assess postrape depressive symptoms.

The results of this initial research (see Frazier, 1990, for more details) suggested that both behavioral and characterological self-blame were significantly related to higher levels of depressive symptoms ($rs = .40$ to $.53$). This may be partly because victims did not seem to make the distinctions between behavior and character implied by the model. That is, very few (7%) individuals blamed their behavior without also blaming their character. It was not surprising, therefore, that the two types of self-blame were not associated with other factors as predicted by Janoff-Bulman's (1979) model. Most important, behavioral self-blame was significantly associated with the belief that the past rape could have been avoided ($rs = .50$ to $.59$) but not with the belief that future rapes could be avoided ($rs = -.15$ to $.06$). According to Janoff-Bulman's model, behavioral self-blame is uniquely associated with the perception that future rapes can be avoided and is adaptive precisely for that reason. Interestingly, the belief that the past rape could have been avoided also was not associated with the belief that future rapes could be avoided ($r = -.04$). Victims who felt they could avoid being raped in the future were significantly less depressed, however ($r = -.38$).

Several other findings also are worth noting. First, blaming society for the rape was as strongly associated with depressive symptoms ($r = .59$) as was self-blame. This suggests that all of the attributions investigated were associated with more distress. In addition, although the data did not support Janoff-Bulman's (1979) model, they did suggest that attributions were strongly related to postrape depression. In a regression analysis, the attribution factors measuring behavioral, characterological, and societal blame accounted for 67% of the variance in depression immediately postrape.

Although intriguing, this research also was limited in several respects. First, the data were collected within 1 week postrape, which is too soon to assess the recovery process. It therefore seemed necessary to examine the relations between attributions and longer term recovery. A second limitation was that the sample was small and consisted of survivors who reported to a hospital-based rape crisis program. Because most survivors do not seek immediate help and may, in fact, not seek help at all, these findings needed to be replicated in more representative samples. Finally, it seemed important to assess whether attributions are uniquely related to depression or whether they also are associated with other psychological symptoms or changes in basic beliefs about the world (McCann & Pearlman, 1990).

Study 2: Attributions, Control, and Long-Term Recovery

Therefore, in the next study (Study 2), we assessed the relations between attributions and symptoms among 59 college women who had been assaulted an average of 8 years prior to participation in the study (Frazier & Schauben, 1994). The goal of this study was to assess the relations among attributions, control beliefs, and long-term recovery in a more representative sample of rape survivors. It was predicted that both behavioral and characterological self-blame, as well as thinking more often about why the rape occurred, would be associated with poorer recovery. Greater perceived control over the future, on the other hand, was predicted to be associated with better recovery. We also predicted that the two types of self-blame would be significantly correlated and that perceptions of control over the past and control over the future would not be strongly related.

Participants rated their current attributions and control beliefs about the rape on six 5-point Likert scales. Questions assessed behavioral and characterological self-blame, past control, future control, likelihood of being raped again, and frequency of thinking about why the rape occurred. Recovery was assessed in terms of general psychological symptoms, via the Brief Symptom Inventory (BSI), and in terms of disruptions in basic beliefs about oneself and others as a result of victimization, via the McPearl Belief Scale (MBS).

Results suggested that both behavioral self-blame and characterological self-blame were associated with more distress, broadly defined in terms of general psychological symptoms and greater disruptions in basic beliefs about self and others (mean $r = .46$). Thinking more often about why the rape occurred also was associated with more distress (mean $r = .37$). Survivors who felt that future rapes were less likely reported fewer symptoms and disruptions in beliefs (mean $r = -.37$), although the belief that future rapes were controllable was not associated with recovery (mean $r = -.14$). As in previous studies, behavioral and characterological self-blame were significantly correlated ($r = .39$). Finally, neither behavioral self-blame nor perceptions of past control were significantly related to perceptions of future control or to the future likelihood of being raped ($rs = -.07$ to .22), supporting our hypothesis that perceptions of past control are distinct from perceptions of control over the future. Thus, these results replicated our previous findings among rape survivors seen immediately postrape in a sample of women who had been raped several years previously, with slightly different measures of attributions and perceived control and a broader assessment of recovery.

Like all studies, this one also has its limitations. The cross-sectional design precluded statements about the direction of the relations between attributions/perceived control and symptoms or changes in these relations over time. In addition, attributions and control beliefs were assessed via single-item measures, and external attributions were not measured.

Study 3: Longitudinal Study of Attributions, Control, and Recovery

The next step in our program of research was thus to conduct a longitudinal study of the relations between attributions/perceived control and postrape symptoms using improved measures of attributions and control. As before, the analyses addressed the relations between attributions/control and postrape symptoms as well as the relations among the attribution/control measures. This study differed from previous studies in that both cross-sectional and longitudinal data were collected and the relations between attributions/perceived control and specific symptoms (i.e., anxiety, depression, hostility, PTSD) were assessed. The predictions were the same, however: All types of attributions (and thinking more often about why the rape occurred) were expected to be associated with more distress, future control was predicted to be associated with less distress, and measures of past and future control were hypothesized to be unrelated to each other. Given the dearth of longitudinal data, no specific hypotheses were made regarding whether attributions/perceived control would predict changes in symptoms over time. The methods and results of this study are described in more detail because the study has not been previously published.

Participants and Procedure

Data were collected from 104 rape survivors seen at SARS in Minneapolis, which is the same agency where Study 1 was conducted. The majority of the participants were Caucasian (80%), and they ranged in age from 14 to 64 years ($M = 25.55$, $SD = 9.17$). Forty-five percent of the participants were raped by strangers. Survivors completed measures of attributions, control, and symptoms at six time periods from 1 week to 1 year postrape and were paid $10 for each assessment. Because not all participants completed question- naires at all time periods, data were combined to form three time periods: early (1 week; $n = 69$), middle (combining the 1- and 3-month time periods; $n = 72$), and late (combining the 6-, 9-, and 12-month time periods, $n = 46$). Before data were combined, paired t tests were performed to ensure that there were no signifi- cant mean differences in scores across the assessment periods being combined (all $ps > .05$). In addition, the median correlation between symptom scores across combined time periods was .78, further justifying the combining of time periods.

Measures

Attributions were examined via three 7-item scales assessing behav- ioral, characterological, and external (society and rapist) attribu- tions about the cause of the rape. Items were developed and then were rated by 11 members of the Violence and Victimization Task Force of Division 35 (Psychology of Women) of the American Psychological Association. All items received high ratings in terms of being realistic, unambiguous, and general enough to apply across situations (i.e., good measures of the constructs). Thus, the attribution measures used in this study were similar to, but improved upon, those used in Study 1. The mean alpha coefficients for the three scales across time periods ranged from .78 to .84. Future control was examined via a 2-item scale that assessed per- ceived control over future assaults and the perceived likelihood of future assaults (alphas = .53 to .65). One item assessed the fre- quency with which the victim thought about why the assault occurred. All items were rated on 5-point scales.

As mentioned, in this study we wanted to assess the relations between attributions/perceived control and measures of specific symptoms. Thus, the symptom measures included the BDI, the anxiety and hostility subscales of the BSI, and a 17-item PTSD checklist developed for this study that assessed the symptoms of PTSD listed in the *Diagnostic and Statistical Manual of Mental Dis- orders* (revised third edition; *DSM-III-R*; American Psychiatric Association, 1987). All scales had good internal consistency reliability (mean alphas .80 to .87). For the PTSD checklist, participants were asked to check the symptoms they had experienced since the rape (e.g., I often have bad dreams about the rape). This checklist was similar to other PTSD self-report measures developed from *DSM-III-R* criteria, such as the PTSD Symptom Scale-Self Report (Foa, Riggs, Dancu, & Rothbaum, 1993), which had not been published at the time we began data collection.

Results

Descriptive Statistics

First, the average scores for the variables at the three combined time periods are described. The means on the behavioral self-blame scale indicated that victims engaged in a moderate amount of self-blame (average $M = 3.05$ on the 5-point scale). Means on the characterological self-blame scale were slightly lower than the scale midpoint at all three time periods (average $M = 2.61$). In contrast, scores on the external blame scale were above the midpoint at each time period (average $M = 3.57$). Three multivariate analyses of variance (MANOVAs) conducted to compare scores on the behavioral, characterological, and external blame scales at each time period were all significant ($ps < .0001$). Follow-up paired t tests revealed that, at all three time periods, victims blamed external factors the most, followed by their behavior and character (all $ps < .01$). Finally, scores on both the future control and "thinking about why" scales were above the scale midpoint at each time period (average $Ms = 3.42$ and 3.95, respectively).

Mean scores on the symptom measures at the three combined time periods indicated that the rape victims in this sample were highly distressed. For example, mean BDI scores were in the moderately depressed range at all three time periods (average $M = 21.35$). Means on the anxiety (average $M = 1.95$) and hostility (average $M = 1.72$) scales also were significantly higher than norm group means for women ($M = 0.37$, $SD = 0.43$, and $M = 0.33$, $SD = 0.42$, respectively) at all three periods. In addition, victims endorsed approximately 60% (11 of 17) of the symptoms on the PTSD checklist at each time period. The percentages of victims who met *DSM-III-R* criteria for a PTSD diagnosis at each of the six time periods were 76% (1 week),

70% (1 month), 69% (3 months), 71% (6 months), 74% (9 months), and 50% (12 months).

Concurrent Analyses: Attributions/Perceived Control and Symptoms

The relations between attributions/perceived control and symptoms at the three combined time periods are summarized in Table 1. As was the case in the previous studies, both behavioral and characterological self-blame were related to higher symptom levels at all three time periods (mean rs = .29 and .33, respectively). The relations between self-blame and depression at the early (1-week) and middle (1- to 3-month) time periods were particularly strong (mean r = .50). External blame was consistently associated with more symptoms (mean r = .37), and, in fact, the relations between external blame and symptoms were somewhat more consistent than those between self-blame and symptoms. External blame also was more strongly related to hostility (mean r = .41) than was self-blame (mean r = .25). Thinking more often about why the rape

TABLE 1 Study 3: Concurrent Relations Between Attribution/Control Measures and Symptom Measures

	BDI	Anxiety	Hostility	PTSD
1 week postrape ($n = 69$)				
Behavioral self-balme	.48***	.27*	.13	.24
Characterological self-blame	.58***	.18	.08	.29*
External blame	.50***	.35**	.35**	.32*
Thinking about why	.32*	.37**	.11	.33*
Future control	−.38**	−.37**	−.12	−.32*
1 to 3 months postrape ($n = 72$)				
Behaviorial self-balme	.43***	.28*	.32**	.26*
Characterlogical self-blame	.48***	.19	.29*	.34*
External blame	.29*	.40***	.45***	.36**
Thinking about why	.30*	.36**	.16	.44***
Future control	−.38***	−.33**	−.22	−.36**
6 to 12 months postrape ($n = 46$)				
Behavioral self-blame	.24	.33*	.27	.22
Characterological self-blame	.39**	.36*	.42**	.34*
External blame	.28	.29*	.43**	.34*
Thinking about why	.38*	.52***	.30*	.54***
Future control	−.39**	−.35*	−.28	−.29

* $p < .05$; ** $p < .01$; *** $p < .001$.

occurred was associated with more symptoms (mean $r = .33$), particularly at 6 to 12 months postrape (mean $r = .44$), and was more
associated with anxiety and PTSD (mean $r = .42$) than with
depression (mean $r = .33$) or hostility (mean $r = .19$). Only future
control was associated with lower symptom levels (mean
$r = -.34$), including less depression, anxiety, and PTSD.

Concurrent Analyses: Attributions and Perceived Control

Correlations also were computed to examine the relations
among the various attribution and control scales at each of the
three time periods. Several results are noteworthy. First, at all
three time periods, behavioral and characterological self-blame
were highly correlated ($rs = .64$ to $.80$). Second, all three types of
attributions (i.e., behavioral, characterological, external) were
associated with thinking more often about why the rape occurred,
particularly at the middle and late time periods (mean $rs = .32$
and $.39$, respectively). Finally, the relations between the attribution measures and the future control scale revealed that behavioral
self-blame was not associated with a sense of future control at any
of the three time periods ($rs = .07$ to $-.16$). However, at 1–3
months and 6–12 months postrape, both characterological self-
blame and external blame were significantly related to lower future
control beliefs ($rs = -.28$ to $-.34$). Thus, individuals who blamed
the assault on their character or on external factors tended to feel
that future assaults were less controllable and more likely.

Longitudinal Analyses: Attributions/Perceived Control and Symptoms

As a means of assessing whether attributions or control beliefs at
one point in time predicted recovery at a later point in time, four
hierarchical multiple regression analyses were performed in which
symptom measures at 1–3 months postrape were regressed on the
attribution/control measures at 1 week postrape, controlling for
symptoms at 1 week postrape. Four similar analyses were performed with the 6–12-month symptom measures as the criterion
variables and attributions/perceived control and symptoms at 1–3
months postrape as the predictors. Because the behavioral and
characterological self-blame scales were highly correlated at each
time period, they were combined into a general self-blame scale. In
seven of the eight equations, symptom levels at one point strongly

predicted symptom levels at a later point in time (standardized betas = .56 to .72). The only exception to this trend was that 1–3-month hostility was not significantly related to 6–12-month hostility (standardized beta = .32). The only attribution/control variable that predicted later symptoms after controlling for earlier symptoms was future control. Specifically, victims who felt they had more control over future rapes at 1 week postrape were less depressed at 1–3 months postrape, after controlling for 1-week depression.

Summary

The results of this study replicated and extended those of the two previous cross-sectional studies. As in both previous studies, both kinds of self-blame were associated with more distress. In this study, self-blame was particularly associated with depressive symptoms. In addition, the measures of self-blame were highly correlated with each other. As in Study 1, external blame was associated with more distress; the relations with hostility were particularly strong. In fact, in both Studies 1 and 3, external blame tended to be more strongly related to symptoms than was self-blame. As in Study 2, more often thinking about why the assault occurred was associated with more symptoms. This relation appeared to increase over time (i.e., the correlations between thinking about "why" and symptoms were highest at the 6–12-month period). In addition, more often thinking about "why" was more strongly related to anxiety and PTSD than to other symptoms. As in both previous studies, an aspect of future control was the only factor associated with lower symptom levels. And, in fact, only future control predicted later symptom levels (i.e., depression) once earlier symptom levels were controlled. This finding underscores the importance of assessing various aspects of perceived control. It also is important to note that, as in the previous studies, although perceived future control was adaptive, it was not associated with behavioral self-blame. Extending previous research, both characterological and external blame were associated with the belief that future assaults were less controllable and more likely.

Like the previous studies, this one also has its limitations. For example, our measure of external blame combined attributions to society and to the rapist. In order to test more directly the adaptiveness of specific attributions, it is important to assess various external attributions separately (e.g., rapist, society, chance). Our perceived control measures also need to be improved both in terms of reliability and in terms of assessing different aspects of present and future control, including control over the recovery process (see, e.g., Thompson, Sobolew-Shubin, Galbraith, Schwankovsky, & Cruzen, 1993). Finally, the sample sizes for some analyses were quite small ($ns = 32$ to 39), resulting in low power to detect significant results. This was a problem particularly in the longitudinal analyses.

Current Studies of Attributions, Control, and Recovery

We have continued this program of research with two additional studies that address these limitations and build on the results of our previous investigations. The first (Study 4) is another longitudinal study of sexual assault survivors conducted at SARS, the site of Studies 1 and 3. The second is a cross-sectional study of long-term recovery among survivors of sexual assault and other traumatic events who were identified through a random digit dialing telephone survey (Study 5). These two studies are described briefly here.

In Study 4, the second longitudinal study at SARS, we built on Study 3 by improving the measurement of key constructs, assessing additional outcomes, and gathering a larger sample. Specifically, in regard to measurement, the assessment of attributions was improved via the development of a 25-item rape attribution questionnaire (Frazier, 1997a) that consists of five 5-item scales assessing two types of self-blame (behavioral and characterological) and three kinds of external attributions (chance, society, and rapist). Future control was assessed via three 5-item measures assessing the likelihood of future assaults, control over the recovery process, and taking precautions to try to avoid future assaults. The same single item assessed the frequency of thinking about why the assault occurred. Symptoms again were assessed via the anxiety, depression, and hostility subscales of the BSI and a 17-item PTSD symptom checklist. In addition, a 20-item measure of positive and negative life changes resulting from the assault was developed and administered. This measure reflects the growing interest in the trauma field in resilience and growth following traumatic events (see, e.g., Tedeschi, Park, & Calhoun, 1998). Measures were completed at 2 weeks and 2, 6, and 12 months after the assault. Participants received $20 for each completed questionnaire. Approximately 90 women completed questionnaires at each of the assessments. Preliminary results of this work have been presented at national and international conferences (Frazier, Byrne, & Klein, 1995; Frazier, Byrne, Klein, & Seales, 1996; Frazier, Iwan, & Glaser, 1998) and currently are being prepared for publication.

Because we are concerned about the generalizability of results obtained from a help-seeking sample, we conducted another study of sexual assault survivors who were identified through a random telephone survey and who have not necessarily sought help. Specifically, we conducted a random digit dialing phone survey that assessed traumatic events and PTSD among a sample of 894 women in Minneapolis and its suburbs. We asked each participant whether she would be willing to take part in a follow-up mail survey for which she would be paid $25. More than 90% agreed to participate, and, from that group, four groups of women were selected as participants: (a) a group that matched the SARS sample in Study 4 in terms of age, race, and education but had not been sexually assaulted ($n = 53$); (b) women who had been sexually assaulted ($n = 132$); (c) a comparison group demographically matched to the second group ($n = 136$); and (d) a group of women whose worst trauma was bereavement ($n = 159$). These data can be used to answer several different questions about posttrauma recovery (see Frazier, 1997b; Frazier et al., 1997; Frazier & Hurliman, 1998a, 1998b). However, only the data relevant to the relations between attributions/perceived control and symptoms are described (briefly) here.

The sample of 132 sexual assault survivors identified through the random phone survey completed questionnaires very similar to those completed by the participants in Study 4 (our second longitudinal study). Exceptions are that the future control measure was slightly expanded and some additional aspects of recovery were assessed, including general health perceptions, social adjustment, substance abuse, and beliefs about the world (i.e., World Assumptions Scale; Janoff-Bulman, 1989). In addition, the "Big Five" personality factors (i.e., Neuroticism, Extraversion, Openness, Conscientiousness, and Agreeableness) were measured.

These data from Study 5 will allow us to assess the generalizability of our findings from the SARS sample who sought help and were assessed immediately postrape (Study 4) to a community sample that had been assaulted many years ($M = 17$ years) previously. The personality data allow us to assess the extent to which the relations between blame and symptom measures are a function of an underlying personality trait such as Neuroticism. Finally, using data from the other Study 5 samples (e.g., women whose worst trauma was bereavement), we can assess whether the relations between control and symptoms identified in sexual assault survivors generalize to other events (see also Frazier & Schauben, 1994).

Summary and Integration

In this section, the results of our program of research on the relations between attributions/perceived control and postrape recovery are summarized and integrated with the results of other relevant studies. As mentioned, at the time Study 1 was conducted, only one study had examined the relations between attributions and recovery among rape survivors (Meyer & Taylor, 1986). At the time this chapter was written, approximately 10 studies had examined these issues (not including our program of research). All of these studies were cross sectional, most assessed longer term (greater than 1 year postrape) recovery, and only about half used standard symptom measures.

First, data from Studies 1, 2, and 3 (and preliminary data from Studies 4 and 5) consistently suggest that both behavioral and characterological self-blame are associated with poorer recovery immediately as well as several years postrape. Other studies that have distinguished between behavioral and characterological self-blame also have shown that both types of self-blame are associated with higher symptom levels (Arata, 1999; Arata & Burkhart, 1996; Hill & Zautra, 1989; Meyer & Taylor, 1986), although two studies have found behavioral self-blame to be unrelated (Regehr, Regehr, & Bradford, 1998) or marginally related (Arata & Burkhart, 1998) to symptom levels. Studies that have assessed internal attributions without distinguishing between behavioral and characterological self-blame have produced somewhat mixed results, with two showing positive relations between internal attributions and symptoms (Katz & Burt, 1987; Wyatt, Notgrass, & Newcomb, 1990), one showing no relation (Mynatt & Allgeier, 1990), and one showing a relation between internal attributions and symptoms only for women who had been victimized in both childhood and adulthood (Ullman, 1997). Some of the nonsignificant relations may be due to the use of one-item measures that may be lacking in reliability and validity (e.g., Mynatt & Allgeier, 1990). Nonetheless, a preponderance of the evidence indicates that self-blame, whether behavioral or characterological, is associated with poorer recovery among victims of rape. However, the longitudinal data from Study 3 do not suggest that attributions predict future symptoms once the effects of earlier symptoms are controlled, which is consistent with results from other domains (see, e.g., Downey, Silver, & Wortman, 1990; Major, Mueller, & Hildebrandt, 1985).

One reason that both types of self-blame are maladaptive is that behavioral self-blame is not associated with other variables as predicted by Janoff-Bulmans (1979) model. For example, in all of our studies, behavioral and characterological self-blame are highly correlated with each other (see also Arata, 1999; Hill & Zautra, 1989; Ullman, 1996). More important, in Studies 1, 2, and 3 (and in preliminary data from Studies 4 and 5), behavioral self-blame is not associated with the belief that future rapes are more controllable, more avoidable, or less likely. In addition, perceptions of past control are unrelated to perceptions of control over the future. Only one other study has tested the mediators of the effects of behavioral self-blame proposed by Janoff-Bulman. Specifically, Hill and Zautra (1989) assessed the perceived changeability of behavioral and characterological attributions and found that, although behavioral attributions were perceived as more changeable, changeability ratings were not associated with symptoms.

Although neither behavioral self-blame nor perceptions of past control are associated with perceived control over the future, the latter is in fact associated with better recovery. Specifically, the beliefs that future rapes can be avoided, are less likely, and are more controllable are associated with less distress in Studies 1, 2, and 3. Importantly, in Study 3, the only factor that predicted later symptoms was a sense of control over being assaulted again. As mentioned, in Studies 4 and 5 we have expanded our measures of future control to explore this aspect of the postrape recovery process more fully. Preliminary data suggest that feelings of control over the recovery process are most strongly related to recovery. This is important because victims actually do have more control over their recovery than over whether they will be assaulted again.

The relations between perceived control and postrape symptoms represent another area that has received very little research attention. Only one other study to date has assessed the relations between perceived control over an assault and recovery (Kushner, Riggs, Foa, & Miller, 1992). In this study, a general sense of control was associated with fewer symptoms, but control over future attacks and control during the attack were not related to symptom levels. However, this sample included victims of both rape and nonsexual criminal assault (e.g., robbery). Thus, additional research on various aspects of past (e.g., control over occurrence), present (e.g., control over the recovery process), and future (e.g., control over recurrence) control definitely is warranted.

Theory and research on attributions and recovery have focused on the role of self-blame. However, our data suggest that victims tend to attribute more blame to external than to internal factors (see also Katz & Burt, 1987; Meyer & Taylor, 1986; Mynatt & Allgeier, 1990). In addition, data from Studies 1 and 3 (and preliminary data from Studies 4 and 5) consistently suggest that blaming external forces is associated with poorer recovery and is, in fact, more strongly related to higher symptom levels than is self-blame. Similarly, three studies have found that societal blame is associated with higher symptom levels (Arata, 1999; Arata & Burkhart, 1996; Regehr et al., 1998), although this relation was not significant in one study (Meyer & Taylor, 1986). Using a measure that combined attributions to society, other people, and other factors, Ullman (1997) also found external attributions to be associated with more symptoms. As mentioned, given the prevalence and negative effects of external attributions, our current work (Studies 4 and 5) explores external attributions more fully by assessing the relations between symptom levels and three separate types of external attributions (i.e., blaming the rapist, chance, and society).

Finally, our data suggest that thinking more often about why the rape occurred is itself associated with more psychological distress. This is consistent with the finding that all kinds of attributions are associated with higher symptom levels and suggests that focusing on the past—on why the assault happened—is not adaptive. The results from Study 3 also indicate that the relation between thinking about why and symptoms increases over time. Preoccupation with the question "Why?" may suggest that a survivor is still trying to make sense of, or find meaning in, the event. As other researchers have shown, individuals who are able to find meaning in tragic events are able to cope more successfully (see, e.g., Silver, Boon, & Stones, 1983; Taylor, 1983). It is important to note that many victims seem to have difficulty answering the question "Why me?" In our studies, few women report that they "never" think about why the rape occurred, even several years after the assault. Thus, this is yet another topic deserving of further attention.

In summary, all types of attributions—including both self-blame and external blame—and thinking more often about why the assault occurred consistently are associated with higher symptom levels. The only factors associated with fewer symptoms are various aspects of future control. Furthermore, perceptions of past control (including behavioral self-blame) are unrelated to perceiving greater control over the future. This lack of relation between perceptions of past and future control is consistent with a framework developed by Brickman and his colleagues (1982) that distinguishes between taking responsibility for problems (i.e., the past) and taking responsibility for solutions (i.e., the future) and indicates that greater attention needs to be paid to aspects of control that may facilitate recovery (vs. the current focus on attributions).

Clinical Implications

Our findings have several implications for clinical work with victims of rape. As noted, all types of attributions are associated with more concurrent distress, including external attributions. This finding is not consistent with the common practice of encouraging victims to blame external factors (the rapist or society) rather than themselves but is consistent with the notion that focusing on the past and on why the rape occurred is not helpful. Although it is natural for rape victims to try to figure out why they were assaulted, no matter how much time they spend trying to apportion blame, they cannot undo the past. Our data suggest that clinicians should help victims to focus on what they can control now and how they might make themselves less vulnerable in the future rather than on why the rape occurred.

Brickman et al. (1982) use the term "compensatory model" to refer to the paradigm in which individuals are seen as having responsibility for the future but not the past. The strength of this model is that "it allows people to direct their energies outward, working on trying to solve problems . . . without berating themselves for their role in creating these problems" (p. 372). In the context of rape, problem solving might mean helping survivors to identify steps they can take to make themselves less vulnerable, such as enrolling in a self-defense course, becoming more aware of their surroundings, or installing a security system. By clearly distinguishing between responsibility for being raped and control over the future, it is possible to talk about decreasing vulnerability without fostering self-blame.

In addition to fostering a sense of control, it is important to help victims make sense of, or find meaning in, the assault. For example, thinking more often about why the rape occurred, which implies that the victim has not been able to find meaning, is associated with higher distress levels. This focusing on finding meaning can also be seen as consistent with the demonstrated effectiveness of cognitive interventions with victims of sexual assault (e.g., Foa, Rothbaum, Riggs, & Murdock, 1991; Resick & Schnicke, 1992). Although finding meaning in an assault may seem like an impossible task, prior research suggests that even 3 days postrape many victims report that they experienced positive changes—a form of meaning making—in their lives as a result of the assault (Frazier & Burnett, 1994). Many of these changes involved gaining a greater sense of control over the future, including being more cautious, reevaluating life and goals, and becoming more assertive (see also Frazier et al., 1995, 1998). Obviously, this does not mean that being raped is a positive event. Rather, finding positive meaning in a traumatic event is one way to make sense of the event and maintain positive assumptions about the world.

Finally, despite our focus on the role of attributions and perceived control in the postrape recovery process, it is important to keep in mind that the best predictors of later symptoms are earlier symptoms. This suggests that early intervention may be important for preventing long-term distress. Resnick and her colleagues (Resnick, Acierno, Kilpatrick, Holmes, & Jager, 1999) have found that a videotaped psychoeducational intervention in the emergency room is associated with lower distress levels over time. In addition, in another of our studies not mentioned here (Frazier, Rosenberger, & Moore, 1999), victims were much more likely to say that they did not seek counseling after an assault because they just wanted to forget about it than that they did not need it. Moreover, those who said they just wanted to forget also reported more symptoms of PTSD. Thus, these data suggest that additional efforts could be made by emergency room staff to provide counseling or to encourage victims to seek counseling soon after the assault in order to prevent long-term distress.

References

American Psychiatric Association. (1987). *Diagnostic and statistical manual of mental disorders* (revised 3rd ed.). Washington, DC: Author.

Arata, C. (1999). Coping with rape: The roles of prior sexual abuse and attributions of blame. *Journal of Interpersonal Violence, 14*, 62–78.

Arata, C., & Burkhart, B. (1996). Post-traumatic stress disorder among college student victims of acquaintance assault. *Journal of Psychology and Human Sexuality, 8*, 79–92.

Arata, C., & Burkhart, B. (1998). Coping appraisals and adjustment to nonstranger sexual assault. *Violence Against Women, 4*, 224–239.

Breslau, N., Davis, G. C., Andreski, P., & Peterson, E. (1991). Traumatic events and posttraumatic stress disorder in an urban population of young adults. *Archives of General Psychiatry, 48*, 216–222.

Brickman, P., Rabinowitz, V., Karuza, J., Coates, D., Cohn, E., & Kidder, L. (1982). Models of helping and coping. *American Psychologist, 37*, 368–384.

Downey, G., Silver, R., & Wortman, C. (1990). Reconsidering the attribution-adjustment relation following a major negative event: Coping with the loss of a child. *Journal of Personality and Social Psychology, 59*, 925–940.

Foa, E. B., Riggs, D. S., Dancu, C. V., & Rothbaum, B. O. (1993). Reliability and validity of a brief instrument for assessing post-traumatic stress disorder. *Journal of Traumatic Stress, 6*, 459–473.

Foa, E., & Rothbaum, B. (1998). *Treating the trauma of rape: Cognitive-behavioral therapy for PTSD.* New York: Guilford Press.

Foa, E. B., Rothbaum, B. O., Riggs, D. S., & Murdock, T. B. (1991). Treatment of posttraumatic stress disorder in rape victims: A comparison between cognitive-behavioral procedures and counseling. *Journal of Consulting and Clinical Psychology, 59*, 715–723.

Frazier, P. (1990). Victim attributions and postrape trauma. *Journal of Personality and Social Psychology, 59*, 298–304.

Frazier, P. (1997a). *The Rape Attribution Questionnaire.* Unpublished manuscript, University of Minnesota.

Frazier, P. (1997b, May). *Trauma experiences and PTSD among a random sample of women.* Paper presented at the annual meeting of the Minnesota Psychological Association, Rochester, MN.

Frazier, P., & Borgida, E. (1997). The scientific status of research on rape trauma syndrome. In D. Faigman, D. Kaye, M. Saks, & J. Sanders (Eds.), *Modern scientific evidence: The law and science of expert testimony* (pp. 414–435). St. Paul, MN: West.

Frazier, P., & Burnett, J. (1994). Immediate coping strategies among rape victims. *Journal of Counseling and Development, 72*, 633–639.

Frazier, P., Byrne, C., Glaser, T., Hurliman, L., Iwan, A., & Seales, L. (1997, August). *Multiple traumas and PTSD among sexual assault survivors.* Paper presented at the annual meeting of the American Psychological Association, Chicago, IL.

Frazier, P., Byrne, C., & Klein, C. (1995, August). *Resilience among sexual assault survivors.* Poster presented at the annual meeting of the American Psychological Association, New York.

Frazier, P., Byrne, C., Klein, C., & Seales, L. (1996, August). *Causal attributions, perceived control, and coping strategies as predictors of postrape recovery.* Poster presented at the XXVI International Congress of Psychology, Montreal.

Frazier, P., & Hurliman, E. (1998a, May). *Issues in diagnosing post traumatic stress disorder.* Paper presented at the annual meeting of the Minnesota Psychological Association, Brainerd, MN.

Frazier, P., & Hurliman, E. (1998b, November). *Prevalence of PTSD following Non-Criterion A events.* Paper presented at the 14th annual meeting of the International Society for Traumatic Stress Studies, Washington, DC.

Frazier, P., Iwan, A., & Glaser, T. (1998, November). *Posttraumatic growth following sexual assault: Prevalence and predictors.* Paper presented at the 14th annual meeting of the International Society for Traumatic Stress Studies, Washington, DC.

Frazier, P., Rosenberger, S., & Moore, N. (1999). *Correlates of help-seeking among recent sexual assault survivors.* Unpublished data, University of Minnesota.

Frazier, P., & Schauben, L. (1994). Causal attributions and recovery from rape and other stressful life events. *Journal of Social and Clinical Psychology, 14*, 1–14.

Hill, J., & Zautra, A. (1989). Self-blame attributions and unique vulnerability as predictors of postrape demoralization. *Journal of Social and Clinical Psychology, 8,* 368–375.

Janoff-Bulman, R. (1979). Characterological versus behavioral self-blame: Inquiries into depression and rape. *Journal of Personality and Social Psychology, 37,* 1798–1809.

Janoff-Bulman, R. (1989). Assumptive worlds and the stress of traumatic events: Applications of the schema construct. *Social Cognition, 7,* 113–136.

Joseph, S., Williams, R., & Yule, W. (1995). Psychosocial perspectives of post-traumatic stress. *Clinical Psychology Review, 15,* 545–566.

Katz, B., & Burt, M. (1987). Self-blame: Help or hindrance in recovery from rape? In A. Burgess (Ed.), *Rape and sexual assault handbook* (Vol. 2, pp. 151–169). New York: Garland.

Kessler, R. C., Sonnega, A., Bromet, E., Hughes, M., & Nelson, C. (1995). Post-traumatic stress disorder in the National Comorbidity Survey. *Archives of General Psychiatry, 52,* 1048–1060.

Koss, M. (1993). Detecting the scope of rape: A review of prevalence research methods. *Journal of Interpersonal Violence, 8,* 198–222.

Koss, M., Goodman, L., Browne, A., Fitzgerald, L., Keita, G., & Russo, N. (1994). *No safe haven: Male violence against women at home, at work, and in the community.* Washington, DC: American Psychological Association.

Koss, M., Koss, P., & Woodruff, J. (1991). Deleterious effects of criminal victimization on women's health and medical utilization. *Archives of Internal Medicine, 151,* 342–347.

Kushner, M., Riggs, D., Foa, E., & Miller, S. (1992). Perceived controllability and the development of posttraumatic stress disorder (PTSD) in crime victims. *Behavior Research and Therapy, 31,* 105–110.

Major, B., Mueller, P., & Hildebrandt, K. (1985). Attributions, expectations, and coping with abortion. *Journal of Personality and Social Psychology, 48,* 585–599.

McCann, I.L., & Pearlman, L. (1990). *Psychological trauma and the adult survivor.* New York: Brunner/Mazel.

Meyer, C., & Taylor, S. (1986). Adjustment to rape. *Journal of Personality and Social Psychology, 50,* 1226–1234.

Mynatt, C., & Allgeier, E. (1990). Risk factors, self-attributions, and adjustment problems among victims of sexual coercion. *Journal of Applied Social Psychology, 20,* 130–153.

Norris, F. H. (1992). Epidemiology of trauma: Frequency and impact of different potentially traumatic events on different demographic groups. *Journal of Consulting and Clinical Psychology, 60,* 409–418.

Regehr, C., Regehr, G., & Bradford, J. (1998). A model for predicting depression in victims of rape. *Journal of the American Academy of Psychiatry and Law, 26,* 595–605.

Resick, P. (1993). The psychological impact of rape. *Journal of Interpersonal Violence, 8,* 223–255.

Resick, P. A., & Schnicke, M. K. (1992). Cognitive processing therapy for sexual assault victims. *Journal of Consulting and Clinical Psychology, 60,* 748–756.

Resnick, H., Acierno, R., Kilpatrick, D., Holmes, M., & Jager, N. (1999). Prevention of post-rape psychopathology: Preliminary findings of a controlled acute rape treatment study. *Journal of Anxiety Disorders, 13*, 359–370.

Silver, R., Boon, C., & Stones, M. (1983). Searching for meaning in misfortune: Making sense of incest. *Journal of Social Issues, 39*, 81–101.

Taylor, S. (1983). Adjustment to threatening events: A theory of cognitive adaptation. *American Psychologist, 38*, 1161–1173.

Taylor, S., & Armor, D. (1996). Positive illusions and coping with adversity. *Journal of Personality, 64*, 873–898.

Tedeschi, R., Park, C., & Calhoun, L. (Eds.), (1998). *Posttraumatic growth: Positive change in the aftermath of crisis.* Mahwah, NJ: Erlbaum.

Thompson, S., Sobolew-Shubin, A., Galbraith, M., Schwankovsky, L., & Cruzen, D. (1993). Maintaining perceptions of control: Finding perceived control in low-control circumstances. *Journal of Personality and Social Psychology, 64*, 293–304.

Thornton, B., Ryckman, R., Kirchner, G., Jacobs, J., Kaczor, L., & Kuehnel, R. (1988). Reaction to self-attributed victim responsibility: A comparative analysis of rape crisis counselors and lay observers. *Journal of Applied Social Psychology, 18*, 409–422.

Ullman, S. (1996). Correlates and consequences of adult sexual assault disclosure. *Journal of Interpersonal Violence, 11*, 554–571.

Ullman, S. (1997). Attributions, world assumptions, and sexual assault. *Journal of Child Sexual Abuse, 6*, 1–15.

Ullman, S., & Siegel, J. (1994). Predictors of exposure to traumatic events and posttraumatic stress sequelae. *Journal of Community Psychology, 22*, 328–338.

Wyatt, G., Notgrass, C., & Newcomb, M. (1990). Internal and external mediators of women's rape experiences. *Psychology of Women Quarterly, 14*, 153–176.

CHAPTER SEVEN

SURVIVORS' NEEDS AND STORIES AFTER ORGANIZATIONAL DISASTERS: HOW ORGANIZATIONS CAN FACILITATE THE COPING PROCESS

MARC ORLITZKY

Organizational Behaviour Cluster, University of New South Wales, Sydney, New South Wales, Australia

For man is born for trouble, As the sparks fly upward.
—Book of Job, 5:7, Old Testament

Research into possible mechanisms preventing disaster (e.g., Hytten, Jensen, & Skauli, 1990; Vaughan, 1996; Weick, 1987, 1993) deserves great attention and praise. Unfortunately, however, organizational disasters cannot be prevented completely, so we must also understand, and prepare for, the social-psychological aftermath of organizational disasters. Despite the common occurrence of manmade and natural disasters, an increasing number of technological disasters (Weisaeth, 1994), and increasing mortality rates in many types of disaster (Ursano, Fullerton, & McCaughey, 1994), individuals, organizations, and institutions are typically ill prepared for the onslaught of massive loss of life because they tend to avoid and deny unpleasant occurrences. Organizational actors must take the aforementioned quotation from the Book of Job seriously or even go a step further and acknowledge the reality of the Buddhist notion of *duhkha*[1] intrinsic in all human life.

This paper extends an earlier article (Orlitzky, 1998) by proposing how organizations can facilitate the coping process among disaster survivors.[2] That is, unlike my previous descriptive review of the research on story telling and long-term coping effectiveness after disasters (Orlitzky, 1998), this paper is primarily prescriptive in tone, especially in the first half. Using recent empirical results, the paper explains what organizations can and should do to facilitate survivors' short- and long-term coping effectiveness. Instead of writing another narrative review of the organizational disaster literature, I decided to draw on my disciplinary roots (organization theory and sociology). The second half of the paper describes the implementation of two organizational coping "cultures" in abstract terms and adds several contingencies and other exogenous independent variables to the previous model.

When organizations such as airlines are faced with the massive loss of human life, they arguably have a moral obligation and civic duty of helping the survivors re-create stories about the meaningfulness of life. Since survivors' short-term postdisaster coping needs differ from their long-term needs, organizations must (have) set up two different internal (including cognitive) processes, "cultures," and resource structures to address these needs. First, an organization affected by a manmade or natural disaster must have incorporated in its organizational culture the emphasis of sociological functionalism on efficiency and expediency in the early stages of coping. Second, a radical-humanist organizational orientation toward existential meaning is necessary to help people cope in the long run (see Burrell & Morgan, 1979, for detailed descriptions of sociological functionalism and radical humanism). Paradigmatic orientations such as sociological functionalism and radical humanism cannot be switched on and off, thus, paradoxically, it becomes necessary for the organization to cultivate apparently incommensurate (i.e., mutually exclusive) paradigms at the same time. My concluding remarks address possible mechanisms of this prescrip-

---

[1] *Duhkha* can be translated as "unsatisfactoriness," "suffering," "pain," or "anguish" (Dalai Lama Tenzin Gyatso, 1966, pp. 142–143).

[2] By disaster survivors, I refer to bereaved families, friends, and organization members who lost significant others and acquaintances in organizational disasters.

tively paradoxical creation of a particular type of organizational culture and the impact of specific contingencies on the mechanisms to be instituted.

Hobfoll's (1998, pp. 59–60) useful classification of resources in terms of their centrality to survival suggests that an organization's social mandate to help with coping after the massive loss of human life must be geared toward the provision of specific resources: primary resources, such as food, shelter, and safety; secondary resources, such as social support, hope, and optimism; and, finally, tertiary resources, such as money, social status, and friendships. In recent research on corporate support in the aftermath of a natural disaster (Sanchez, Korbin, & Viscarra, 1995), tangible primary support (transportation, financial assistance, housing, emergency supplies, and meals) was a significant inverse predictor of state anxiety and post-traumatic stress disorder (PTSD) symptoms 30 days after a hurricane. However, 90 days after the hurricane, social support (counseling, information, and company-sponsored social gatherings) replaced tangible primary support as a negative determinant of PTSD symptomatology. These findings suggest (at least) a two-stage model of corporate support in which organizations must recognize existential cognitions (i.e., those cognitions concerned with the meaning of life) as psychological resources that have to be replenished as well. Thus, organizations cannot only meet survivors' immediate physiological and informational needs. To address both types of needs (for information and material resources on the one hand, and existential meaning on the other), organizations, including airlines, must develop a culture integrating functionalist and radical-humanist paradigmatic aspects, as argued subsequently.

Addressing Survivors' Short-Term Coping Needs Through Sociological Functionalism

Following the realist (in its ontological assumptions) and positivist (in its epistemological assumptions) conservation of resources (COR) stress model (Freedy et al., 1994; Hobfoll, 1998), most organizations and governments have come to realize that resource loss of any kind causes stress. Resources are broadly

defined in COR theory as "objects, conditions, personal characteristics, and energies that are either themselves valued for survival,
directly or indirectly, or that serve as a means of achieving these
ends" (Hobfoll, 1998, p. 54). Arguably, the government and
organizations, which are concerned with a broad base of constitu-
ents, have a mandate to replenish lost resources after organizational disasters. Effective resource replenishment can often be
accomplished in the early stages of postdisaster strains (Sanchez et
al., 1995).

The "next-of-kin rule," which was passed by the 105th U.S.
Congress and prescribes notification mechanisms and procedures
for foreign air carriers, follows the regulative logic of sociological
functionalism. The bill, which took effect on October 1, 1998,
stipulates the submission of detailed plans for addressing the needs
of families of passengers involved in a foreign aircraft accident
resulting in a significant loss of life. Foreign air carriers must transmit disaster relief plans to both the secretary of transportation and
the chairman of the National Transportation Safety Board. The
plan is to contain information on the airline's toll-free contact
number for families, efficient and effective notification procedures,
passenger lists, consultation regarding disposition of remains and
effects, return of possessions, unclaimed possessions retained, consultation of families regarding monuments, equal treatment of passengers, compensation to service organizations, coverage of families'
travel and care expenses, and resource allocation for the plan's
implementation. Furthermore, the bill contains a subsection that
places a limitation of liability on foreign air carriers in a federal or
state court procedure. Air carriers are responsible only for grossly
negligent behaviors and intentional misconduct. Thus, the "next-
of-kin" rule is primarily concerned with the efficient implementation of resource replenishment plans immediately upon the
occurrence of an air traffic disaster. Without a doubt, this bill has
helped, and will help, solve many problems relating to notification
of bereaved families, but a review of its contents also shows that it
is clearly functionalist in orientation.

Unfortunately, the attribute "functionalist" has over time
acquired pejorative connotations, especially in sociology. I use the
term *functional* or *functionalist* in this context to characterize, rather
than evaluate, the needs and mechanisms that are most called for

in the immediate aftermath of an airplane crash or any other type of organizational disaster. Following Parsonian functional analysis (Parsons, 1959), organizations must be able to (a) *adapt* quickly to a disaster situation, (b) establish *goal attainment* mechanisms to meet intra- and extra-organizational survivors' coping needs, (c) *integrate* coordination (including communication) patterns during and after disasters, and (d) maintain *latency*, that is, supply disaster assistance personnel with necessary motivation. Organizations that fulfill these functional requirements will be more successful in meeting survivors' short-term coping needs than organizations that do not.

One concrete example illustrating the requirements of functional preparation for disaster was already mentioned, the "next-of-kin" rule. Another functional mechanism that is primarily centered on the integration dimension of Parsons's scheme is an analysis of the postdisaster service delivery network for poor linkage cracks, which occur when sectors of the organizational network are not adequately connected (Gillespie & Murty, 1994). Isolated and peripheral clusters of organizations must be avoided. Otherwise, the accessibility to essential disaster assistance resources would be restricted and the effective provision of postdisaster help impeded. Isolates have no interorganizational relations to the rest of the disaster relief network (i.e., they have mean network centrality scores close to zero), while peripherals have only indirect relations with the most central organizations in the network. Community planning councils and other government bodies can strengthen postdisaster relief networks by helping peripheral and isolated organizations become more coordinated with the network, encouraging peripherals and isolates to initiate contacts and participate with central network activities, and helping isolates and peripherals overcome network restrictions and barriers (Gillespie & Murty, 1994).

Preventive psychiatry, almost by definition, can also be classified as a functionalist way of reducing PTSD among disaster survivors (Weisaeth, 1995). Here, instead of postdisaster reconstruction of existential meaning, the focus is on providing individuals with the necessary psychological resources, before the disaster, in order to enhance disaster preparedness and thus lower the probability of PTSD symptomatology among individuals affected by disaster. Weisaeth's (1995) idea of establishing an information-support center is also geared toward an efficient solution to the common postdisaster gaps and lack of information available to bereaved families.

The aforementioned examples illustrating a functionalist solution to the problem of disaster coping share an emphasis on efficient ways to meet organizational disaster survivors' basic (immediate) needs for information and material and psychological resources. They have in common the assumption that coping effectiveness can be coordinated and regulated a priori or at least immediately after the occurrence of a disaster. It is further assumed that what is most called for in the immediate disaster aftermath is tangible support. In other words, the functional approach acknowledges one particular type of postdisaster story, a story line that ignores, for the most part, bereaved families' and friends' difficulty with finding life meaningful in the midst of frequently sudden and traumatic loss of significant others. Functionalist approaches alleviate suffering in the short term, but for full postdisaster recovery the following radical-humanist approaches to coping are probably necessary as well.

Addressing Survivors' Long-Term Coping Needs Through Radical Humanism

> You cannot tell people what to do. You can only tell them parables. (W. H. Auden, cited in Harvey, 1996, p. 9)

This quotation reflects the radical-humanist or existentialist orientation toward grieving well. In its emphasis on subjective personal experience, radical humanism regards human consciousness as a major change agent (Burrell & Morgan, 1979). Therefore, it does not assume that external observers or a third party can predict possible psychopathologies in response to the loss of significant others and use this expectation, or knowledge, in restoring the predisaster status quo, which is exactly the orientation of sociological functionalism. To express it in a slightly oversimplified manner, functionalism assumes that there is one right way, one right story, that will help survivors cope with strains resulting from disaster, while radical humanism acknowledges the open-endedness, the equifinality, of the social-psychological grieving process. One single party does not have responsibility for the creation of a "correct" healing story. Instead, meaningful stories are socially constructed.

Obviously, radical humanism emphasizes the construction and restoration of meaning. There is not one meaning that can be imposed on bereaved families and friends; rather, there are many meanings that grow out of the stories that disaster survivors, according to radical humanism's voluntarist assumptions about human nature, choose to tell themselves and significant others. The content of the stories is secondary to the existential void they fill: Stories (re)connect the bereaved with the dead and with each other. In an earlier review (Orlitzky, 1998), I outlined some generalizations that can be drawn from the previous theoretical and empirical postdisaster grief literature and presented a number of antecedents of effective story telling and long-term coping. Note that the previous article did not suggest there is one best story to be told after disasters (e.g., stories about life after death); what matters more is that a story, any narrative, is told and shared.[3]

Through the creation and co-creation of stories, we feel and, in fact, know that we have pieced together many unrelated, confusing, and often horrifying bits of information into a meaningful holistic account. The social-psychological act of story telling increases our perceived control over our destiny. For example, Solomon and Smith (1994) stress the impact of social support and perceived control on survivors' responses to disaster. The belief that we are not at the mercy of some unforgiving Fate but can use interpersonal loss as a creative motivator (Harvey, 1996) may be the key to successful coping and healing. Research shows that health care providers' and rescue workers' exposure to the grotesque is particularly stressful (Brandt et al., 1995). Feeling helpless and adrift in an absurd reality appears to be a major hindrance to postdisaster healing. Since most organizational disasters are technological disasters, which, in theory at least, are "preventable" (Ursano, McCaughey, & Fullerton, 1994), the total breakdown of

---

[3] It must be noted, however, that in argumentative strucure and model building effort, Orlitzky (1998) had clear functionalist overtones by relying on the conceptualization and measurement of objective social variables. Radical humanism would typically avoid all objectivist generalizations.

a technological system, such as a plane crash, frequently seems particularly absurd to the bereaved.

One radical-humanist suggestion to facilitate effective coping is the provision of opportunities for victims to create (tell) and co-create (listen and respond to) stories. Frequently, though, we tend to avoid the victims of trauma and disaster because the bereaved are reminders of our own vulnerability to unforeseen terrors (Ursano, McCaughey, & Fullerton, 1994). In other words, we would rather continue living in a story (a fantasy?) of personal control than be robbed of this psychological security blanket ourselves. However, in the interest of the survivors, it would be advisable to refrain from the stigmatization of survivors and accept death as a natural part of the human condition (Kierkegaard, 1843/1954). Organizations can institutionalize in their cultures the ever-present awareness of loss by eliminating communicative patterns that would lead to denial and avoidance.[4] Absolute honesty and authenticity would be required from all employees in all interactions, akin to the belief of Andy Grove, former CEO of Intel, that constant reminders of lurking organizational failure and decay spur managers' motivation and job performance. Suffering is at the core of human existence (Dalai Lama Tenzin Gyatso, 1966; Moulyn, 1982). Following Kierkegaard, we must realize that true vitality emerges from our acknowledgment of the fragility of our lives and the "preciousness of time as an antidote to existential despair" (Harvey, 1996, p. 173).

Unlike functionalism, radical humanism is not concerned with the quick and efficient administration of postdisaster support services. According to radical humanism, disaster relief efforts can be judged successful if they help survivors re-create meaning, regardless of the time and costs consumed by these efforts. Seen from this perspective, radical humanism is an orientation that may be alien to managerial values, especially in the aftermath of disaster. For this reason, it may be advisable to not only distinguish and separate the functionalist helpers from the humanist ones but to "outsource" the radical-humanist disaster relief work to consul-

---

[4] The long-term coping benefits of supposedly advantageous denial, repression, and avoidance (Lazarus, 1982) have not been demonstrated empirically. To the contrary, in the case of reexposure, those who seek information tend to fare better than those who avoid it (Shalev, 1994).

tants trained in psychiatry and clinical psychology. "Outsourcing" external help immediately after the disaster may appear confusing to bereaved families and friends, who are likely to identify the organization (e.g., an airline) closely with the disaster (e.g., a plane crash). On the other hand, individuals' acceptance of external expert counseling will be much greater two or three months after the disaster.

One of the positive effects of story telling (and the creation of meaning) is due to (re)appraisal, the process of cognitive (re)assessment of an event (Lazarus & Folkman, 1984). Cognitive schemas can be changed (but, according to radical humanism, should not be imposed) after disasters in order to modulate post-event recollections (Loftus, 1979). These cognitive modulations in turn can lead to persistent changes in emotions. Hence, internal pre-story-telling cognitions can affect how, and what, personal meaning is created while the bereaved individual tries to make sense of the disaster. Hence, story telling involves reason and emotion.

Viewed from a psychoanalytic perspective, a disclosed narrative can have another desirable side effect. Greenberg and Van der Kolk (1987) suggest that traumatic memories are stored as iconic collections, which preclude further processing of the traumatic experience. Through verbalization, a narrative discloses and controls iconic memories. Empirical results show that poor health can result from the failure to express and disclose traumatic experiences (Pennebaker & Susman, 1988).

An organizational culture inspired by radical humanism would privilege dyadic and group relations affecting interpersonal change after disaster over objective, systemic realities, such as inter-organizational disaster networks and their analysis. This shift in emphasis toward personal and interpersonal cognitions is necessary because meaning, according to radical humanism, is always subjective. There is no higher system-immanent authority that can be invoked for the imposition of meaning. Arguably, even invocations of religious figures can ultimately be regarded as human constructions (Becker, 1973; Freud, 1949). Since the nominalist ontology of radical humanism implicitly denies the existence of objective social reality, the veridical content of the stories that survivors tell is less consequential than the degree to which they (re)create subjective

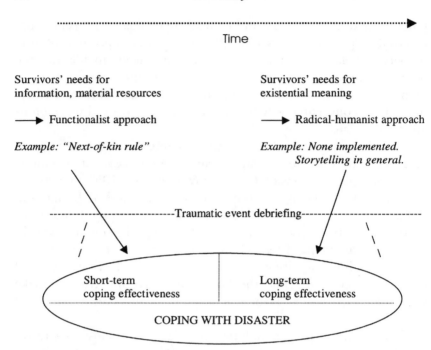

FIGURE 1 Postdisaster relief efforts: A typology of organizational coping support.

existential meaning. Especially in later stages of the healing process, those involved in helping individuals cope with disaster may be well advised to pay more attention to the mental (including emotional) states created by the stories they share than to the objective verifiability of the stories' contents. Figure 1 presents a graphical overview of this model of organizational mechanisms set in place to improve disaster coping effectiveness.

Implementing the Paradox

Radical humanism is generally regarded as the antithesis of sociological functionalism (Burrell & Morgan, 1979). While the former has a nominalist ontology and an antipositivist epistemology, makes voluntaristic assumptions about human nature, and uses ideographic methodology, functionalism is characterized by realism, positivism, determinism, and nomothetic methods (Burrell

& Morgan, 1979). From a general perspective as well as from the specific arguments mentioned in the context of organizational disasters, it may follow that implementing both coping mechanisms, or cultures, may be difficult. At the same time, both mechanisms are postulated as essential ingredients of short-term coping (functionalism) and long-term coping (radical humanism) with disaster.

One way of resolving this paradox of incompatible mental models has already been mentioned. While functionalist assistance should be provided in-house at early stages of postdisaster coping, radical-humanist efforts can rely on outsiders, that is, expert counselors who are not part of the organization involved in the disaster. The temporal, geographic, and organizational separation of functionalist relief effort providers from radical-humanist ones makes the implementation of both paradigmatic orientations possible.

It is also important to note that the incompatibility emerges at one level of analysis, the organizational level (or higher). However, it is also known that organizational cultures are differentiated and fragmented and that organizations typically consist of several different subcultures (Van Maanen, 1991; Van Maanen & Barley, 1985). The individuals contributing their assumptions, values, and artifacts to the whole that is traditionally called "organizational culture" are likely to differ with respect to the lenses through which they view the world. Some individuals and teams will feel a strong urge to exercise control and address coping problems efficiently, while others will be more concerned with the long-term emergence of meaning from tragic loss. For managers of disaster-prone organizations, it would be important to know a priori the ontological and epistemological assumptions of employees who are the key decision makers when disaster strikes. The assignment of individuals to certain roles should conform to their "natural" inclinations. For instance, existentialists like Frankl and Sartre would never see and implement solutions to anxiety and trauma within a functionalist framework.

In addition, Howard (1998) argues that paradoxes apparent within the organizational culture construct may in fact constitute attitude dualities of criterial referents. In other words, the reasons some disaster relief workers stress efficiency values (functionalism) may be different from the reasons others emphasize meaning (radical humanism). Furthermore, the integration of functionalism and radical humanism may appear paradoxical, but in reality these two orientations may just be cultural expressions and acknowledgments of different human needs at different stages in postdisaster coping. Viewed from this perspective, the great cognitive and behavioral complexity usually attributed to resolving "paradoxes" (Denison, Hooijberg, & Quinn, 1995) may not be necessary after all. Howard (1998) examined the "paradoxes" of mutually exclusive value dimensions of structural control versus flexibility, focus on internal versus external stakeholders, and means versus ends. With respect to the three aforementioned "paradoxes," Howard (1998) suggests that the forces influencing one choice may not preclude an alternative choice, even though it might appear that they would. One current example with which he illustrates the argument of attitude duality of criterial referents is organizations' move toward decentralization paired with the simultaneous pursuit of efficiency of operations.

Moreover, paradoxes may be inherent in all organizational cultures but cannot be managed, explained, or understood by self-conscious rational minds (Linstead & Grafton-Small, 1992). If paradox is intrinsic in many emergent supra-individual processes, then the identification and suggestion of yet another one will not so much pose an epistemological or ontological problem as a problem of current human understanding. For can individual scholars really rationally comprehend systems that transcend the individual? Or is our full rational comprehension of complex systems and dynamic processes limited to that systematic level at which we are able to think? More important, can we identify a concrete solution to coping with disaster, transcending the functionalism versus humanism paradox (or duality)?

One postdisaster service delivery design that comes closest to bridging the functionalist and radical-humanist orientations to disaster relief efforts is traumatic event debriefing (TED; Bell, 1995; Mitchell, 1983). TED is divided into seven functionally delimited phases. However, the content of at least four phases (fact phase, thought phase, reaction phase, and symptom phase) reflects TED's concern with the psychological effects and, in fact, meaning of the traumatizing disaster. On the one hand, TED's approach to postdisaster support is very structured and, in its stated goals (e.g., "traumatic conditioning"), has regulative overtones (Shalev, 1994). On the other hand, TED focuses on emotional processing. The argument that humanist assistance to disaster survivors ought to come later than functionalist assistance is supported by Chemtob et al.'s (1997) personal communications with Raphael and Mitchell in 1995. These two researchers assume that survivors need to be psychologically ready for existential questions.

Contingencies and Revisions of the Earlier Model

In this paper, I argued for the desirability of the implementation of both functionalist and radical-humanist cultural orientations to facilitate postdisaster coping processes. Other contingencies may require adjustments of the integrative model, which was presented in Orlitzky (1998). While the original model postulated several direct relationships between antecedent variables, story telling (mediator), and long-term coping effectiveness (see Figure 2), another look at studies undertaken since the early 1990s would also suggest moderating (i.e., interaction) effects of some variables. For instance, Hodgkinson and Shepard (1994, p. 587) report a "complex interaction" between personality characteristics (coping style/hardiness), factors related to disaster relief work (impact of client contact and role issues), and factors not related to disaster relief work (prior life events). Also, variables at the community level may interact with several of the predictors presented in my earlier literature review (Trickett, 1995). In general, organizations need to be aware of the disaster context and survivor character-istics that influence story telling.

Individual-level variables may act as moderators of the degree to which story telling and PTSD are related. For example, the age of the affected individual may determine the extent to which story telling leads to coping effectiveness (Honig et al., 1993; Norris, Phifer, & Kaniasty, 1994). Alternatively, age may have to be added as an exogenous antecedent of story telling and long-term-coping effectiveness, although the sign of the relationship (i.e., positive or negative) is debatable and the relationship possibly curvi-linear (inverted U shape).

National culture has been suggested as a mediator between the disaster experience and the traumatic responses of individuals

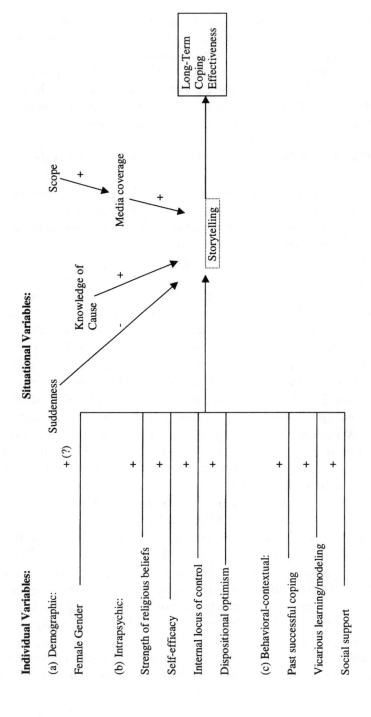

FIGURE 2 Model of long-term coping effectiveness (Orlitzky, 1998).

140

(Figley, Giel, Borgo, Briggs, & Haritos-Fatouros, 1995). I, on the other hand, would instead suggest that national culture acts as a contingency (i.e., a moderator) because it may influence the salience of behavioral-contextual and situational variables (see Orlitzky, 1998, for a differentiation of these two types of independent variables). For instance, in collectivist national cultures, social support may be more highly related to long-term coping effectiveness than in individualist cultures, which often stress and institutionalize the importance of autonomy, independence, and emotional "toughness."

In a similar vein, the sex of the bereaved individual might make a difference in coping effectiveness because society rewards expression of emotions to a different extent in boys and girls (Anderson & Manuel, 1994; Yule, Ten Bruggencate, & Joseph, 1994). Whether sex differences in stress levels are real or simply the outcome of different reporting levels is open to debate. What the results in the disaster coping literature suggest, however, is the fact that my earlier conclusion regarding women's greater aptitude for story telling and, thus, higher long-term coping ability (in comparison with men) needs to be revised. In 1998, I was hedging when suggesting female gender as an independent variable but still expected a positive correlation between female gender, story telling (mediator), and long-term coping effectiveness. Varying previous findings do not lead to firm conclusions, so more longitudinal studies with greater sample sizes or a meta-analysis of previous studies may be the only avenues for reaching closure with respect to gender.

In contrast to the increasing questions about gender effects, the findings of Ursano et al. (1995) underline the importance of social support as a precursor to effective coping. These authors found that single body handlers reported more avoidance and somatization than did married body handlers. Avoidance and especially somatization probably indicate poor coping with disaster. Therefore, marital status may have to be added as yet another variable to the model, either as a precedent of social support or as an independent demographic variable (like sex and age).

The research report written by Ursano and his colleagues (1995) also emphasizes the necessity to include not only bereaved families, friends, and organization members but also disaster and rescue workers in any theoretical model of disaster coping effectiveness (see also Ursano, McCaughey, & Fullerton, 1994). The routine of coping with disaster may not increase coping effectiveness. Quite to the contrary, the constant exposure to traumatic events may consume valuable psychological resources, which cannot be replenished before the next disaster. Despite disaster and rescue workers' unlikely personal acquaintance with the victims, coming in contact with corpses and body parts can be extremely traumatizing. In the development of a theoretical model of coping effectiveness, scholars must not forget these constant victims of disaster.

This paper extended my previous first attempt of a comprehensive model of long-term coping effectiveness (Orlitzky, 1998) in several ways. First and most important, it introduced—at a rather abstract level—the coping mechanisms that organizations likely to be affected by organizational disasters can institutionalize in their organizational cultures. Second, it conceptualized time as an important influence on the relative importance of functionalist versus radical-humanist organizational coping "cultures." Third, it discussed a number of variables that either moderate or lead to revisions of the previous model of coping effectiveness. From a theoretical standpoint, future work must make these suggestions more concrete in terms of implementation. From an empirical standpoint, we must start to operationalize the variables and test the comprehensive model within a disaster situation (individual variables; as far as those tests are possible) and across disaster situations (situational variables; see Orlitzky, 1998, for a description of the difference between the two sets of variables).

Coping with organizational disaster is not simply a rational exercise in resource provision or supplementation. What organizations need to incorporate in their cultures are radical-humanist characteristics that counterbalance attributes of sociological functionalism. As depicted in Figure 1, survivors' coping needs will differ over time, so organizations must be able to cope with both types of coping needs. It is important to have proper coordination mechanisms in place and to distribute disaster information as efficiently as possible, but it is equally important to help survivors fill the existential void left behind by such frequently traumatizing events as organizational disasters. Resource provision and story telling must go hand in hand.

References

Anderson, K. M., & Manuel, G. (1994). Gender differences in reported stress response to the Loma Prieta earthquake. *Sex Roles*, 30, 725–733.

Becker, E. (1973). *The denial of death*. New York: Free Press.

Bell, J. L. (1995). Traumatic event debriefing: Service delivery designs and the role of social work. *Social Work*, 40, 36–43.

Brandt, G. T., Fullerton, C. S., Saltzgaber, L., Ursano, R. J., & Holloway, H. (1995). Disasters: Psychologic responses in health care providers and rescue workers. *Nordic Journal of Psychiatry*, 49, 89–94.

Burrell, G., & Morgan, G. (1979). *Sociological paradigms and organisational analysis: Elements of the sociology of corporate life*. London: Heinemann.

Chemtob, C. M., Tomas, S., Law, W., Cremniter, D., et al. (1997). Postdisaster psychosocial intervention: A field study of the impact of debriefing on psychological distress. *American Journal of Psychiatry*, *154*, 415–417.

Dalai Lama Tenzin Gyatso. (1966). *The opening of the wisdom eye*. Wheaton, IL: Quest Books.

Denison, D. R., Hooijberg, R., & Quinn, R. E. (1995). Paradox and performance: Toward a theory of behavioral complexity in managerial leadership. *Organization Science*, *52*, 540–561.

Figley, C. R., Giel, R., Borgo, S., Briggs, S., & Haritos-Fatouros, M. (1995). Prevention and treatment of community stress: How to be a mental health expert at the time of disaster. In S. E. Hobfoll, et al. (Eds.), *Extreme stress and communities: Impact and intervention* (pp. 401–419). Dordrecht, the Netherlands: Kluwer Academic.

Freedy, J. R., Saladin, M. E., Kilpatrick, D. G., Resnick, H. S., & Saunders, B. E. (1994). Understanding acute psychological distress following natural disaster. *Journal of Traumatic Stress*, 7, 257–273.

Freud, S. (1949). *The future of an illusion*. New York: Liveright.

Gillespie, D. F., & Murty, S. A. (1994). Cracks in a postdisaster service delivery network. *American Journal of Community Psychology*, *22*, 639–660.

Greenberg, M. S., & Van der Kolk, B. A. (1987). Retrieval and integration of traumatic memories with the "painting cure." In B. A. Van der Kolk (Ed.), *Psychological trauma* (pp. 191–216). Washington, DC: American Psychiatric Press.

Harvey, J. H. (1996). *Embracing their memory: Loss and the social psychology of storytelling*. Needham Heights, MA: Allyn & Bacon.

Hobfoll, S. E. (1998). *Stress, culture, and community: The psychology and philosophy of stress*. New York: Plenum.

Hodgkinson, P. E., & Shepard, M. A. (1994). The impact of disaster support work. *Journal of Traumatic Stress*, 7, 587–600.

Honig, R. G., Grace, M. C., Lindy, J. D., Newman, C. J., et al. (1993). Portraits of survival: A twenty-year follow-up of the children of Buffalo Creek. *Psychoanalytic Study of the Child*, 48, 327–355.

Howard, L. W. (1998). Validating the competing values model as a representation of organizational cultures. *International Journal of Organizational Analysis, 6*, 231–250.

Hytten, K., Jensen, A., & Skauli, G. (1990). Stress inoculation training for smoke divers and free fall lifeboat passengers. *Aviation Space and Environmental Medicine, 61*, 983–988.

Kierkegaard, S. K. (1954). *Fear and trembling and the sickness unto death.* New York: Doubleday. (original work published 1843).

Lazarus, R. S. (1982). The costs and benefits of denial. In S. Bereznits (Ed.), *The denial of stress* (pp. 1–30). Madison, CT: International Universities Press.

Lazarus, R. S., & Folkman, S. (1984). Cognitive appraisal processes. In R. S. Lazarus & S. Folkman (Eds.), *Stress appraisal and coping* (pp. 22-52). New York: Springer.

Linstead, S., & Grafton-Small, R. (1992). On reading organizational culture. *Organization Studies, 13*, 331–350.

Loftus, E. F. (1979). *Eyewitness testimony.* Cambridge, MA: Harvard University Press.

Mitchell, J. T. (1983). When disaster strikes . . . *Journal of Emergency Medical Services, 8*, 36–39.

Moulyn, A. C. (1982). *The meaning of suffering.* Westport, CT: Greenwood Press.

Norris, F. H., Phifer, J. F., & Kaniasty, K. (1994). Individual and community reactions to the Kentucky floods: Findings from a longitudinal study of older adults. In R. J. Ursano, B. G. McCaughey, & C. S. Fullerton (Eds.), *Individual and community responses to trauma and disaster: The structure of human chaos* (pp. 378–400). Cambridge, England: Cambridge University Press.

Orlitzky, M. (1998). One night, everything disappeared: Toward a model of coping effectiveness after organizational disasters. *Journal of Personal and Interpersonal Loss, 3*, 53–84.

Parsons, T. (1959). *Economy and society.* London: Routledge & Kegan Paul.

Pennebaker, J. W., & Susman, J. R. (1988). Disclosure of trauma and psychosomatic processes. *Social Science and Medicine, 26*, 327–332.

Sanchez, J. I., Korbin, W. P., & Viscarra, D. M. (1995). Corporate support in the aftermath of a natural disaster: Effects on employee strains. *Academy of Management Journal, 38*, 504–521.

Shalev, A. Y. (1994). Debriefing following traumatic exposure. In R. J. Ursano, B. G. McCaughey, & C. S. Fullerton (Eds.), *Individual and community responses to trauma and disaster: The structure of human chaos* (pp. 201–219). Cambridge, England: Cambridge University Press.

Solomon, S. D., & Smith, E. M. (1994). Social support and perceived control as moderators of responses to dioxin and flood exposure. In R. J. Ursano, B. G. McCaughey, & C. S. Fullerton (Eds.), *Individual and community responses to trauma and disaster: The structure of human chaos* (pp. 179–200). Cambridge, England: Cambridge University Press.

Trickett, E. J. (1995). The community context of disaster and traumatic stress: An ecological perspective from community psychology. In S. E. Hobfoll et al. (Eds.), *Extreme stress and communities: Impact and intervention.* Dordrecht, the Netherlands: Kluwer Academic.

Ursano, R. J., Fullerton, C. S., Kao, T.-C., & Bhartiya, V. (1995). Longitudinal assessment of posttraumatic stress disorder and depression after exposure to traumatic death. *Journal of Nervous and Mental Disease, 183*, 36–42.

Ursano, R. J., Fullerton, C. S., & McCaughey, B. G. (1994). Trauma and disaster. In R. J. Ursano, B. G. McCaughey, & C. S. Fullerton (Eds.), *Individual and community responses to trauma and disaster: The structure of human chaos* (pp. 3-27). Cambridge, England: Cambridge University Press.

Ursano, R. J., McCaughey, B. G., & Fullerton, C. S. (1994). The structure of human chaos. In R. J. Ursano, B. G. McCaughey, & C. S. Fullerton (Eds.), *Individual and community responses to trauma and disaster: The structure of human chaos* (pp. 403–410). Cambridge, England: Cambridge University Press.

Van Maanen, J. (1991). The smile factory: Work at Disneyland. In P. Frost, L. Moore, M. Louis, C. Lundberg, & J. Martin (Eds.), *Reframing organizational culture* (pp. 58–76). Newbury Park, CA: Sage.

Van Maanen, J., & Barley, S. R. (1985). Cultural organization: Fragments of a theory. In P. Frost et al. (Eds.), *Organizational culture* (pp. 31-54). London: Sage.

Vaughan, D. (1996). *The Challenger launch decision: Risky technology, culture, and deviance at NASA*. Chicago: University of Chicago Press.

Weick, K. E. (1987). Organizational culture as a source of high reliability. *California Management Review, 29*, 112–128.

Weick, K. E. (1993). The collapse of sensemaking in organizations: The Mann Gulch disaster. *Administrative Science Quarterly, 38*, 628–653.

Weisaeth, L. (1994). Psychological and psychiatric aspects of technological disasters. In R. J. Ursano, B. G. McCaughey, & C. S. Fullerton (Eds.), *Individual and community responses to trauma and disaster: The structure of human chaos* (pp. 72–102). Cambridge, England: Cambridge University Press.

Weisaeth, L. (1995). Preventive psychosocial intervention after disaster. In S. E. Hobfoll, et al. (Eds.), *Extreme stress and communities: Impact and intervention* (pp. 401–419). Dordrecht, the Netherlands: Kluwer Academic.

Yule, W., Ten Bruggencate, S., & Joseph, S. A. (1994). Principal components analysis of the Impact of Events Scale in adolescents who survived a shipping disaster. *Personality and Individual Differences, 16*, 685–691.

CHAPTER EIGHT

THE AGING OF GRIEF: PARENTS GRIEVING OF ISRAELI SOLDIERS

RUTH MALKINSON and LIORA BAR-TUR

School of Social Work, Tel Aviv University, Ramat-Aviv, Israel

This chapter examines long-term parental grief of soldiers within the context of the Israeli society. Parental grief is discussed along the life span, commencing at the immediate phase following the loss through the bereavement process in middle to late adulthood and its manifestations in aging. Interviews with a group of elderly bereaved parents whose sons were killed during military service give further support to previous findings regarding the notion that the passage of time has no diminishing effect on their grief nor does it relinquish their attachment to the deceased. With aging, there appears to be an increase in internalized involvement with the long-lost child, fears of fading memories, and the need to eternalize the deceased. In reviewing the past, parents reevaluate their coping with the loss and their relationship with the surviving children. The parents' preoccupation is twofold: On one hand, the strong attachment seems to continue in inner representations of the lost child, and, on the other, this preoccupation is enhanced externally owing to Israeli society's attitude toward dead soldiers. An intersection is therefore established between society and bereaved families. Grief is apparently a central theme in aging parents who are preoccupied with the "aging" of their grief rather than their own aging.

Bereavement and Culture

For me grief is like rocking the cradle with my dead baby. (Mr. Y., a
78-year-old bereaved father for almost 30 years)

Israel is a small country with a population of approximately 6
million: 80% Jewish, 15% Muslim, 3% Christian, and the
reminder divided among Druze and other religious groups. The
United Nation voted to establish the state of Israel in 1948 after
several decades of Arab-Jewish tension and following the Nazi
Holocaust. During the 50 years of Israel's existence, it has experienced four wars and many military actions and terrorist attacks.
During this time, almost 19,000 young Israelis have been killed,
and this number increases as more soldiers are killed in military
actions, terrorist attacks, and accidents.

Israeli society's attempts to preserve the memory of those who
fell in the struggle to establish the state and in its subsequent wars
represent a means of coping with severe trauma and loss and
support for the process of mourning and grief. Commemoration has
been organized to take place both at the national, social, and personal levels of society. A national Memorial Day, when ceremonies
are conducted throughout the country at military cemeteries, was
instituted and falls in the 10-day period between Holocaust Memorial Day and Independence Day. A special law enacted for this
purpose includes a detailed addendum addressing memorialization
at the individual level, such as inscriptions on tombstones in
military cemeteries.

Over the years, with the growing number of fallen soldiers, a
"bereavement culture" has emerged reflecting the importance that
Israeli society accords to the death of its young people. It views this
death as a sacrifice, while the sense of heroism associated with such
mortality confers an existential meaning at the national and social
levels. The phrase "family of the bereaved" embodies this concept
and is used to refer to those directly affected by the loss of loved
ones in military service. In addition to the Memorial Day and
memorial ceremonies as a way of commemorating the dead soldiers, other forms of remembering such as the erection of monuments, publication of memorial albums, and solemn assemblies are
widespread. These various frameworks express the collective representations that society has developed as part of the meaning

attached to the death of its sons in combat (Malkinson & Witztum, in press; Witzum & Malkinson, 1993). These collective representations also establish a relationship between personal mourning and national bereavement.

Throughout the years, prolonged wars in Israel have seemingly brought about a change in the pattern of grief expression by the bereaved families. Rather than a more inhibited and private experience of grief, many bereaved families are expressing nowadays more open and uninhibited emotions of pain and anger, in protesting against the never-ending wars, the army, and the politicians. More recently bereaved parents characteristically voice such protest, while the voices of veterans and older bereaved parents remain mostly unheard publicly. The question is whether this silence reflects compliance with the sociopolitical reality or is part of aging processes reflected in disengagement, the shift from activity to passivity, less energy, and increased focus on interiority and on inner representations of the deceased (Bar-Tur Levy-Shiff, & Burns, 1997; Cumming & Henry, 1961; Gutmann, 1977; Neugarten, 1977). Without empirical evidence, it is our assumption that the differences between the younger, recently bereaved parents and the older veterans are a result of both the social and the aging processes. This question remains open for future investigation.

This chapter focuses on long-term bereavement processes along the life cycle. We propose that the effects of a child's loss on parental bereavement can be viewed from three main developmental phases of the life cycle: the immediate phase following the loss, the long-term phase of the bereavement process through middle and late adulthood, and the aging phase.

Loss of a Child Along the Life Span

The grief of a parent over a lost child is lonely and like a heavy burden; it becomes heavier as one ages and weakens in body and spirit. Yehudah Amichai (1985), an Israeli poet, describes a parent who loses a child in the war as a pregnant woman who carries a dead fetus in her womb.This description of a lonely bereaved parent, carrying the deceased child in a private inner world, is a vivid image of the "family of the bereaved." It is a metaphor for what the literature identifies as an increase in the intensity of grief from early pregnancy loss to loss of an adult child (Archer, 1999;

DeVries, Davis, Wortman, & Lehman, 1997; Klass, Silverman, & Nickman, 1996; Malkinson & Bar-Tur, in press; Rubin & Malkinson, in press).

In comparison with other types of bereavement, parental bereavement is particularly intense, complicated, and long lasting (Rando, 1993). The increase in grief with age is consistent with the increase of reproductive value of the offspring from conception to early adulthood and the decline in parental reproductive value, identified by the evolutionary perspective (Archer, 1999).

It has been suggested that grief and adaptation to loss following death of a child be examined from a life-course perspective. In addition to the circumstances of the loss, the developmental stage of parenthood in the family's life cycle is also considered: Will a loss of an infant child to younger parents differ from a loss of a young child to parents in their midlife stage and that of an adult child during middle and late adulthood (Rubin & Malkinson, in press)? Another the question is, what effect does time have on the grief process, alongside the normative developmental processes in the life cycle?

The Immediate Phase

During the immediate phase, also referred to in the literature as the initial period or the acute stage (Bowlby, 1980; Lindemann, 1944), the bereaved parents are in a state of shock, search, and acute grief. They are required to accept the reality of the loss and its effect on the relationship with the deceased (Raphael, 1983; Rubin, 1985, 1990, 1993, 1996; Sanders, 1989; Tahka, 1984). This phase is characterized by psychophysiological as well as behavioral, emotional, and social changes. Support for this intense phase in bereavement is given by the Jewish tradition "The Shiva" (the first 7 days following the loss), which is a period of official mourning, socially recognized, during which relatives, friends, and acquaintances express their condolence by visiting the mourners' home. The first 30 days are traditionally viewed as the acute mourning phase. To mark its end, the family unveils the stone with a special memorial service. Toward the end of the first year of the mourning process, a memorial service is conducted at the cemetery, which is then repeated each year. This traditional framework corresponds to the universal grief process with its diminishing intensity during the first year or so.

As time passes, the acuteness of the response subsides; there is generally a reduction in the intensity of the focus upon the reworked attachment to the deceased, as well as a reduction in the extent of the somatic and behavioral changes characterizing the bereaved. At this time (sometimes referred to as the stage of depression or disorganization), there is an ever-deepening appreciation that the living relationship to the deceased is no longer possible (Bowlby, 1980). Some of the changes that buffered the bereaved will have disappeared, and others will recede with time.

Bereavement Process Through Middle and Late Adulthood

The impact on life qualities and history transforms this loss into a combination of lost relationships and lost potentials. As life continues, the living siblings and friends of the deceased child mature and develop, while the bereaved parents experience the loss from other perspectives. In the words of a bereaved mother: "When I received the invitation for his friend's wedding, I experienced a pang, realizing that my son will never marry, will never have children, will never be a lawyer, as he wished to be . . . so many lost opportunities, lost hopes and dreams that will never come true."

During middle adulthood (for most parents, this is the initial phase of bereavement following a death of a child in the army) and continuously into late adulthood, the parents are involved in various activities aimed at finding meaning to their dead child, either on the individual level or community at large. "Typically this involves a newfound appreciation of their lives and a consequent reordering of priorities" (Janoff-Bulman & Berg, 1998, p. 42). The parents are active and engaged in external activities and roles as parents to their living children and other roles in the extended family. Most of them are involved in their career, work, education, social activities, and the like. At the same time, they also continue to be preoccupied in their engagement with the deceased child in the inner world. In research evaluating parents who had lost sons 4 and 13 years previously (in the 1973 Yom Kippur War and in the 1982 Lebanon war), Rubin (1990, 1993,

1996) found that bereaved parents experienced their deceased children as being closer and more involved with them than non-bereaved parents experienced their living children. The results pointed to a paradoxical feature of bereavement; the death of the son and the loss of living contact with him often led to an increase in the strength of the relationship to the now internalized and remembered son. In many cases, the investment and involvement with the deceased remained disproportionately elevated for many years, and at considerable cost to the interpersonal relationships with other children (Rubin, 1993, 1996). Similar findings by Florian (1989–1990) and Sanua (1983) indicate that almost all war-bereaved parents in Israel lead a psychologically painful life, regardless of the time that has lapsed since the loss.

The extensive clinical and research literature on the impact of losses of school-aged, adolescent, and adult children is consistent with the picture of a pervasive, overwhelming, and persistent response to loss (DeVries, 1966; DeVries et al., 1997: Lehman, Wortman, & Williams, 1987; Rando, 1983, 1986, 1993; Trait & Silver, 1989; Videka-Sherman, 1982; Wortman & Silver, 1987).

These reports indicate that, even 23 years later, a considerable proportion of the bereaved reported an ongoing cognitive and emotional involvement in the loss event. It seems, therefore, that time has no effect on moderating the impact of the loss. Some individuals were unable to relinquish their attachment to the loss and remained distressed much longer than expected (Edelstein, 1984; Goodman, Rubinstein, Baine, & Luborsky, 1991; Levav, 1989–1990; Lesher & Berger, 1988; Levav, Friedlander, Kark, & Peritz, 1988; Moss, Lesher, & Moss, 1984; Rando, 1986).

Possible social implications of the continuing cognitive and emotional involvement with the deceased child may be reflected in what Riches and Dawson (1996) refer to as the "culture of bereaved parents" who continue to be involved with their deceased children. They suggest that, as a result of the loss of a child, some bereaved parents feel isolated and misunderstood. Therefore, they form their own community where they feel that they can release their personal grief and painful emotions and search for meaning through a network of new social and alternative relationships.

Regardless of the developmental stage or time, parents continuously construct meaning in their interaction with their inner and outer world. Daily experiences are perceived and evaluated within the context of a new framework, one that includes their own past traumatic loss. By rebuilding their inner world and maintaining the possibility of tragic loss, parents can experience gains (Janoff-Bulman & Berg, 1998). Silverman, Klass, and Nickman (1996) suggest that people seek to make meaning of death continuously throughout their life and look for rituals and language that will enable them to maintain the bond with the dead and absent. The focus on facilitating mourning should be, therefore, on how to change connections and view the relationship in a new perspective, rather than on how to separate.

As mentioned earlier, conceptions of grief cannot be separated from the sociocultural context of which they are part and the systems meanings that are imposed by society. For example, in Israel, the Department of Rehabilitation of the Ministry of Defense supports memorialization of deceased soldiers as a way of representing society's obligation to its dead heroes and is so involved in meaningful activity on the social level. Thus, memorialization of deceased soldiers or victims of terror attacks (as opposed to "unheroic" death in car accidents or from illness) often includes publishing a book, making a film, or printing a Torah scroll. These engagements are typically carried out during the first years following the loss, when "young" bereaved parents (mostly in middle adulthood) are characteristically involved in more active and social engagements concerning the loss. It seems that with their aging process, they shift into a more inner, private, and passive mode of engagement.

The Aging Phase

Aging is a phase in which many changes and losses are expected in major life domains. Older bereaved parents may experience a diminishing external world, decreases in social and professional roles and engagements, loss of health, and loss of a spouse, siblings, and friends. With increased isolation and loneliness and more time available, many older adults are engaged in long-term memories, reviewing their life (Butler, 1963). For older bereaved parents, there is an added component, that of reviewing the process of grieving throughout the years. As they approach the end of their own life, their search for meaning takes another shift. They are searching for ways to eternalize their dead child's memory. Their greatest fear is that as time goes by, and with the decline in their memory, their child's memory will fade away. Moreover, they fear that on their own death, the child will die forever.

There are few reports regarding the continuing bond of elderly bereaved parents. Various questions are raised: How do losses as a result of the aging process intertwine or affect the grief process? Are there any changes in grief patterns over the years? How does collective bereavement, so uniquely manifested in Israeli society, interact with the parents' personal grief?

To explore these questions, a group of elderly war-bereaved parents was formed to discuss their aging process and share their life experiences and feelings of grief and loss (Malkinson & Bar-Tur, 1999). The group consisted of 29 bereaved parents (17 mothers and 12 fathers). Their ages ranged from 60 to 87 years ($M = 74$). Five were in their 60s, and the rest were in their 70s and over. The length of bereavement was 11 to 33 years; about 60% had been bereaved more than 20 years. Forty percent were widowed. There were four couples, and the rest were single parents. Most of them came from kibbutzim or villages in the north of the country. Some had previous contacts in meetings or ceremonies of the "Yad Labanim" (Memorial for the Sons) organization. There were also two younger mothers, aged 46 and 55, who joined the older group and shared their experiences with a support group they had established for younger bereaved parents.

Analysis of the discussion with parents who had, lost children as long as 33 years previously shed additional light on this process. In addition to the losses often associated with aging, many parents also told of continued difficulties in coming to terms with the loss of the child. They described grief as a personal process that continues along the years, and its emotional impact does not diminish with time. One of the issues that concern elderly parents is the change in memory of the deceased child. Although they think of their child every day, they feel guilty as his or her image is fading over time: "As my body shrinks, so do my memories of him; I worry that I may lose him." Sadly, some expressed their fear that the deceased sons would "die forever" when they themselves die. The actual death of the son awaits the second symbolic death—the loss of the child's inner representation, which would occur with the death of the parents themselves. Interestingly, they are concerned with their child's second symbolic death rather than with their own death and their eternalization.

The older bereaved parents tended also to reevaluate their grief as experienced shortly after the death and years and decades later (Malkinson & Bar-Tur, 1999). Central themes dealt with the naming of a grandchild after the deceased, marital relationships, the relationship with the surviving children, and the impact of other losses on their lives. In retrospect, few parents bemoaned their intense emotional involvement with the deceased son rather than with the living children. They realized how difficult their grieving and response to loss had been for the other members of the family. Many felt that the continued emotional involvement with the lost son had gone on disproportionately and had affected their ability to fully engage with their families, which themselves were developing and changing (Rubin, 1996). Responsibility to the deceased child coexisted alongside that of the surviving children, even though the parents expressed greater guilt toward the living children. These older bereaved parents seemed to live in two separate worlds: the real and the virtual. In aging, for some parents, it is the deceased child who is perceived as the more accessible and the more real of the children. As one parent put it, "Our children have left home. We are at home with Danny [the deceased child]. He is the only one left with us" (Malkinson & Bar-Tur, 1999).

Grief as a Lifelong Task

The death of a child is considered, in comparison with other losses, to be more intense, complicated, and long lasting. In fact, the multidimensionality of grief and its outcomes, especially the prescribed endpoint or recovery from the loss, was reexamined following studies of parental grief and other types of losses (Rando, 1993; Sanders, 1989). Empirical and clinical evidence shed light on the continuing inner relationship with the deceased child, questioning the "grief resolution" hypothesis, especially when the death involved an older child. It seems that bereaved parents carry within themselves the memories of the child throughout their lives. As they age, they face in addition to the identified normative end of life tasks one more task, that which is considered by them as the most difficult: approaching their own death. They are confronted with a major task that of leaving behind them a memorial for the dead child.

This image of a lonely bereaved parent, carrying the deceased child in a private inner world, was described in our group meeting by both mothers and fathers (Malkinson & Bar-Tur, 1999). Despite the common destiny of the group members and their openness and ability to share their intimate and painful experiences, the theme that was overshadowing and interwoven during the 3-hour group process was that grief is a private, isolating inner process. The isolation is not only from the nonbereaved but also within the community of bereaved parents and often between two parents sharing the grief of their child. It seems that grief continues along the life span unaffected by other developmental processes or life events and that the inner attachment to the deceased child is not relinquished. This may suggest reevaluation of parental grief resolution. It seems that older bereaved parents who look back on their life without the deceased child and on their adjustment to the loss may have a somewhat different perspective on their grief process. In retrospect, there may be second thoughts and somewhat different perspectives on their actions, emotions, attitudes, and decisions. Thus, it is suggested that parental grief resolution should be viewed as a temporary and a phase-related outcome rather than as an end to a process. Grief resolution, as defined in the literature, is somewhat static and unchangeable. In this group, it was expressed as a dynamic and an ongoing process. Time is not a healer, nor does the pain ease when a new generation is born and carries the name of the deceased child. It is related to the paradox of the inner representation of the deceased (Dietrich & Shabad, 1989): one that is both frozen in time and also timeless, simultaneously immortalized and lost.

Aging of bereaved parents may, therefore, be difficult and different from that of nonbereaved elderly people. A diminishing outer world and multiple losses in various life domains may increase parental preoccupation with the inner world, and so grief may become more painful. Moreover, because life consists of developmental processes, where time brings changes and is characteristically future oriented, one can consider the grief process as almost contradictory to vital processes. Grief relates to death and is characteristically past oriented, with a tendency to freeze and not to change the image of the dead person. These conflicting tendencies between moving forward and looking back may be viewed as an integral part of the bereaved parents' life.

Recently, Lomranz (1998), in discussing coping strategies of older survivors of traumatic losses, coined the term "A-integration." According to him, A-integration is conceived as an individual's potential to experience well-being without necessarily having integrated all of the biopsychosocial levels, including traumatic losses and experiences. This perspective sheds light also on bereaved parents' coping along the life span, arguing that despite conflicting tendencies, their unique adaptation to losses may be further understood.

In old age, when the future orientation decreases and people may become more engaged in the past, their involvement with grief may increase. As bereaved parents approach their final stage in life, the inner world and outer world may no longer have conflicting tendencies. Older parents may become concerned with the fact that their own death involves yet another death: that of their lost child, who for many years was, and still is, alive in their inner private world.

Considering the sociocultural environment of the bereaved parents and the circumstances of the death, we assume that the loss of an adult child as a soldier may be somewhat different from losses of other adult children. The deceased child belongs not only to his family; symbolically he also belongs to the Israeli society. The death often has heroic elements, and the social and cultural habits, ceremonies, and expectations from the bereaved parents may encourage a never-ending, eternal grief. This tendency is embedded in Israeli literature, poetry, art, and theater. The parents and the deceased soldier-child become a symbol of sacrifice, and their personal and social grief intertwines (Malkinson & Witztum, 1995; Tamir, 1993). Parents' grief over their soldier-child may be regarded and understood in relation to this unique culture.

Conclusions

The bond between the parent and the dead child remains powerful and alive throughout the entire life span, in inner thoughts, feelings, and memories. Parental grief of Israeli soldiers along the life cycle seems to have an added unique dimension. Sustaining, retaining, and nurturing the image of the deceased child for so many years is seen as a normal and adaptive coping mechanism that is accepted and even encouraged by society. Parental preoccupation with the lost child may therefore be supportive rather than destructive, especially in older parents, as they become more isolated and self-centered. Society has to accept the culture of bereaved parents as a unique and personal coping lifestyle that may be different from normative life processes and, therefore, cannot be fully integrated with other developmental processes. Cross-cultural studies are recommended to further understand the impact of differences in psychosocial context on long-term outcomes of parental bereavement.

In comparison with younger bereaved parents who take a more active part in various forms of social meaning construction ("Bereaved Parents for Peace"), elderly parents are more passive and engaged in their inner private world. Their limited social engagement is manifested mostly in their concern about society's remembrance of their soldier sons. That concern may explain their involvement, more than anything else, in a search for ways to eternalize their child's memory as they approach their own death. For them, the important issue is who will remember the dead child after their death. In other words, they are preoccupied with the "aging" of their grief rather than their own aging. Elsewhere (Malkinson & Bar-Tur, 1999) we have proposed the term "aging of grief" to describe this unique experience.

> When the body weakens the burden of grief becomes heavier, but I must carry on. My grief is aging and only when I die will my child die. (Mr. S., a 77-year-old bereaved father for almost 40 years)

References

Amichai, Y. (1985). *And behind all that hides a great happiness.* Tel Aviv: Shocken.

Archer, J. (1999). *The nature of grief: The evolution and psychology of reactions to loss.* London: Routledge.

Bar-Tur, L., Levy-Shiff, R., & Burns, A. (1997). Past traumatic losses and their impact on the well-being of elderly men. *Journal of Personal and Interpersonal Loss, 2*, 379–395.

Bowlby, J. (1980). *Attachment and loss: Vol. 3. Loss: Sadness and depression.* Cambridge, England: Cambridge University Press.

Butler, R. N. (1963). The life review: An interpretation of reminiscing in the aged. *Psychiatry, 26*, 65–76.

Cumming, E., & Henry, W. E. (1961). *Growing old.* New York: Basic Books.

DeVries, B., Davis, C. G., Wortman, C. B., & Lehman, D. R. (1997). Long-term psychological and somatic consequences of later life parental bereavement. *Omega, 35*, 97–117.

DeVries, M. W. (1996). Trauma in cultural perspective. In B. A. van der Kolk, A. C. MacFarlane, & L. Weisaeth (Eds.), *Traumatic stress: The effects of overwhelming experiences on mind, body and society* (pp. 338–413). New York: Guilford Press.

Dietrich, D. R., & Shabad, P. C. (1989). *The problem of loss and mourning: Psychoanalytic perspectives.* Madison, CT: International Universities Press.

Edelstein, L. (1984). *Mental bereavement.* New York: Praeger.

Florian, V. (1989–1990). Meaning and purpose in life of bereaved parents whose son fell during active military service. *Omega, 20*, 91–102.

Goodman, M., Rubinstein, R. L., Baine, B. A., & Luborsky, M. (1991). Cultural differences among elderly women in coping with the death of an adult child. *Journal of Gerontology: Social Sciences, 6*, 321–325.

Gutman, D. L. (1977). The cross cultural perspective: Notes towards a comparative psychology in aging. In J. E. Birren, & K. W. Schaie (Eds.), *The handbook of the psychology of aging* (pp. 302–326). New York: Van Nostrad.

Janoff-Bulman, R., & Berg, M. (1998). Disillusionment and the creation of value: From traumatic losses to existential gains. In J. Harvey (Ed.), *Perspectives on loss: A sourcebook* (pp. 35–47). Washington, DC: Taylor & Francis.

Klass, D. (1996). The deceased child in the psychic and social worlds of bereaved parents during the resolution of grief. In D. Klass, P. R. Silverman, & S. L. Nickman (Eds.), *Continuing bonds.* Washington, DC: Taylor & Francis.

Klass, D., Silverman, P. R., & Nickman, S. L. (1996). *Continuing bonds: New understandings of grief.* Washington, DC: Taylor & Francis.

Lehman, D. R., Wortman, C. B., & Williams, A. F. (1987). Long-term effects of losing a spouse or child in a motor vehicle crash. *Journal of Personality and Social Psychology, 52*, 218–231.

Lesher, E. L., & Berger, K. J. (1988). Bereaved elderly mothers: Changes in health, functional activities, family cohesion, and psychological well-being. *International Journal of Aging and Human Development, 26*, 81–90.

Levav, I. (1989–1990). Second thoughts on the lethal aftermath of a loss. *Omega, 20*, 81–90.

Levav, I., Friedlander, Y., Kark, J., & Peritz, E. (1988). An epidemiological study of mortality among bereaved parents. *New England Journal of Medicine, 319*, 457–461.

Lindemann, E. (1944). Symptomatology and management of acute grief. *American Journal of Psychiatry, 101*, 141–148.

Lomranz, J. (1998). An image of aging and the concept of A-integration. In J. Lomranz (Ed.), *Handbook of aging and mental health: An integrative approach* (pp. 217–250). New York: Plenum.

Malkinson, R., & Bar-Tur, L. (1999). The aging of grief. *Death Studies, 23*, 403–431.

Malkinson, R., & Witztum, E. (in press). Commemoration and bereavement: Cultural aspects of collective myth and the creation of national identity. In R. Malkinson, S. Rubin, & E. Witztum (Eds.), *Traumatic and non-traumatic loss: Clinical theory and practice*. Madison, CT: Psychosocial Press.

Malkinson, R., & Witztum, E. (1995). From "Magash Hakesef" to Mi. Yizkor et Hazochrim: Psychological aspects of bereavement in historical and literature analyses. *Alpaim, 12*, 211–239 (in Hebrew).

Moss, M. S., Lesher, E. L., & Moss, S. Z. (1984). Impact of the death of an adult child on elderly parents: Some observations. *Omega, 17*, 209–218.

Neugarten, B. L. (1977). Personality and aging. In E. Birren, & K. W. Schaie (Eds.), *Handbook of the psychology of aging* (pp. 616–649). New York: Van Nostrand.

Rando, T. A. (1983). An investigation of grief and adaptation in parents of children who have died from cancer. *Journal of Pediatric Psychology, 8*, 3–20.

Rando, T. A. (1986). *Parental loss of a child*. Champaign, IL: Research Press.

Rando, T. A. (1993). *Treatment of complicated grief*. Champaign, IL: Research Press.

Raphael, B. (1983). *The anatomy of bereavement*. New York: Basic Books.

Riches, G., & Dawson, P. (1996). Communities of feelings. *Mortality, 1*, 143–162.

Rubin, S. S. (1985). The resolution of bereavement: A clinical focus on the relationship to the deceased. *Psychotherapy: Theory, Research, and Practice, 22*, 231–235.

Rubin, S. (1990). Death of the future: An outcome study of bereaved parents in Israel. *Omega, 20*, 323–339.

Rubin, S. (1993). The death of a child is forever: The life course impact of child death. In M. S. Stroebe, W. Stroebe, & R. O. Hansson (Eds.), *Handbook of bereavement*. Cambridge, England: Cambridge University Press.

Rubin, S. S. (1996). The wounded family: Bereaved parents and the impact of adult child loss. In D. Klass, P. R. Silverman, & S. L. Nickman (Eds.), *Continuing bonds: New understandings of grief* (pp. 217–232). Washington, DC: Taylor & Francis.

Rubin, S. S., & Malkinson, R. (in press). Parental response to child loss across the life cycle: Clinical and research perspective. In M. S. Stroebe, W. Stroebe, R. O. Hansson, & H. Schutt (Eds.), *Handbook of bereavement research: Consequences, coping, and care*. Washington, DC: American Psychological Association.

Sanders, C. S. (1989), *Grief: The mourning after*. New York: Wiley.

Sanua, V. (1983). War bereavement in Israel. *Midstream, 29*(3), 23–27.

Silverman, P. R., Klass, D., & Nickman, S. L. (1996). Introduction: What's the problem? In D. Klass, P. R. Silverman, & S. L. Nickman (Eds.), *Continuing bonds: New understandings of grief*. Washington, DC: Taylor and Francis.

Tahka, V. (1984). Dealing with object loss. *Scandinavian Psychoanalytic Review, 7,* 13–33.

Tamir, G. (1993). Long term adjustment among war bereaved Israeli parents. In R. Malkinson, E. Witztum, & S. R. Rubin (Eds.), *Loss and bereavement in Jewish society in Israel.* Jerusalem: Cana.

Trait, R., & Silver, R. C. (1989). Coming to terms with major negative life events. In J. S. Uleman, & J. A. Bargh (Eds.), *Thoughts: The limits of awareness, intention and control* (pp. 351–382). New York: Guiford Press.

Videka-Sherman, L. (1982). Coping with the death of a child: A study over time. *American Journal of Orthopsychiatry, 52,* 688–699.

Witztum, E., & Malkinson, R. (1993). Bereavement and commemoration: The dual face of the national myth. In R. Malkinson, S. Rubin, & E. Witztum (Eds.), *Loss and bereavement in Jewish society in Israel* (pp 231–294). Jerusalem: Cana.

Wortman, C. R., Silver, R. C. (1987). Coping with irrevocable loss. In G. Van den Bos, & B. K. Bryant (Eds.), *Cataclysms, crises, and catastrophes* (pp. 185–235). Washington, DC: American Psychological Association.

CHAPTER NINE

COPING WITH LOSSES AND PAST TRAUMA IN OLD AGE: THE SEPARATION-INDIVIDUATION PERSPECTIVE

LIORA BAR-TUR

School of Social Work, Tel Aviv University, Ramat-Aviv, Israel

RACHEL LEVY-SHIFF

Department of Psychology, Bar-Ilan University, Ramat Gan, Israel

Old age is a stage in life in which numerous changes associated with loss can be expected to occur in major life domains. Deterioration of health; retirement; relocation; occupational and financial loss; loss of social roles, identity, status, and support; and the loss of spouse and significant others (siblings, friends) pose an ongoing threat to everyday functioning, forcing the individual to adapt. Thus, effective functioning in daily life represents a major developmental task for the aging (Baltes & Carstensen, 1996; Marsiske, Lang, Baltes, & Baltes, 1995). There is marked variability in adjustment among the elderly, and despite the numerous losses associated with aging, many elderly people are well adjusted and report experiencing high levels of well-being (George & Clipp, 1991; Wetle, 1990).

Researchers have addressed the factors that determine the capacities of some elderly people to maintain or even improve their well-being in the face of accumulating loss. Two major interrelated factors associated with adaptation have been discussed recently: resilience and resources (Baltes & Lang, 1997; Hobfoll & Wells, 1998; Ryff, Singer, Love, & Essex, 1998). Resilience, as postulated by Ryff et al. (1998), is defined as maintenance, recovery, or improvement in mental and physical health following change

163

(often experienced as loss). Resilience is an outcome of an individual's resources operating as protective factors at the socio-demographic, psychological, social, and biological levels. Baltes and Lang (1997) assert that older individuals' adaptation to loss depends on the availability of resources in the sensorimotor, cognitive, personality, and social domains of functioning. Thus, the more resources that are available, the easier it is for the individual to anticipate, confront, and adapt to aging losses. Indeed, research has identified a number of factors associated with enhanced or impaired adjustment among the elderly, such as quality of marital relations, health, and financial status, yet a significant measure of variance remains unexplained (Larson, 1978). The question arises as to what adaptive processes are activated to counteract external stressors and increase resilience when other resources are in decline.

As numerous resources (social, physical, and cognitive) are increasingly depleted, we suggest that the inner, psychological resources become of major importance at this stage of life. The association between psychological resources and the process of adaptation of the elderly to loss has not been widely investigated.

The present perspective proposes that successful adjustment to losses in aging is associated with the development of a rich inner world based on mental and emotional engagements. These engagements act as inner adaptive processes that help moderate the negative impact of aging losses, facilitate adaptation, and even ensure developmental gains. This perspective corresponds to the life-span developmental view, which places an emphasis on the interplay between internal and external factors, present and past experiences, and gains and losses in adult development (Baltes, 1987).

Losses and Gains Along the Life Span

The experience of loss is an inherent part of human development and is associated with various life transitions. As individuals mature, they enter new social contexts and leave others, often experiencing an accompanying sense of loss (Rosenblatt, 1993). In recent years, the view of how people deal with major loss has been reconceptualized, suggesting that with change there is also a potential for gain (Miller & Omarzu, 1998). Whereas previous perspectives assumed that successful coping with loss was attained by returning to a balanced preloss state, more recent perspectives suggest that individuals who suffer loss never completely return to their preloss state, as loss alters one's self-identity or self-schema (Harvey, 1998). Furthermore, this may not even be an optimal goal. The developmental goal is to survive loss, come to terms with change, and integrate oneself into a new social context and identity.

This new perspective is in line with Baltes's (1987) developmental model emphasizing the complexity, plasticity, and multidirectionality within the life span, with internal and external factors continuously influencing each other. Old age, according to Baltes's model, can be a dynamic and important phase in which intrapsychic processes are modified through physical and environmental changes. Ontogenetic development suggests also that there is no gain without loss and no loss without gain. Baltes (1987) nevertheless suggests that there is a systematic script to life-span changes in the relative allocation of resources. During childhood, the primary allocation of resources is directed toward growth; during adulthood, the predominant allocation is toward maintenance and recovery. In old age, more and more resources are required to regulate loss.

We suggest that inner adaptive processes such as separation-individuation may affect both the regulation of loss and the interplay between losses and gains in the internal and external world. Loss imposes separations. Each separation, however, also bears potential for growth, which can be achieved through further individuation. The focus of this chapter is on losses and gains associated with inner processes of separation-individuation and the role they play in the adjustment of the elderly.

Separation-Individuation Along the Life Span

The theory of separation-individuation developed by Mahler (Mahler, 1968; Mahler, Pine, & Bergman, 1975) suggests that separation-individuation is a lifelong process. This process begins with psychological birth, which, unlike its biological counterpart, involves a slowly unfolding intrapsychic dynamic. This dynamic is first manifested in early childhood and is later active as the intrapsychic process of adolescence, described by Blos (1967) as second individuation. After subsequently reappearing in young adulthood, the elaboration of these processes is later manifested with the inevitable crises, challenges, and tasks of middle adulthood (Colarusso, 1997). Colarusso argues that, in each phase of adulthood, there are specific adult developmental tasks to be negotiated. He proposes that the third individuation occurs in young adulthood, the fourth in middle adulthood, and the fifth in aging.

Few have elaborated on the processes of separation-individuation during old age. Colarusso suggests that, among the elderly, there are various common tasks, such as adapting to new types of relationships, the changing of one's goals, facing the decline of physical vigor, and ultimately the separation of death. Coping with losses among the elderly is determined by previous separation-individuation resolutions and may be moderated by the fulfillment of grandparenthood and by engagement with and idealization of grandchildren. According to Colarusso, separation-individuation at this stage in life serves a number of defensive and developmental purposes.

Cath (1997) has also noted that becoming a grandparent activates aspects of the first individuation and may bear potential for late-life emotional refueling. Discussing the separation-individuation process in old age, Cath describes how the human being moves from the early experience of learning to be with and attach to others to the challenge in old age of separating from imperfect others and from unfulfilled aspirations. Cath suggests that the essence of separation-individuation in old age is reflecting on life, seeking universal wisdom. Thus, personal growth often comes through reminiscence, reflection, and consolidation.

Elaborating on the separation-individuation process in aging, we suggest that despite multiple losses and separations, there are potential gains for personal development beyond grandparenthood and wisdom. Since aging often involves a diminution in the social sphere as well as a decline in biological processes, we contend that it is the inner world, which includes present and past representations of experiences, relationships, and objects, that bears the primary potential of development and growth.

Separation processes in aging involve emotional independence from external societal forces, achieved through selective disengagement from roles and objects that were part of the individual's past reality and are no longer relevant and rewarding. Individuation is achieved through mobilization of inner resources for mental and emotional engagements, some of which cannot be fully expressed and observed in the outer world. Mental engagements comprise activities and interests with which the individual is cognitively involved and that occupy the mind. Emotional engagements include relationships with significant others during the life cycle and their representations in the inner world. Mental and emotional engagements may be interrelated, containing components of both the past and the present. These engagements with significant others, in the outer and the inner world, affect the older person's well-being. Gains in aging may therefore be attained via emotional independence from external forces and through an increase in inner resources. This conceptualization is in line with Jung's (1933) concept of individuation, Butler's (1963) suggestion of life review, Neugarten's (1977) findings on increased introversion with age, and Erikson's (1963, 1984) concept of integrity and wisdom.

Levinson, Darrow, and Kline (1978) have maintained that the primary developmental task of late adulthood is to find a new balance between involvement with society and involvement with the self. Wisdom regarding the external world can be gained through a stronger focus on the self, as the individual becomes less interested in rewards offered by society. Through the creation of a new form of self-in-world, late adulthood can be a season as full and rich as previous ones. Ryff (1989), in viewing the possibility of continued growth and development in the later years, suggests that old age has its unique responses and challenges. Autonomy and self-determination, components of well-being, thus can be achieved through the processes of separation-individuation without necessarily having active social roles and relationships.

According to Kernberg (1987), dealing with loss and separation is possible if individuals sense that their creativity has contributed to the strength and permanence of "good" internalized object relations and that they have fulfilled their duties toward their loved ones. The ability to separate emotionally depends on reorganization of the inner world so that there are representations of significant objects from the present and past with which relations can continue. A strong world of internalized object representations offers enrichment and support to the self. It enables one to accept loss and failure with a sense of sufficient inner resources to continue accepting oneself and to trust one's own capacity to reconstitute a meaningful life. Narcissistic gratification from external sources is augmented by secondary narcissistic gratification from internal resources. It also allows elderly people to maintain a sense of mastery and autonomy during the reversal of generational roles when they become dependent on children or grandchildren. In terms of the balance between gains and losses, we posit that, in old age, engagements in the inner world can complement and sometimes replace diminishing external physical and social resources. Furthermore, since well-being is based on the meaning that a person attributes, rather than on the concrete experience (Ryff, 1989), a subjective feeling of well-being can prevail, despite significant loss. Separation frees the elderly from preoccupation with the past, enabling them to attain individuation by focusing on significant engagements in the present.

The process of separation-individuation is thus the adaptive mechanism in aging that helps reduce the impact of loss often experienced through many of the imposed changes in the last phase of the life cycle. The ability to disengage mentally and emotionally from certain aspects of life and to fill the gap with alternative content helps the elderly retain integrity and self-esteem and thus maintain a high level of well-being (Bar-Tur, Levy-Shiff, & Burns, 1998). Gains in aging may be achieved through individuation, as the individual continues to develop through enrichment of the inner world while the external world is gradually shrinking. The following vignette is one such example.

> Mrs. B. is 90 years old and lives in a nursing home. Old age took its toll 8 years ago, when her husband became ill and she could no longer continue her daily activities. Seven years ago, her husband passed away, and she decided to move into the home 2 years after her husband's death, following a major deterioration in her own health. Numerous losses accompanied her relocation, including the loss of a large home, familiar environment, respect and status, and friends and neighbors. Following a period of bereavement, Mrs. B. gradually adjusted to her new life and came to appreciate her new friends, lectures she attended, meals she received hassle free, and especially the medical care and security she felt at the nursing home. All of these were perceived as gains, compensating for the attendant losses. Despite her restricted mobility and autonomy, she maintained an active social life. She read a newspaper daily, listened to the radio, and watched television. She

spoke on the telephone with her grandchildren almost every day and supported them financially. The role of grandmother provided her with satisfaction and pride, and she regarded her grandchildren's successes as the fruits of her life and that of her husband.

Mrs. B. has successfully disengaged from aspects of her past life, including objects, friends, and roles, and reengaged in new roles as an active member of the nursing home's committee and as a proud grandmother, with new friends. In her inner world, she still maintained memories of her beloved husband and friends, her old home and her past. However, she realized that, at the age of 90, she was lucky to have found love, shelter, and care. Her individuation has been achieved, despite past and present losses, through the gains of grandparenthood, through her activities in the nursing home, and through representations of life achievements, manifesting itself in feelings of well-being, autonomy, and self-esteem.

Past Traumatic Loss and Its Impact on the Elderly

Unlike Mrs. B., there are many elderly who experience traumatic losses from which they do not disengage. People who have experienced traumatic losses mobilize their resources to counter their effects and may therefore suffer from extreme resource loss and from a diminished resource reservoir when coping with later loss (Hobfoll & Wells, 1998). Hence, the question arises as to the particular effects of loss associated with previous traumatic experience on the elderly. Two issues can be addressed: whether past traumatic losses have long-term effects in aging, interacting with those losses associated with aging, and whether elderly people who have experienced traumatic loss in the past cope better or worse with the normative losses of aging.

Miller and Omarzu (1998) contend that the occurrence of multiple losses can greatly affect one's definition and perception of future loss experiences, as well as how well one copes with such events. They also postulate that individuals may use previous losses as yardsticks by which they "measure" their current level of grieving; however, the operations of such processes are still unknown. Past traumatic losses, according to this view, thus interact with coping with aging losses.

A substantial body of theory, often grouped as the "vulnerability perspective," maintains that prior experience with extreme stress reduces the ability of individuals to withstand additional stress (e.g., Selye, 1976). This view is supported by a range of findings related mostly to loss of a family member (Lehman, Wortman, & Williams, 1987). The loss of a child has been found to have a pervasive impact, sometimes marked by chronic grief (Raphael, 1983), and by constant thoughts and feelings about the deceased accompanied by pain and guilt (Lehman et al., 1987; Rando, 1996; Rubin, 1993; Videka-Sherman, 1982).

On the other hand, the "inoculation perspective" (e.g., Eysenck, 1988) maintains that stress contributes to the development of useful coping strategies. This perspective holds that each stressful event increases familiarity, thereby leading to a decline in perceived stress, enabling a more successful adaptation to future stressful events. In their review of coping with traumatic life events, Janoff-Bulman and Timko (1987) conclude: "The benefits derived from negative events include a new-found appreciation of life and a recognition of what is really important, as well as a more positive view of one's own possibilities and strengths" (p. 155). Pearlin and Skaff (1996) suggest that people may use their success in dealing with past stressful experiences to help them feel competent in mastering current adversity.

A discussion of the effects of past traumatic loss may be enhanced by focusing on two types of such loss: the loss of a single significant other and losses related to massive trauma, such as the Holocaust. How do Holocaust survivors, having experienced massive traumatic losses that no doubt depleted their resource reservoir, cope with losses in aging?

Five decades of research and clinical studies yield a broad array of indicators. Numerous factors have been found to be involved in determining the coping and well-being of elderly survivors, including prewar personal history, personality characteristics, age of survivors, nature of traumatic experience (primarily concentration camps, labor camps, and hiding), and postwar experience. These factors present complex models of adjustment, both along the life span and in old age, suggesting an interaction between past and present loss and between inner and external processes of adjustment.

Late-Life Effect of Holocaust Losses

Reports related to coping of Holocaust survivors in old age are incongruent and diverse and may be classified within the two opposing perspectives of vulnerability and inoculation. A significant body of data views aging survivors as a high-risk group for emotional pathology, suggesting that old age, with its multiple losses, may be particularly difficult for survivors (e.g., Eitinger, 1980; Nadler & Ben-Shushan, 1989). Dasberg (1987) argues that individual's stressful events and losses in aging may be symbolically reminiscent of their earlier losses in the Holocaust. Danieli (1981, 1994) even suggests that, for some survivors, old age in itself is particularly traumatic.

Many survivors are particularly vulnerable to the changes that are part of the aging process. Unstructured time reduces defenses and may reactivate intrusive thoughts, nightmares, somatic problems, guilt, and agitated depression, symptoms that are now recognized to be components of post-traumatic stress disorder (Danieli, 1981; Robinson, Rapaport, & Durst, 1990; Safford, 1995; Steinitz, 1982).

Steinitz's (1982) findings, based on 550 noninstitutionalized survivors, reveal that, for many survivors, daily coping requires an individual to fill a meaningful family role, to participate in various activities, and to be employed. These activities seem to provide a sense of self-worth as well as an opportunity to focus on present and future concerns rather than on the past. However, these coping strategies are often inadequate when the losses and disabilities associated with aging interact with Holocaust-related psychic wounds and chronic health problems. Memories, fears, and other psychological residual effects of the Holocaust may resurface for the first time in years, suggesting that survivors' coping strategies are particularly vulnerable to the normal experiences of aging.

Despite these findings, studies of community-dwelling, nonclinical survivor populations also reveal strong indicators of adaptation and coping in major life domains during adulthood, with numerous survivors working, maintaining economic stability, and raising families. Some studies have concluded that there is no serious psychological impairment to be found among survivors or among their children (e.g., Carmill & Carel, 1986; Eaton, Sigal, & Weinfeld, 1982). In one study, Helmreich (1992) contends that most of the survivors interviewed were well adjusted, resourceful, and resilient. More than half of the elderly survivors (55%) whom Kahana, Harel, and Kahana (1988) queried reported that their Holocaust experience either had no impact or made it easier for them to cope with aging. Fully 26% of Kahana et al.'s (1988) Holocaust survivor interviewees said that their Holocaust experience made it easier for them to cope with the aging process (e.g., "Once you survive the Holocaust, you can survive normal aging").

Sadavoy (1997) argues that the more convincing data suggest that emotional reactivity may remain intense and dysphoric without affecting measures of adaptation and overt behavior.

Shmotkin and Lomranz's (1998) study comparing Israeli Holocaust and non-Holocaust survivors also supports the assertion that the trauma of the Holocaust may impair well-being but may also promote reactions of accomplishment and a desire to place a stronger grip on life. Thus, impairment and mental suffering do not contradict successful coping and adjustment among survivors.

Lomranz (1990) argues that the Holocaust experience helped prepare some survivors to respond appropriately to future loss. He (1998) suggests the concept of A-integration, which may explain these contradictory findings. A-integration is conceived as an individual's potential to experience well-being without necessarily having integrated all of the biopsychosocial levels, including traumatic losses and experiences. Moreover, many people feel that their traumatic experience is incongruent with the prevailing cultural value system or ongoing modes of daily life (Janoff-Bulman & Berg, 1998), yet they live with this contradiction, are aware of it, and nevertheless lead productive, well-functioning lives.

We may conclude that the gains revealed in the functioning and coping of many survivors enhance their external daily life, whereas in the inner world many continue their emotional engagements accompanied with the unresolved pain and grief associated with traumatic loss that cannot be healed. The losses of old age may act as a trigger for past traumatic repressed losses, and aging Holocaust survivors may therefore be more vulnerable and resource depleted.

Whereas the long-term effects of massive trauma, such as the Holocaust, on the elderly have been demonstrated, the question arises as to how other discrete traumatic loss in the past, such as the loss of a child, affects the process of coping with the losses of aging.

The Traumatic Loss of a Child and Old Age

The traumatic effects of the death of a child have been described as pervasive, with patterns of chronic grief. Edelstein (1984) has discussed three unique qualities associated with the loss of a child: the loss of a part of oneself, of a link to the future, and of illusions regarding life, death, and existential issues. Rando (1996) has also discussed "survival guilt" and "out of turnness," often experienced by bereaved parents. Both Edelstein and Rando suggest that the death of a child may be the most difficult loss to resolve, with the intensity of grief lasting longer than in other types of bereavement. Rubin (1993) found parents to be highly involved with their deceased child at the relational level, with their responses to loss occurring along two tracks: biobehavioral and ongoing attachment to the deceased. Pain is dominant in their lives. An examination of the long-term effects of the death of a young or an adult child reveals a continuing engagement in thoughts and feelings concerning the deceased, sometimes accompanied by pain and guilt (Lehman et al., 1987; Rando, 1996; Rubin, 1993; Videka-Sherman, 1982).

Trait and Silver (1989) found that even 23 years later, a considerable proportion of parents who had lost a child reported an ongoing cognitive and emotional involvement in the loss event. It appears that time has little effect on moderating the impact of the loss. Some individuals were unable to relinquish their involvement with loss and remained distressed much longer than might have been expected. All of these studies point to the absence of a relationship between the time elapsed since the death and the well-being of bereaved parents (Edelstein, 1984; Moss, Lesher, & Moss, 1984).

For elderly parents, the death of an adult child is a most difficult event, requiring the highest degree of adjustment. This experience turns into a dominant theme in their later life (Rubin, 1993; Tamir, 1993). Lesher and Berger (1988) found that elderly bereaved mothers suffered from a significant level of prolonged psychological distress. None of the mothers interviewed indicated that they had resolved or adjusted to their child's loss. The themes that emerged in a group discussion with 29 elderly bereaved Israeli parents whose sons were killed during military service (between 11 and 33 years in the past) support previous findings that the passage of time has little effect on diminishing a parent's grief or on relinquishing attachment to the deceased.

The loss of a child is experienced as unnatural, unexpected, and always traumatic. Aging appears to increase internalized involvement with the long-lost child, triggering fears of fading memories as well as a need to eternalize the deceased. This strong attachment seems to continue in both external and inner representations of the lost child (Malkinson & Bar-Tur, 1999). Despite functioning normally and adequately, elderly bereaved parents bear the scars of traumatic loss in their inner world, supporting the concept of a distinction between the external and inner world.

Klass, Sliverman, and Nickman (1996) have asserted that the bereaved hold the deceased in memory, often forever, and that such maintenance of inner representation is normal rather than abnormal. The authors suggest that these relationships can be described as interactive, despite the physical absence of the other. With time, this bond can take on new forms, yet the connection is maintained. As people mature and develop over the life cycle, their internal representations change.

Adaptation to loss refers to how people reorganize their lives and their sense of self in a way that enables them to live in the present, including learning to deal with the extreme sadness and pain associated with loss. Resolution of grief is described by the authors as a process that continues beyond adaptation and coping with loss, as the memory and representation of the deceased continue across the life cycle.

The results of our study (Bar-Tur, Levy-Shiff, & Burns, 1997) indicated a significant interaction between past traumatic losses and aging losses in predicting well-being among the elderly. However, while losses related to the massive trauma of the Holocaust seem to impair the individual's ability to cope with later losses, traumatic personal loss of a significant other seems to inoculate the individual against the effects of later loss and even to contribute to personal growth. The evidence gleaned from interviews suggests that individuals who experienced a single traumatic loss (such as the death of a child) came to regard the losses of aging as secondary, enabling them to better cope with aging losses and, in some cases, to turn these into opportunities to develop. These gains were achieved despite continued emotional and mental engagements with the deceased in the inner world. Our findings are consistent with the concept whereby people who weather a severe stressor may develop enhanced perceptions, a more positive view of their strengths, and a different perspective on future events (Janoff-Bulman & Berg, 1998; Janoff-Bulman & Timko, 1987).

Nevertheless, despite the psychological and social reorganization manifested in the well-being and coping with loss among numerous elderly survivors of discrete trauma such as the loss of a child or of multiple massive traumas such as the Holocaust, many continue to experience pain and grief in their inner world. This is consistent with recent perceptions of bereavement (Klass et al., 1996; Rubin, 1993).

While bereaved parents live their lives side by side with the trauma, the traumatic effects of the Holocaust on survivors were repressed for years. Survivors did not undergo a legitimate mourning process and were unable to experience acute grief while trying to survive. Grief is perhaps manifested through physiological or mental symptoms such as post-traumatic stress disorder, yet Holocaust survivors are not yet posttrauma, since mourning is designed for loss, not for catastrophe (Roth, 1988).

Aging-related losses may lead to various attempts to maintain continuity and self-esteem by turning to past memories. However, the supportive elements of reminiscence are often unavailable to survivors, as remembrance evokes traumatic memories (Sadavoy, 1997). Nadler and Ben-Shushan (1989) also assert that since the manifestation of psychological effects of massive victimization depends on the victims' life circumstances, most survivors repressed trauma and coped with the world by trying to rebuild what was lost. In old age, with the completion of such tasks, survivors focus less attention on the external world, and the psychological effects of traumatization resurface. Furthermore, the particular emphasis that survivors place on the integrity of the family unit may increase their vulnerability to stress associated with the natural process of family disintegration.

The following vignettes present two different modes of adaptation to aging losses as manifested in a Holocaust survivor and in a survivor of a discrete traumatic loss, the death of a child.

Mrs. M., aged 95, is the sole survivor of a prominent family from Poland. She lost her parents, younger brother, husband, and son in the Holocaust. Her survival during the war included horrific traumatic experiences. She emigrated to Israel in 1949, married a man who was also a lone survivor, and lived with him until his death in 1971. Her love and longing for her first husband, and especially for her son, never diminished. She thought and dreamt about them throughout her life. She rebuilt her life, becoming a teacher and then a headmistress, giving love and care to young children. Her emotional survival was achieved through a mission she took upon herself to bear witness to the Holocaust. She wrote books, poems, and newspaper articles; lectured, testified, and gave interviews; and built memorials to her family and those who perished. In her later years, while sick and weak, living alone in a small room in an old age home, she continues with her mission writing poems and letters and telling young students her story and that of the loved ones whom she still carries in her inner world. She does not disengage from them or from her traumatic past. Despite her advanced age, loneliness, traumatic past losses, and accumulating present losses, she is not depressed, is in fact well adjusted, possessing a sense of mastery. Such active and public engagement with the losses of the past represents a major gain that helps in sustaining hope and coping with both past and present losses (for more details, see Bar-Tur & Levy-Shiff, 1994). Mrs. M.'s well-being is manifested in her individuation, achieved through continued mental and emotional engagements with the Holocaust and its traumatic losses, in the inner and outer world.

Mr. L., aged 74, whose son was killed in 1975 while serving as an officer in an elite army unit, was an active member of an organization of bereaved parents in Israel. After his son's death, Mr. L. was involved in community activities aimed at helping bereaved families. At the age of 65, a malignant tumor was removed from his bowel. Soon after his operation, while in remission, he formed a support group for cancer patients. In addition, at the age of 72, despite his deteriorating health, he formed yet another support group, for elderly bereaved parents. When asked how he deals with his deteriorating health, he replied: "As long as I am active, I live; if I stop, I'll die. Aging losses are not the issue; I can deal with them—compared to the loss of my son with which I deal with all my life. It made me stronger. The pain and weakness are only inside." Like Mrs. M., Mr. L. is also engaged, mentally and emotionally, with activities related to the traumatic loss of his son. Active mental engagements in the outer world with bereaved and sick people enhance his well-being and individuation, despite continued emotional and mental engagements with the deceased in the inner world.

Conclusions

The present chapter proposes that separation-individuation processes operate as inner adaptive processes, regulating the interplay between losses and gains in aging. These processes are triggered by external changes and losses that require internal reorganization and resource regulation. Use of one's inner resources can create an inner world rich with mental and emotional engagements, compensating for the diminishment of the external world. The processes of disengagement and individuation help moderate the negative impact of aging losses, facilitate adaptation, and even ensure developmental gains.

Regulating the effects of loss is more complicated for those elderly people who have experienced past traumatic losses. Multiple traumatic losses in the past deplete the resource reservoir, impairing adaptation and well-being. In terms of separation-individuation processes, we suggest that survivors of significant traumatic loss or massive trauma such as the Holocaust can never fully disengage from the representations of their beloved ones. Thus, the inner world remains of major importance in old age and is likely to become more significant with time. Older survivors tend to function on two levels. In the external, functional world, many are well adapted; however, in the inner world, they continue to be emotionally engaged with the deceased and may experience increased pain. Despite these engagements, findings reveal that individuals who previously experienced a discrete traumatic loss often came to regard aging-related losses as secondary, enabling them to better cope with those losses and, in some cases, to turn them into opportunities for further development.

However, it appears more difficult for Holocaust survivors, as compared with bereaved parents or survivors of other discrete traumatic losses, to regulate and compensate for aging losses, as they carry in their inner world memories of an ongoing traumatic experience that defies mourning. For such survivors, disengagement from a diminishing outer world and increased engagement with their inner world may be too painful to tolerate.

References

Baltes, M. M., & Carstensen, L. L. (1996). The process of successful aging. *Aging and Society, 16,* 397–422.

Baltes, M. M., & Lang, F. R. (1997). Everyday functioning and successful aging: The impact of resources. *Psychology and Aging, 12,* 433–443.

Baltes, P. B. (1987). Theoretical propositions of life-span developmental psychology: On the dynamics between growth and decline. *Developmental Psychology, 23,* 611–626.

Bar-Tur, L., & Levy-Shiff, R. (1994). Holocaust review and bearing witness as a coping mechanism of an elderly Holocaust survivor. *Clinical Gerontologist, 14,* 3–15.

Bar-Tur, L., Levy-Shiff, R., & Burns, E. (1997). Past traumatic losses and their impact on well-being of elderly men. *Journal of Personal and Interpersonal Loss, 2,* 379–395.

Bar-Tur, L., Levy-Shiff, R., & Burns, E. (1998). Mental engagements as a moderator of losses of elderly men. *Journal of Aging Studies, 12,* 1–17.

Blos, P. (1967). The second individuation process of adolescence. *Psychoanalytic Study of the Child, 14,* 113–121.

Butler, R. N. (1963). The life review: An interpretation of reminiscing in the aged. *Psychiatry, 26,* 65–76.

Carmill, D., & Carel, R. (1986). Emotional distress and satisfaction in life among Holocaust survivors: A community study of survivors and controls. *Psychological Medicine, 16,* 141–149.

Cath, S. H. (1997). Loss and restitution in later life. In S. Akhtar & S. Kramer (Eds.), *The seasons of life: Separation-individuation perspectives* (pp. 128–156). Northvale, NJ: Jason Aronson.

Colarusso, C. A. (1997). Separation-individuation processes in middle adulthood. In S. Akhtar & S. Kramer (Eds.), *The seasons of life: Separation-individuation perspectives* (pp. 75–94). Northvale, NJ: Jason Aronson.

Danieli, Y. (1981). The aging survivor of the Holocaust: On the achievement of integration in aging survivors of the Nazi Holocaust. *Journal of Geriatric Psychiatry, 14,* 191–210.

Danieli, Y. (1994). As survivors age, Part II. *NCP Clinical Quarterly,* Spring, 20–24.

Dasberg, H. (1987). Psychological distress of Holocaust survivors. *Israel Journal of Psychiatry and Related Sciences, 24,* 243–256.

Eaton, J., Sigal, J., & Weinfeld, M. (1982). Impairment in Holocaust survivors of the Nazi Holocaust. *American Journal of Psychiatry, 139,* 773–777.

Edelstein, L. (1984). *Mental bereavement.* New York: Praeger.

Eitinger, L. (1980). The concentration camp syndrome and its late sequel. In J. Dimsdale (Ed.), *Survivors, victims and perpetrators* (pp. 127–162). New York: Hemisphere.

Erikson, E. (1963). *Childhood and society.* New York: Norton.

Erikson, E. H. (1984). Reflections on the last stage. *Psychoanalytic Study of the Child, 39,* 155–167.

Eysenck, H. J. (1988). Stress, disease and personality: The inoculation effect. In C. L. Cooper (Ed.), *Stress research* (pp. 121–146). New York: Wiley.

George, L. K., & Clipp, E. C. (1991). Subjective components of aging well. *Generations, 15,* 57–60.

Harvey, J. H. (1998). The connection between grief and trauma. In J. H. Harvey (Ed.), *Perspectives on loss: A source book* (pp. 3–17). New York: Brunner/Mazel.

Helmreich, W. B. (1992). *Against all odds—Holocaust survivors and successful lives they made in America.* New York: Simon & Schuster.

Hobfoll, S. E., & Wells, J. D. (1998). Conservation of resources, stress, and aging. In J. Lomranz (Ed.), *Handbook of aging and mental health: An integrative approach* (pp. 121–134). New York: Plenum.

Janoff-Bulman, R., & Berg, M. (1998). Disillusionment and the creation of value: From traumatic losses to existential gains. In J. H. Harvey (Ed.), *Perspectives on loss: A source book* (pp. 35–47). New York: Brunner/Mazel.

Janoff-Bulman, R., & Timko, C. (1987). Coping with traumatic life events: The role of denial in light of people's assumptive world. In C. R. Snyder & C. E. Ford (Eds.), *Coping with negative life events* (pp. 135-155). New York: Viking. (Original work published 1933).

Jung, C. G. (1933). *Modern man in search of a soul.* New York: Harcourt, Brace, & World.

Kahana, B., Harel, A., & Kahana, E. (1988). Predictors of psychological well-being among survivors of the Holocaust. In J. Wilson, Z. Harel, & B. Kahana (Eds.), *Human adaptation to extreme stress* (pp. 171–192). New York: Plenum.

Kernberg, O. (1987). *Internal world and external reality.* London: Aronson.

Klass, D., Silverman, P. R., & Nickman, S. L. (1996). Continuing bonds: New understandings of grief. Washington, DC: Taylor & Francis.

Larson, R. (1978). Thirty years of research on the subjective well-being of older Americans. *Journal of Gerontology, 33,* 109–125.

Lehman, D. R., Wortman, C. B., & Williams, A. F. (1987). Long-term effects of losing a spouse or child in a motor vehicle crash. *Journal of Personality and Social Psychology, 52,* 218-231.

Lesher, E. L., & Berger, K. J. (1988). Bereaved elderly mothers: Changes in health, functional activities, family cohesion, and psychological well-being. *International Journal of Aging and Human Development, 26,* 81–90.

Levinson, D. J., Darrow, C., & Kline, E. (1978). *The seasons of man's life.* New York: Knopf.

Lomranz, J. (1990). Long-term adaptation to traumatic stress in light of adult development and aging perspectives. In M. A. Perris, S. Crowthet, S. E. Hobfoll, & D. L. Tennenbaum (Eds.), *Stress and coping in later life families* (pp. 99–121). Washington, DC: Hemisphere.

Lomranz, J. (1998). An image of aging and the concept of integration. In J. Lomranz (Ed.), *Handbook of aging and mental health: An integrative approach* (pp. 217–250). New York: Plenum.

Mahler, M. S. (1968). *On human symbiosis and the vicissitudes of individuation.* New York: International Universities Press.

Mahler, M. S., Pine, F., & Bergman, A. (1975). *The psychological birth of the human infant.* New York: Basic Books.

Malkinson, R., & Bar-Tur, L. (1999). The aging of grief: A perspective of bereaved parents in Israel. *Death Studies, 23,* 413–432.

Marsiske, M., Lang, F. R., Baltes, P. B., & Baltes, M. M. (1995). Selective optimization with compensation: Life-span perspectives on successful human development. In R. Dixon & L. Backman (Eds.), *Psychological compensation: Managing losses and promoting gains* (pp. 35–79). Hillsdale, NJ: Erlbaum.

Miller, E. D., & Omarzu, J. (1998). New directions in loss research. In J. H. Harvey (Ed.), *Perspectives on loss: A source book* (pp. 3–20). New York: Brunner/Mazel.

Moss, M. S., Lesher, E. L., & Moss, S. Z. (1984). Impact of the death of an adult child on elderly parents: Some observations. *Omega, 17,* 209–218.

Nadler, A., & Ben-Shushan, D. (1989). Forty years later: Long-term consequences of massive traumatization as manifested by Holocaust survivors from the city and the kibbutz. *Journal of Consulting and Clinical Psychology, 57,* 287–293.

Neugarten, B. L. (1977). Personality and aging. In E. Birren & K. W. Schaie (Eds.), *Handbook of the psychology of aging* (pp. 616–649). New York: Van Nostrand.

Pearlin, L. I., & Skaff, M. M. (1996). Stress and the life course: A paradigmatic alliance. *Gerontologist, 2,* 239–247.

Rando, T. (1996). Complications in mourning traumatic death. In K. Doka (Ed.), *Living with grief after sudden loss* (pp. 139–160). Washington, DC: Hospice Foundation of America.

Raphael, B. (1983). *The autonomy of bereavement.* New York: Basic Books.

Robinson, S., Rapaport, J., & Durst, R. (1990). The late effect of Nazi persecution among elderly Holocaust survivors. *Acta Psychiatrica Scandinavica, 82,* 311–315.

Rosenblatt, P. C. (1993). Grief: The social context of private feelings. In M. S. Stroebe, W. Stroebe, & R. O. Hansson (Eds.), *Handbook of bereavement* (pp. 102–111). New York: Cambridge University Press.

Roth, S. (1988, May). *The shadow of the Holocaust.* Paper presented at the Fourth Conference of the Freud Center of the Hebrew University of Jerusalem.

Rubin, S. (1993). The death of a child is forever: The life course impact of child loss. In M. S. Stroebe, W. Stroebe, & R. O. Hansson (Eds.), *Handbook of bereavement* (pp. 285–299). New York: Cambridge University Press.

Ryff, C. D. (1989). Beyond Ponce de Leon and life satisfaction: New directions in quest of successful aging. *International Journal of Behavioral Development, 12,* 35–55.

Ryff, C. D., Singer, B., Love, G. D., & Essex, M. J. (1998). Resilience in adulthood and later life. In J. Lomranz (Ed.), *Handbook of aging and mental health: An integrative approach* (pp. 69–96). New York: Plenum.

Sadavoy, J. (1997). A review of the late-life effects of prior psychological trauma. *American Journal of Geriatric Psychiatry, 5,* 287–301.

Safford, F. (1995). Aging stressors for Holocaust survivors and their families. *Journal of Gerontological Social Work, 24,* 131–153.

Selye, J. (1976). *The stress of life.* New York: McGraw–Hill.

Shmotkin, D., & Lomranz, J. (1998). Subjective well-being among Holocaust survivors: An examination of overlooked differentiations. *Journal of Personality and Social Psychology, 75,* 141–155.

Steinitz, L. Y. (1982). Psycho-social effects of the Holocaust on aging survivors and their families. *Journal of Gerontological Social Work, 4,* 145–152.

Tamir, G. (1993). Long term adjustment among war bereaved Israeli parents. In E. Malkinson, R. Witztum, & S. R. Rubin (Eds.), *Loss and bereavement in Jewish society in Israel.* Jerusalem: Cana.

Trait, R., & Silver, R. C. (1989). Coming to terms with major negative life events. In J. S. Uleman & J. A. Bargh (Eds.), *Thoughts: The limits of awareness, intention and control* (pp. 351–382). New York: Guilford Press.

Videka-Sherman, L. (1982). Coping with the death of a child: A study over time. *American Journal of Orthopsychiatry, 52,* 688–699.

Wetle, T. (1990). Successful aging: New hope for optimizing mental and physical well-being. *Journal of Geriatric Psychiatry, 20,* 3–11.

CHAPTER TEN

HOLOCAUST TRANSMISSION: PERVERSE OR LIFE AFFIRMING?

HARVEY PESKIN

Department of Psychology, San Francisco State University, San Francisco, California, USA

NANETTE C. AUERHAHN

Bellefaire/Jewish Children's Bureau, Cleveland, Ohio, USA

Instructions for Getting Across the Border

Fictitious man, get going. Here's your passport.
Remember, you are forbidden to remember.
These are the particulars you must answer to
(your eyes are already blue).
And don't try to escape
with the sparks and the smoke
through the locomotive chimney
You are a man, and you'll sit in a coach. Relax.
After all, the suit's respectable,
the body patched,
the new name ready on your tongue.
Get going. Remember, you are forbidden to forget.
Remember, you are forbidden to forget.

—Dan Pagis, Israel

Bridging Worlds

Pearl grew up in Czechoslovakia, the daughter of two deaf parents, with a deaf sister. Pearl was her family's bridge—its translator—to

the hearing world. Once the war came, her role as translator
became life saving. As a blond, blue-eyed child, age 8, she was
initially able to roam freely, passing for Christian, scouting the city
and then returning home to report on the progress of the war and
the dreaded deportations. At one point, both parents were picked
up by the Nazis. Pearl and her younger sister were left to fend for
themselves. They sought shelter as Pearl took her sister to several of
her parents' neighbors and acquaintances, knocking on doors,
hoping to be let in. One by one they slammed doors in the girls'
faces. With nowhere to hide, they turned themselves into the
police, hoping to be sent to where the parents had been taken.
They were sent to Auschwitz, where Pearl's knowledge of Polish
and German as well as her resourcefulness allowed her to continue
in the role of scout, forewarning her sister and others of impending
danger, including medical experimentation. Whenever a new
transport of women would arrive at Auschwitz, Pearl would call
out her mother's name, knowing that Mother could not hear her
but hoping that someone who knew Mother would alert her to the
fact that her name was being called. This irritated a guard who hit
Pearl so savagely that she temporarily lost her hearing. It eventually returned, but to this day she suffers a hearing loss in the
affected ear. While in the camps, Pearl kept a diary on the only
paper she could find: toilet paper. One day a guard found her
treasure. She watched helplessly as he unrolled it and read what
was written on it, laughing as he read. To her horror, the guard
tore up her "diary." At the time of liberation, she was near death
from typhus. She states that one of the saddest facts of her life is
that she has no recollections of liberation. She remained ill for
quite some time and needed to be hospitalized, precipitating a first
separation from her sister, who had been totally dependent on her
for translation and as a bridge to the world. Lacking contact with
someone who could be such a vehicle for her, the sister totally
withdrew into her own mute silence. Later the sisters were reunited
and sent to live with religious relatives in the United States who
did not wish to listen to their stories and, upon hearing them, tried
to relegate them to other tragedies in Jewish history, as if no new
categories or liturgical accommodations needed to be made—as if
the Holocaust could be assimilated into prior Jewish traumas.
Pearl eventually resolved not to speak of her experiences and came

to the conclusion that she existed in two worlds: the prewar and war self separated from the postwar self. These two selves and two worlds could be neither integrated nor reconciled.

The theme of being the messenger between two worlds abounds in this narrative. Pearl negotiates between the world of the hearing and the world of the deaf, between the prewar world and the post-Holocaust world, between the world that is supposed to be and the world that is (the care vs. the cruelty of doctors, neighbors, police), between being a Jew and passing as a Christian. Missing the joyful moment of liberation represented the loss of a momentously imagined bridging link between her various worlds. Such a link is forever yearned for. But the yearning itself stands as a portent of what will be forever denied her. Pearl concludes that she must keep each world separate from the other to preserve their authenticity. This reality is ambivalently accepted only after several failed attempts at witnessing. The diary on toilet paper was an attempt at witnessing for herself all her fears and yearnings. The guard's scorn constituted a betrayal of witnessing made into an internal robbery of witnessing by the temporary loss of hearing—cut off from others as sister, at the end, is eventually cut off from all human contact. At that point sister epitomizes the survivor who, thus cut off from the world, has lost even her internal witness. The impossibility of testifying is made clear in the uncomprehending remarks of American family members, as Pearl later turns to writing poetry about mute eyes. But her struggle with writer's block shows that she remained uncertain about her right to bridge both worlds through artistic integration. The witness that would have allowed for a creative bridging of the two worlds was not to be found among her relatives or in the larger community in which they lived.

The presence of two worlds—the attempt to bridge them as well as the failure to bridge them—is a theme that runs through the lives both of survivors and children of survivors (succinctly expressed in one woman's description of herself as a dead survivor, and in a child survivor's portrayal of her mother as being buried alive). The survivor lives in both worlds simultaneously, yet with an impassable border between them. The transmission of Holocaust trauma usually refers to the psychological consequences exacted by this impasse that spreads pathologically within the intra- and intergenerational structures of survivor-families. Normally, transmission from one generation to the next is expected to be in the service of historical continuity that is essential for human development. Such healthful transmission is traditionally open, generative, and sustaining. The legacy that parents owe their children for identity formation normally includes the sharing of an informed history of family and community experience. The child is neither made to feel overincluded as a peer who is absorbed in the parents' issues or underincluded as an outsider or one so fragile as to be unable to bear the meaning of events. Transmission of a normal world respects the natural order and rights of heritage, especially the right to know what is known by an older generation. When sponsored by the right to know, transmission grants to the next generation the spirit of survival and love of life itself (Valent, 1998). Living normally and healthfully means the right and duty to transmit to loved ones a legacy of care, even in the face of its imagined impossibility. The recent Holocaust movie *Life Is Beautiful* depicts such a transmission through a work of imagination in which a parent strives to act as a protective screen for the child and to communicate the message that life is worth living. The movie stands in relationship to the Holocaust as a certain kind of dream stands to life: It is a fantasy that represents not naive wishful thinking but the reality of wishes that generational transmission can reanimate life. In actuality, the true horrors of the Holocaust shattered parents' ability to protect their children and to believe, let alone transmit, that, after all, life is beautiful.

The first world of the survivor is the extraordinary world of the past—of war and prewar—wherein the self that "is the sum of everything we remember" (Kundera, 1997 p. 234) resides. This world is recalled in both prewar and war memories that are intermingled, so that early positive memories are associatively linked with the circumstances of their destruction, creating contaminated, compromised images. The past as was is thus unrecoverable in memory. Indeed, we have found that the pre-traumatic past is recalled only as an idealized, paradisical state about which details are not retrievable. When attempting to recollect it, only schematic, stereotyped memories that are neither unique nor personal are produced, together with vague memories that consist more of a feeling tone than fully structured experiences. When remembered, this past is regarded by the survivor as fantasy (Auerhahn & Laub, 1984), The traumatic past too (despite the concreteness of its horrific details) feels strangely unreal; as many a survivor has admitted, "I don't believe it myself," or "I can't believe what my eyes have seen." This is due, in part, to the fact that trauma is registered in fragments that defy integration or narratization into a whole. To remain solely in this first world is to be continually confronted with the horror of its destruction, while to transmit a legacy from that world is to communicate the consequences of shame, degradation, and unbridled aggression. In the Holocaust past, the natural order of informed transmission from one generation to the next risks maiming, for how can Holocaust reality be transmitted without also communicating the message that evil predominates over good and life without loved ones is not worth living?

The second world of the survivor is the normal, everyday one of the present. It is a world that has fantasy, art, and symbols at its disposal—all ways of dealing with trauma that had been lacking in the Holocaust world where the immediacy of unpredictable events overwhelmed any chance of normal mastery. This world, too, feels unreal and strangely abnormal, as the signs of evil that have defined reality for the survivor are absent. Stated one survivor of the post-Holocaust selves of her peers. "I think we are not normal because we are so normal." In this second world, the scaffolding of reality and normalcy is present, but the landscape is devoid of people—those relationships by which the self was originally defined are absent, while the survivor feels profoundly disconnected from those who are present owing to their lack of familiarity with that other world. Thus, the "normal" self is unrecognizable and fractured by loneliness and the guilty abandonment of all those whom the survivor had loved but who perished.

The question arises: How does the survivor transmit his Holocaust world to his family and community, and how does he transmit his normal world, which is not experienced by him as normal at all? The difficulty of this task is compounded by the frequent contamination—and fear of contamination—of one world by the other, as in this stark example: Faye Sholitan (personal communication) tells us about a survivor who responded to the question "What was the Sabbath like in your home?" with a series of impressions (my father's chair, fish cooking, cleaning home) that collapsed, with unbidden and inexplicable suddenness, into a description of a pogrom where he watched his mother hung and his sister raped. Thus, to know the Holocaust risks resurgence of the Holocaust reality rather than allowing historical and generational distance from the Holocaust to develop. For these reasons, injunctions against knowing the Holocaust are often invoked to halt the transmission of trauma. In fact, the horrific reality of the Holocaust cannot be barred by such fiat but, rather, stays lurkingly present, in a manner leading to unaccountable or obscure action. One lives in the half-life of uninvested, forbidden, or forsaken identities far from either shore of past trauma or present adaptation. We have elsewhere called this half-life a Second Holocaust (Peskin, Auerhahn, & Laub, 1997) of ennervated existence where one wards off the liveliness and passion of experience. Life is copied rather than lived.

The survivor finds herself in the near unresolvable struggle to transmit a normal reality over the sinister pull of her Holocaust world, because she personally does not feel grounded in the reality of a normal existence. Since everything has changed, the old self is no more. The movement from pathological transmission (of the Holocaust) to life-affirming transmission (characterized by the normal world) can be made only if the rift between the survivor's "before" and "after" selves (Auerhahn & Laub, 1990) is healed by locating a bridge between her two worlds. This bridge must be provided by a witness in the present who exists simultaneously in both worlds, creating a passageway wherein the self of the past can be united with the present self. Only then can the survivor reclaim her self, once it is known to a witness who validates and acknowledges the reality of both worlds and both selves. In many situations, this may be accomplished without a therapist.

In this regard, we understand one survivor's explanation of why she remained with her husband after the war: "The man I married and the man he was after the war weren't the same person. And . . . I was not the same person either. . . . But . . . we had a need for each other because he knew who I was and I knew who he was. . . . You feel like you come from nothing, you are nothing. Nobody knows you. You need some contact; you need some connection. He knew who I was and I knew who he was." The knowing that on first reading covers over the lack of continuity does not in fact prevent its recognition, but it does support traffic between the survivor's two worlds in such a way as to keep both in place. It involves being a witness to the other's identity by keeping in perspective past and present inner and outer reality, in such a way that neither eclipses nor contaminates the other. For this to occur, the other must know something about the survivor's extraordinary world so as to guarantee the continuance of the basic landmarks according to which the survivor's self was originally established (Auerhahn & Laub, 1990). Indeed, being a virtual witness of the spouse's Holocaust existence helps lift a crucial doubt held by many survivors (especially child survivors) concerning the credibility of their traumatic memories. The joint work of remembering means that both partners help each other move beyond being shut down by anxiety, guilt, and shame to a growing confidence that one's memories are not only acknowledged but believed, rather than enthralled to what others can bear.

A case in point is the survivor who mistakenly thought he had told his wife about a traumatic Holocaust incident that beleaguered his artistic work. But when, in fact, he did finally tell his wife, his work inhibitions and other symptoms vanished miraculously and have never returned. Such witnessing must also be firmly rooted in the normal world of abiding care and love to convince the survivor that he can return to normalcy. Only then can he permit himself to enter the Holocaust world. If a witness knows, then the survivor regains the hope of discovering such capacity for knowing in himself—the capacity to render both worlds equally authentic by the establishment of traffic between them. Without such traffic, the survivor feels either false (trapped in the unreality of the normal world) or fragmented (compromised by trauma). Thus, the urge to bear witness in order to have a witness is intended ultimately to create knowledge in oneself so that life may be reinvested, living can proceed, and generational continuity can be reestablished (Auerhahn & Laub, 1990). It is in this context that we understand the declaration of a survivor interviewed by Spielberg's Shoah project that the taping of his testimony was "the happiest moment of my life." "There he was in his Spielberg-style redemptive ending, surrounded by his wife, children, and grandchildren, taking almost childlike pleasure in his achievement. 'I told my story on tape,' he said. 'Now maybe I won't be crazy anymore.'" (Sholitan, personal communication).

From Pathological to Life-Affirming Transmission

The following examples of pathological and healthful Holocaust transmission illuminate the conditions that allow for movement from one to the other in therapeutic settings.

1. In survivor families, one finds at times a fear of being so absorbed by Holocaust trauma that generational boundaries are fragile and easily breached. The situation is paradoxical in that family members are at once overincluded by absorbing so much and underincluded by knowing so little. Fonagy's (1999) case presentation is prototypical of this unknowing enmeshment: A third-generation adolescent with little knowledge of his family's Holocaust victimization clings to Holocaust fantasies of Nazi terror (like being a camp commandant). His imaginings are kept to himself, just as Holocaust reality has been kept from him, sealed off from intrafamily acknowledgment, correction, verification, and witness. The Holocaust is known only dissociatively, with images of horror transposed into the self in moments of nonresponsiveness on the part of the caregiver. The only continuity in Fonagy's case is the direct infiltration ("colonization") of unconscious traumatic images from grandmother (the survivor) to mother (the child of a survivor) and from mother to son created by the absence of maternal care under the child's press for emotional contact. We encounter here an example of family traumatic pathology that reveals a prototypical disjunction between knowing, affect, and action, which is itself a legacy of the Holocaust. Silence in the survivor generation, beyond being a stunning effect of trauma, may also be an attempt at self-cure that, by a dissociative splitting of consciousness, counts on the inattention of self and others to eradicate traumatic memory. Staying hidden long enough behind silence becomes finally the silence of having nothing to remember. With psychodynamic irony, however, the outcome is often otherwise, namely, the transmission of inattention and amnesia itself. A sense of emptiness and unreality becomes symptomatic of perverse transmission where a part of the self fails to bear witness to what is real.

Besides the silence of survivor family members, the feeling of unreality—as discussed earlier—has several sources: the unreality that infiltrates the pretraumatic and traumatic states of the past world and the post-traumatic "normal" world.

But notwithstanding his cogent formulation of Holocaust dissociation in the patient's family, Fonagy's presentation is also prototypical of clinical reports of therapeutic work with Holocaust families insofar as they do not enlighten us about patients' development from such perverse transmission (or "transposition" in Kestenberg's apt [1982] term) to a rightful grasp and conveyance of knowledge to the next generation about the Holocaust history and identity of the family. One is left uncertain about whether the therapy had allowed new and creative integrations of Holocaust reality to supplant dissociative mechanisms. In effect, the important issue of the resources available to each succeeding generation to make such integrations remains unattended. The therapy, then, may unwittingly reprise the family silence. Indeed, the concept of dissociation, by pathologizing Holocaust memories that the next generation patient could not have had, overlooks that such dissociated fantasies, when properly acknowledged and witnessed in the therapy as the child's initial reach for personal knowledge that has been denied her, provide a starting point for distinguishing true personal identity from false memory. Personal identity moves the child beyond either forgetting or repeating history to finding out what part of the Holocaust belongs authentically to her. Merely to disabuse the child of false memory leaves her with an equally false perception that she has no right to personal knowledge of family history. Personal identity presupposes a child in her own right who does not dissociatively mimic or purloin the Holocaust memory of her significant others but cogently holds and preserves their memory as personal knowledge. The personal identity of the children's generation serves to bridge Holocaust memory and Holocaust history. This transmission is a life-affirming transformation of experience that binds yet differentiates the generations.

2. Often enough, one must turn to personal memoirs to hear the full unfolding of the transmission process from Holocaust dissociation to integration. In Fremont's (1999) memoir, two American daughters of survivors, raised Roman Catholic by Jewish survivor parents who transposed their wartime pose of being Catholic into

present-day reality, overcome years of denial by confronting each other and their parents with irrefutable proof of the family's Jewishness. The chronic suppression of this forbidden knowledge had kept the family huddled loyally together in a kind of co-dependent pseudo-ignorance but never far from a tentativeness about who they were and what they believed that expressed a suspended yet longed-for connection with other Jewish survivors. The memoir itself is a culminating act of healthy transmission, because it makes known to the world what the family members were finally able to disclose to each other. Disclosure was hardly seamless. Openness is at first precarious, ridden with suspicion of personal exposure. Helen Fremont's mother, confronted by her daughters with proof of her Jewish past, initially accuses them of being like Nazis hunting her down. These hard-won disclosures constitute knowledge-as-action ("action knowledge" as described by Auerhahn & Peskin, 1999) that recognized the indisputable reality of liberation and the family's entitlement to restore its lost identity. Before, the family had stayed hidden in a time-frozen, unwitnessed Holocaust past that violated and withheld the truths of the parents as survivors and the daughters as rightful heirs of their survival.

The vital role of witnesses in fostering life-affirming transmission is well shown in Fremont's story. The resolving evidence of Jewishness that the daughters brought to their parents came from actual testimony by witnesses from the mother's Polish hometown, made available by Yad Vashem, the Holocaust research center in Israel. Beyond that, the parents were able to acknowledge and resume their lost identities when they were rendered as gifts of their children's love and devotion to truth, not as accusations of withheld birthright. Thus, the external witnessing (by Yad Vashem) established the conditions necessary for witnessing on the part of the daughters, which in turn allowed for the parents' own internal witnessing. In initiating this restitution of identity, the children were not being perversely "parentified"; rather, by acting as the parents' witnesses, they restored to mother and father the lost legacy of parenthood: the right, duty, and joy of believing and fostering a child's birthright and heritage. In the liberation that these children and parents brought to each other, one sees that the Holocaust loses its ghostly domination of family life in the grim symptom picture of the Second Holocaust (Peskin et al., 1997).

Instead, a clarity of vision puts the Holocaust in a historical and psychological context that allows one to be in the world and lay claim to one's own experience. The ardor of caring that binds family members together in pathological transmission of blind loyalty is, however, the same ardor that sustains healthy transmission of one's truly lived experience. What is different is that loyalty and obedience are now no longer the only conditions for caring and feeling cared for; braving the unpredictable course of restoring a truer selfhood also expresses the bonding of love.

3. The transmission of blind loyalty necessarily means sacrificial blindness to one's own needs even beyond devotion to parents' well-being. A case in point is the daughter of survivors who was convinced that her mother would be retraumatized if she married her non-Jewish partner. Hence, she and her partner agreed that their relationship was so strong that marriage could easily wait until the parent's death. To this, the therapist remarked: "Do you know that if you hold off marriage until your mother dies, you'll be finding yourself wishing for her death?" The intervention was meant to stop a pathological transmission that was driven by the death imprint of the Holocaust that still held sway in the family. By the daughter's reckoning, her personal fulfillment could only be joyless for the parent. Yet, the daughter's personal sacrifice might just as likely spell a lost opportunity for parent and child to share the birth of grandchildren and bring forth hopes for family continuity that had fallen by the family wayside. Following this therapeutic intervention, the couple did indeed marry, with a fully alive and happy mother and father in attendance. Perverse transmission of deadness had turned open, generative, and sustaining: in short, life affirming (Peskin et al., 1997).

4. The Holocaust death imprint of murder and genocide courses through perverse transmission, subverting the right to live fully for oneself and for those whom one loves. Perhaps nowhere is the self-deprivation of this right to possess the creative uniqueness of one's own life more poignant and more unjust than when members of the survivor's family give up their right to mourn the death of a loved one. Instead, the unique grief for the lost person collapses into the anonymity of the countless murdered. Ilany Kogan (1989) reports on her psychoanalysis of a child, Rachel, of a survivor father who came to Israel to reincarnate his lost family. The

patient followed her parents' injunction to stay loyal to their
absorption in the world of the dead. The witnessing that her
parents seemingly craved had collapsed under the weight of their
greater need to press Rachel into being both their proxy of the
abandoned survivor and their memorial to the dead, unknown
children of the extended family. Either way, such moribund enactments denied Rachel the truth of belonging to the next generation
as a child of a survivor rather than the falsehood of being a survivor (or a victim) herself. One day, her caring lover died while
they were making love. As an ineffable, suicidal sense of doom
closed rapidly around her, she heard from the analyst—
overcoming her own fright and helplessness at Rachel's unspeakable terror—that "his death resembled his birth—he was born
from a woman and died, in the midst of love, inside one" (Kogan,
1989, p. 665). To acknowledge such a death as a life-giving experience remarkably lifted the Holocaust shadow of nonrelatedness
that had consumed the patient. Rachel began thereafter to work
on breaking away from her mother and establishing a life of her
own. Such a separation no longer evoked crippling guilt from a
victimizing mother. After the analysis ended, Rachel married and
had a child with a man whom mother came finally to accept in a
new rapprochement with daughter. Here again, transmission had
become open, generative, and sustaining. The treatment had been
interminable as long as Rachel remained stagnated in the belief
that self-sacrifice was the only face of love and loyalty that would
be acceptable to her lost and living family. The therapist's intervention acknowledged that the patient's loss of her lover evoked
and deserved her own autonomous and regenerative feelings of
grief and attachment to a person special to herself. A death, not a
murder; a loss of her own, not to be added to the undifferentiated,
bewildering, and nameless guilt of family losses that beckoned her
to take her own life (Peskin et al., 1997).

The Role of the Witness in Moving From Pathological to Life-Affirming Transmission: An Oral Testimony of a Child Survivor

For years, Menachem refused to talk about the Holocaust. Finally,
one day he decided to give an oral testimony to the Fortunoff

Video Archive for Holocaust Testimonies at Yale University. As he sat down before the cameras, he explained to the interviewer:

In my personal experience, this was a subject that was never brought up in my father's household . . . because it was something that you have to forget. It's not something that you have to talk about. I think what is really significant is that for many years now people were trying to deny that it ever happened, that it ever happened to them, or if it did happen, that it afflicted them in any way. So that it's better to forget about it. Then when you bring it up, you bring up all kinds of repressed emotions that were never dealt with, so you get upset, you get your nightmares back, you become emotional, sleepless, depressed. . . . So you just didn't deal with it. I have talked with a few of my friends lately, and it was always the same. You shouldn't be talking about it. Father will get upset, Mother will cry, so let's pretend it's never been, it's never happened. Personally speaking, I was unable to read any books, for instance, about the Holocaust. Until very recently, I didn't read one word about it. I was never able to watch any movies on the Holocaust, and I was pretending very hard that it never happened to me; it just wasn't there. And oddly enough, I wasn't able to talk about this with my children, so I realize now; but I never realized that I never talked about it, neither with my wife nor with my children. I mean she knew, but going into the feelings—never. Now, a few things have changed lately: I've been talking to some friends and this is how I got here. . . . You know Manuel [another survivor]? Now I know him for years, but we've never talked about it [the Holocaust]. We talked about hundreds of subjects but we've never touched upon it. Then one day we were sitting in our house and Arthur . . . [another survivor] was there and somehow we started to talk about it and realized we have something in common, very much in common. Then he was talking about it to . . . [people involved in the videotaping project, who] asked me if I'd be willing to come and I said, "No way." Anyway, to cut a long story short, my wife said, "You know, you've been trying to run away for a long time, why don't you confront it?" . . . For the first time there was the Holocaust movie on television [NBC's 1978 miniseries "Holocaust," authored by Gerald Green]. . . . For the first time I decided to watch it with my family. It was a moving experience. At one point, by the end of it, we were all crying, and my nine-year-old said to me, "Hey, Daddy, you're crying," and I said, "Yeah, you're crying too." She said, "I cry from time to time, but I've never seen you cry." I answered, "Well, I do cry from time to time. Not as much as you do, but I can remember times when I cried." Then I asked her, "Why are you crying here?" and she said, "I cry for all those poor people. Why do you cry?" I said, "Well, I really cry for myself." She said, "What do you mean, for yourself?" "Well, you know, I was a part of it. I went through those miseries." She looked at me and said, "Daddy, I never knew. Why didn't you tell me?" For once in my life I was speechless. I realized I wasn't able to tell her. My daughter and I have very good communication; we talk about almost everything there is, but somehow I wasn't able.

In his testimony, Menachem described how, as a Polish child of 4, his parents smuggled him out of a labor camp, hoping that thereby he would have better chances of surviving.

> They told me that, the times being what they were, I would have to go. We would have to part. They promised me that when the war was over they would come and look for me, no matter where I'll be. . . . My mother gave me her student ID, which speaking logically was a stupid thing to do. But to me it really meant everything, the ID with her picture in it. . . . [She] said, "You keep my picture, so when we meet again. . . ." They said to me, that when the war will end, and they made a promise, that they will come for me. . . . To me, if they say they are coming for me, they will come. This is something that kept me going.

For the next year, Menachem lived first in a brothel and then as a vagabond on the streets. He describes himself at that time: "Today this sounds like a joke, but to me, it's serious. At that point, I was like 70 years old. I was really an old man. I was short, but I was old. I had the whole responsibility of the whole world for myself. I knew that what I finally had to rely upon was myself." Eventually an elderly woman took him in during the winter and passed him off as her grandson.

> So I had to do a few things that I didn't know how to do, like to pray . . . to go to church. The prayers I found I didn't like to do. . . . As primitive as this lady was, I saw she had a wonderful sense of what's important and what's not important. By this time I had revealed to her that I had a treasure, and this was the picture of my mother's. So she agreed that every night before bedtime, I would pray to the picture of my mother rather than to the crucifix . . . I used to take this picture out and pray to God to make this war end and please let my mother come back and get me.

Lacking food, the elderly woman eventually sent Menachem to live with her sister and brother-in-law in the country. One night,

> the woman who I was staying with . . . said to her husband, "We are not going to sleep at home; we are going to our neighbors." [Her husband] . . . said, "You crazy woman, what do you mean?" She said, "Well, I had this dream in which my mother came to me and said that this house is unsafe." You know, it was a primitive Polish setting. Once a parent appeared in a

dream, it was a command; you can't do anything about it. So we left everything and went to sleep with the neighbors. The house was destroyed [that night]. A bomb or an artillery shell fell on it and it was wiped out.

Eventually, after the war, Menachem was reunited with his parents.

It was a very traumatic meeting. I had the picture of my mother, but of course she didn't resemble my mother at all. They were still dressed in their prison camp clothes, with the wide stripes. My father is six foot two, and he weighed . . . less than 100 pounds. They were really emaciated, and my father looked terrible. He was tortured, and he had all his teeth hanging out. It was terrible. . . . I just couldn't believe it, that they were my parents . . . I think that this was the hardest part of it all, to accept them again. They were my parents logically, but emotionally, I didn't feel anything towards them. For some period, I used to address them by calling them Mister and Missus. I just couldn't bring myself to accept them . . . this was really the first time that I started to realize what has happened. Until then, I was preoccupied with everyday life. I knew that I could take care of myself. . . . But then, first of all, I had to become a child again, which I resented. Of course . . . they came back different. It took me awhile until I was able to accept this. It haunted me for many, many years. Once I was safe again . . . I disintegrated. I developed fevers; I couldn't sleep. I started having nightmares, nightmares that were totally abstract, always repeating themselves. They eventually boiled down to a surrealistic, abstract representation of a feeling of helplessness. It was like a conveyor belt on which I was moving toward a press which was rolling, and there was no power whatsoever to stop it. I couldn't move; I was just rolling closer and closer, and I would wake up totally disoriented, crying my head off, screaming, sweaty and shaking. I could never go back to sleep. This went on for many years. As a matter of fact, I would never go to sleep without taking some sort of sleeping pill. . . . Until at one point, I stopped dreaming. I know that this sounds weird, because you never stop dreaming, but I somehow managed to totally repress all dreams.

[When I was asked to give my oral testimony] my initial reaction was "No." My wife said, "Well, why don't you think it over?" I said "Okay," but I was resolved at that time that I would not do it. The fear of once again trying to revive the things that I was trying so hard to repress. My wife asked me what it was all about and I told her, and she said, "Well, what are you afraid of?" I said, "I'm scared that everything will come back, my nightmares. . . ." She said, "Well you've been living with this thing for 34, 35 years after the war and you're still afraid. You never talked about it. It's because you're still afraid, still anxious. Why don't you try the other way?" We spent a lot of time talking about it. I began to see the logic. This particular night, we went to bed very early in the morning because we had talked very far into the night. . . . The next night, I had my nightmares again. But this time it was different. It was again the conveyor belt; it was again the rolling presses; it was again the feeling of helplessness and of terrible anxiety. But for the first time in my life, I stopped the conveyor belt. I woke up, still feeling anxious, but the anxiety was turning into a wonderful sense of fulfillment and satisfaction. I got up; for the first time I wasn't disoriented; I knew where I was; I knew what happened; and somehow for the first time I was able to do it. I feel strongly that it has to do with the fact that I decided to open up, to discuss, and it has to do with the fact that it's been repressed too long. It had to come up. We had to talk about it.

Menachem concluded his testimony with the following:

In many ways, everything was really shaped by those experiences. It took me a while to realize. One of the things that I am trapped with right now is, if we don't deal with our feelings, we don't understand our experiences, then what are we doing to our children? I realized that when my first daughter was born. For a very short moment, I suspected there might be something that I'm doing as a reaction. This was right after I delivered her. (I delivered my children myself, being a gynecologist. This privilege was very important to me.) So I went on a kind of a buying spree, binge. I spent a couple of hundred pounds on toys. I bought all kinds of toys that you really don't buy for a newborn: an electric train, a pedal-car. I very proudly prepared everything in the room for my daughter, who came home three days later with my wife. My wife looked at the things and she said to me, "Why did you buy all this?" I said, "What do you mean, why did I buy all this? A child needs to have toys." She said, "Yes, but it will take years before she is able to play with them." "What do you mean, it will take years? A child needs toys. I just bought some toys. What's wrong with a child having toys?" And it took me a long time to realize what I was doing. I was finally buying toys for myself. This was the start of my wondering: What are we doing to the next generation? We are as we are. We can change some. We will never be able to eradicate what happened. We might try to understand some of the dynamics, but we will never be able to wipe it out. It will always live with us and let's face it. I'm facing it now. The big question is, what will become of those? Are we transferring our anxieties, our fears, our problems to the generations to come?

Menachem frames his narrative with concerns around Holocaust transmission: He begins by acknowledging the difficulty of telling his story to his daughter and ends with the fear of transferring his anxieties to her. His own ability to withstand, know, and tell his experience is made possible, submerged, and then reinstated by the status of the maternal witness. What kept him going when he was alone as a "70-year-old" five-year-old was the image of his mother as represented in her student ID and as embodied in the women who took him in and gave him shelter (first the prostitutes and then the elderly ladies). Mother's protective, sheltering function reached its magical pinnacle when another mother, that of the Polish peasant with whom he lived, appeared in a dream and saved their lives through forewarning of an attack. This image was shattered by the reunion with the real mother, who no longer looked like Mother and who is not even described (the loss of the pretraumatic mother being unspeakable) but whose appearance is inferred as the mirror image of Father, who *is* described as tortured and emaciated. Mother is lost, as is sleep, and years of nightmares ensue until finally the absence of she who watches over the sleeping child is accompanied by the absence of dreaming and of the transitional world itself expressed in the function of dreaming, which borrows its value and safety from the protective function of the maternal introject. That is, it is the connection with Mother that makes possible the entrance into the transitional world (Auerhahn & Laub, 1987). This world is longed for and sought after, especially when Menachem becomes a parent and attempts to reconnect with his own capacity to play via projective identification with the mothering experience of his daughter.

Menachem offers us a rich narrative in which life-affirming transmission has been prefigured in his repeated Holocaust rescue by female care and nurturance. Menachem's wife activates these prior rescues by becoming his witness and the vehicle by which the maternal introject is reinstated. His choice of profession had been an attempt to connect with the maternal introject by internalizing its function of giving birth. Menachem's wife becomes his bridge to the normal world, recovering his faith in talking and recognizing the intrusion of his Holocaust world into his new world. She is the one to whom he discloses his past even while trying to live in her present. After staying up all night talking, his faith in the possibility of a witness is restored and he is able to regain a sense of mastery over his experience. At that point he can begin to recognize the pernicious effects of Holocaust transmission and concern himself with the legacy bequeathed to future generations. Acknowledgment by a witness leads to knowing his own experience (Auerhahn & Peskin, 1999), which in turn establishes the conditions for rendering transmission a conscious process and allows him to move from testimony about "mere" survival and a death-in-life that invokes repetition (symbolized by the repetitive dream of the crushing machine) to testimony about the resumption of living (symbolized by his ability to stop the machine).

Social Influences on Perverse and Healthy Transmission

While the family of the survivor has an important role to play in helping reestablish the conditions necessary for internal witnessing, which in turn allows the survivor to move from unconscious transmission of pathological and negative life themes (Laub & Auerhahn, 1993) to the conscious transmission of a life-enhancing message, the survivor family cannot succeed in such a task without the witness of the larger community as well. Indeed, Menachem's dialogue with his family and then himself begins with watching the television series "The Holocaust," which in itself was a form of public acknowledgment of events. Society's role as a necessary witness has been underestimated in the psychological literature, which in turn has underestimated the impossibility and inappropriateness of a child serving as sole witness for the parent. The burden on such children is beyond their developmental capacities. Indeed, by so forcing the child (like Rachel) to suspend her own development, children unknowingly assume a posture of maturity that ironically plays into the community's Holocaust inattention, insouciance, and amnesia.

Models for life-affirming or pathological transmission are first learned and incorporated from living in the community, the nation, and the world. The social forms of Holocaust denial are legion: obtrusive or subtle, innocent or disingenuous. Together they prefigure the survivor's own proclivity to face or flee Holocaust knowledge. Clinicians are likely to consider societal causes of traumatic transmission—however true in the abstract—neither compelling nor useful in their urgency to alleviate this suffering. Is this professional stance part of the problem or part of the solution? We believe that without reflecting on society's part in dissociating survivors from their trauma, the psychotherapist of Holocaust victims perpetuates the alienation, leading to the constriction, passivity, and aloneness that brought the survivor to treatment. The intrusion of societal views of the Holocaust into the treatment will go undetected to the extent that such reflection is avoided. Such intrusions, of course, are just as operative in the treatment of non-survivors, especially in nations that perpetrated the Holocaust (Bergmann & Jacovy, 1982). The privacy and confidentiality of individual therapy is then hardly protection against the infiltration of deep-seated silences about the Holocaust. We propose that such silence in the therapies of survivors and their families is more pregnant than empty because common dissociative processes in patient and therapist may be silently but powerfully at work.

The absence of Holocaust material in a survivor's therapy may mean many things. But what often escapes notice is that such absence may enact the doubt or disbelief that a patient expects will greet his traumatic experience. Such fears of not being believed are likely to be inseparable from the trauma itself. Indeed, inculcating these fears was a primary intention of perpetrators of massive human evil who ultimately sought to persuade the world that the evil had never happened (Arendt, 1973). Primo Levi's (1978) discovery at Auschwitz that his unusual dream of being disbelieved was common among fellow inmates may serve as a striking commentary on the meaning of silence in the treatment of survivors. In the throes of Auschwitz, Levi had already anticipated how we would all be prey to Holocaust denial in his nightmarish dream where his sister back home gets up without listening to him and walks out. Alfredo, his friend, confides to Primo Levi that this dream of not being believed is also his dream "and the dream of many others, perhaps everyone" in Auschwitz. The carryover of such a situation into the treatment setting leads to a perverse therapeutic process in which the patient's own unvoiced doubts about being believed are displaced and mislaid onto unrelated areas of the patient's life. In turn, the absence of such material in the child-of-survivor's therapy represents a transmission of the survivor-parent's own fears of being discounted by the outside world.

Yet, the silence is complex, representing not only hiding, fleeing, or resignation but also waiting and challenging. The therapist who wraps himself in the garment of neutrality by waiting for the patient to introduce the Holocaust will miss that the patient too is waiting, now for the therapist to accompany the patient empathically through the impasse of society's injunction against disclosure that their mutual silence had embodied. Indeed, because of the potent dynamics of silence that Holocaust trauma creates therapeutic neutrality calls for a revised and broader scope to include the therapist's explicit willingness to raise and be faced with the patient's need to be believed without compromising awareness of countertransferential suggestion. Identifying the issue of not being believed, especially when it involves a traumatic history, is itself a complex issue, with a paucity of defining landmarks and interventions in the therapy literature. In general, not being believed has no ready vocabulary in clinical practice but, rather, is revealed by obscure enactments as diverse as disdaining support or trusting excessively. Yet, patient and therapist may need first of all to confront the issue of the therapist's capacity to believe in order to create for the patient the equivalence in treatment of a witness whose listening helps the patient remember rather than repeat the abandonment of the traumatic state. The trauma of the Holocaust itself, including the patient's own self-doubts about traumatic memory, can then be approached without undue fears of personal discredit by self-blame or the retribution of others.

A clinical case report by Chaseguet-Smirgel (1999) illustrates with dramatic poignancy the importance of the therapist's own confrontation with belief before the patient can turn safely inward toward entrusting the therapeutic process with his unfinished grief. The patient is a child survivor who had been exposed to ghastly and eyewitnessed losses. The treatment had come to a point where the patient could openly doubt that the analyst believed his Holocaust memory. Perhaps, ventures Chasseguet-Smirgel to her patient (making the classical intervention of turning the patient's attention inward), it is the patient who doubts himself. This the patient rejects angrily and vehemently. But the issue stays alive, and the analyst finds a second chance to meet this impasse: Chasseguet-Smirgel responds this time by recalling Primo Levi's Auschwitz dream of not being believed. What followed is so sparing as to be ineffably moving: The patient indicates how much he wishes to acknowledge that the analyst is able after all to countenance the issue of her capacity to believe; he asks her for the name of the statuette of a prone boy that sits in the analyst's waiting room. Chasseguet-Smirgel answers: "Kaddish" (the Hebrew prayer for the dead).

We present the following situations to illuminate the wider social context affecting Holocaust transmission.

1. Some years ago, an informal, qualitative study was undertaken (Peskin & Karr, 1982) that revisited 15 offspring of survivors who had been first interviewed as adolescents in coffee-klatch group discussions (Karr, 1973) at a time when media silence about the Holocasut prevailed. The follow-up individual interviews occurred about 10 years later under the sway of the new media openness about the Holocaust. The acclaimed TV docudrama and miniseries "The Holocaust" was the flagship of this new era. All of those interviewed had watched it. The purpose of the inquiry was shared with these children of survivors: to determine whether family communication about the Holocaust had noticeably improved with the greater media attention to Holocaust programming. In the follow-up interview, the children were asked to reflect on their own participation in the transmission of parents' suffering. Although the children lived in the same neighborhood of a large American city and often knew each other in junior or senior high school, none knew each other as children of survivors.

Relistening to the audiotapes of the earlier group discussion underscored the children's underinclusion and distinct remoteness from their parents' Holocaust suffering. This remoteness could be characterized as seemingly uninformed, incurious, and unempathic, even to the point of obliviousness and condescension. Parents were described as vaguely "odd" or "weird" because of what "happened" to them in the war. The children chose to remain mystified by rather than aware of the difficulty of disclosure. They affected minimal interest in what befell their parents, as well as feeling minimal interest from the parents in conveying their past.

A decade later, the situation had changed considerably for most of the children. Being a child of survivors now held a visible place in their sense of personal identity. Even if held ambivalently, being survivors' children became open to discussion, as if now, also 10 years more mature, they had woken up to its unavoidability. There was now more activity between parents and children (and between siblings) to acknowledge the Holocaust past and to give each other the right to experience and to have known what belonged to each generation: the parents' life in the camps or in hiding and in postwar rehabilitation; the children's life as offspring often bewildered by the silent trauma that hung in the family air. Like Helen Fremont's family, the children, much more than the parents, initiated discussion and inquiry into parents' Holocaust and postwar past. For several children, such knowledge illuminated their parents' punitive child-rearing practices that before had been confusing, frightening, and humiliating. These children became more aware of what clinicians describe as still unmastered aggression aroused in the camps and in hiding. The family discussions helped the children realize how much such perverse parenting also signified the dissociation and the transmission of Nazi traumatization. In most of the families, media programming was cited as an important catalyst for such new interaction. Several reported planning family get-togethers around a media Holocaust event or Holocaust commemoration. One child in a family that had been absolutely mute about the Holocaust reported how family members went to their separate rooms to watch a TV Holocaust documentary, all reconvening during commercial breaks for a brief, cautious talk about what they saw and heard.

The media's "permission" to allow explicit interest in the Holocaust helped breach the amnesic surface of parent/child interaction. Perverse transmission, therefore, may often be undetected until stirred from its apparent invisibility by potent social catalysts, like the media. (We next discuss the social support emanating from survivor organizations.) In the relative safety of the social approbation conferred by the media (and by our interview process as well), the children, now 10 years older, frequently let themselves disclose to the interviewer what lay beneath the surface of indifference: for example, preoccupying fantasies and worried suppositions about the rectitude of parents' behavior during the Holocaust. In the derogative portrayal of their parents, one sensed that the children's images of the Holocaust carried parents' survivor guilt and self-doubts about their upstandingness and faithfulness in fighting for survival. Such withheld moral misgivings, left to fester in the tight confines of a nuclear family that often felt socially tangential, added the anguish of stigma to the fear of retraumatization. We offer the informed opinion that the personal and family disclosures encouraged by the new societal openness to the Holocaust helped alleviate the insular self-blame that feeds on unmitigated silence, for this openness allows hope that the impossible circumstances of enslavement and hiding will finally be acknowledged by the world.

2. The dark side of social influence on transmission of the Holocaust remains in the public's readiness to be swerved to disbelieve, especially by the media. The public's credibility toward Holocaust reality is problematic where there are few survivors to validate and contextualize memory, as in the case with aging survivors whose peers are dying off or with those survivors, especially children, who alone remained alive from among whole families and communities. A recent case in point is the controversy surrounding the authenticity of a child-survivor memoir, *Fragments: Memories of a Wartime Childhood* by Binjamin Wilkomirski (1996). The memoir received multiple honors until it was exposed as a hoax. Rather than living in the hell of the notorious Majdanek death camp when he was 3 or 4 years old, as his memoir claims, Wilkomirski has been widely accused of living out the war in peacetime Switzerland as a Swiss-born, non-Jewish child. Since the expose, the media—from the *New York Times* to *60 Minutes*—have built a case against Wilkomirski that is devastating and appears to be irrefutable, with barely any person or scrap of evidence proffered to defend him. Yet, there is enough such evidence to question the media's rush to judgment (Peskin, 1999). This adversarial judgment against Wilkomirski will make it even more difficult for child survivors to trust in their own memories and to dare cross the border between knowing and making known. Without the experience of making known, the fear of not being believed festers, and memory itself loses coherence—preconditions for pathological transmission (Auerhahn & Peskin, 1999). The disproportionate death of children in the Holocaust conspires with society's greater disbelief in child memory to indicate that childhood may never fully cross over into Holocaust history. Such transmission of disbelief, initiated and carried by tabloid journalism and left barely countered or debated by other community agencies, suggests that Holocaust denial has found fertile soil in doubting child victims—the most decimated of all—with relative impunity.

3. Because of the singular problems of self-recognition and self-identity, child survivors have doubtless been the most marginalized of survivor groups. Most in need of community support and

respect, they have been least visible. Building their own community, apart from other survivor organizations, has been a crucial
step in rescuing their memory and their identity, thus the Hidden
Child Conference in 1991. Child survivors have often lived in the
limbo of others' definitions of their experiences. By virtue of their
uncertain memories from an early age, their vulnerability to per-
suasion that their memories were wrong, and the absence of witnesses to confirm their memories, child survivors have had little
societal support for believing in the truth of their own recollections.
Indeed, the fear of not being believed—common even to adult survivors, as Primo Levi learned—is widespread enough among child
survivors that they often closet and dismiss the memory of the suffering itself. Nowhere else has Hitler's plan to leave no witnesses of
the Holocaust come closer to being realized than in separating the
young from their own experience. We know of many child survivors, especially those who were hidden, who have not considered
themselves survivors. The doubt about one's right to the identity of
a child survivor is exacerbated when one has lived out the war in
safe hiding and thus survived when the rest of the family had been
annihilated. The participants of the 1991 conference helped each
other revive and animate the lost feelings of these tragic war years
in which forgotten parts of the self still survived. "Before the conference," said Paul Valent, a hidden child, "it had never struck me
that I, who was the little abandoned boy, should be felt sorry for"
(Valent, 1994, p. 128).

4. The First International Conference of Children of Holocaust
Survivors in 1979 (Peskin, 1981) was groundbreaking in building a
social network of self-help groups that now comprise a cohesive
community to support the identity formation of those in the second
and later generations who seek their own Holocaust consciousness
against the inroads of perverse transmission. Witness the following,
overheard at the conference's registration desk: Two college fresh-
men query each other on how their mothers felt about their
attending the conference. Exclaims the first young woman, "I'd
never tell her. She'd kill me if she knows I'm here." Then she asks
her friend, "Did you tell your mother anything?" The friend
answers: "When I told her last week I was going, she said, 'What
do you want to go to such a silly thing for?' But today when I left,
she told me it was okay." For these young women and doubtless

many of the 600 in attendance, a positive identity meant to risk or accept struggle within themselves and with parents over a course of action no longer moored to conditioned family loyalties.

The program of the two-day conference reviewed expertly the psychological injuries suffered in the silence and nondisclosure of survivor families. But unplanned were the spontaneous, uneasy, and vigorous interactions between the first and second generations (at the open microphones and in small groups) that asserted the need of children-of-survivors to be listened to and taken seriously. Finding their own voice shined through the formal program, making the conference itself an arena of life-affirming transmission between children and parents. An unplanned metaphor of surrendering parental control came in the person of Henry Krystal—an invited psychiatric expert on Holocaust transmission and himself a survivor and parent—who discarded a prepared speech because of little time left to him by the prior, well-regarded speaker of the younger generation. He began straightaway with a whole-hearted embrace of the children for their ardor ("You're wonderful")—an embrace, he allowed, that they might dismiss as "just words," sharing with their parents the belief that they do not deserve to be loved. Identifying himself as survivor and parent, Krystal held a rapt audience in a warm sense of family that, beneath the tension between generations, bore witness to the lovability of survivor families (Peskin, 1981).

Peskin's initial report of the 1979 conference was refused by a Jewish mental health association newsletter out of concern that the report was subjective and inflammatory, likely to cause dissension among the membership. The association's own subsequent debate about the prudence of refusing publication led to an important healing gesture in the newsletter's later acknowledgment of its editorial refusal and the association's need to tolerate controversy. We add here that it is no small accomplishment for an organization to endorse the airing of Holocaust testimony that might at first sight seem to weaken its firm resolve to memorialize the Holocaust.

Conclusion

Since the act of genocide was born—by fear, indifference, or active collaboration—in the larger community, the healing of Holocaust trauma must also begin in the larger community. Clinical preoccupation with traumatic symptomatology impedes awareness of the crucial role of society and culture in facilitating or impeding passage from the Holocaust world to the world today. Witnessing begins in the community. It follows that the quality of Holocaust transmission is a measure of the community's capacity to acknowledge the reality of the Holocaust and to create conditions for listening. The listener is the witness before the survivor-narrator can be her or his own witness. A community's resistance to Holocaust awareness may be counted both as an identification with and as a post-traumatic symptom of the Nazis' injunction against knowing and bearing witness—and may be felt as such by the survivor. In this process, of course, the adult offspring inevitably discount the significance of their own experiences and relationships to the Holocaust. The therapist who lets such fears of disbelief go by represents the community's parallel wishes to disbelieve. Whether the survivor repeats the unknowability of trauma in the perversity of hidden transmissions or repeals it in the full light of witness and acknowledgment depends enormously on the extent that we are ready to know how much the Holocaust still courses through our lives. The doleful remarks of a Jewish psychiatrist in Prague, himself a child of survivors whom we met in a Prague synagogue in 1998, still echo: Even today in the Czech Republic, he said, almost nothing of the Holocaust is spoken in psychotherapy or psychoanalysis. The differential availability of Holocaust material for therapeutic work in different communities and countries doubtless indicates the power of societies to effect—to prolong or mitigate—the perverse transmission of Holocaust trauma. The issue of Holocaust transmission, having produced a well-known clinical psychology, needs now to build an experience-near social-clinical psychology in which the distinction of perverse and healthful transmission might usefully apply.

References

Arendt, H. (1973). *The origins of totalitarianism.* New York: Harcourt Brace.

Auerhahn, N., & Laub, D. (1984). Annihilation and restoration: Post-traumatic memory as pathway and obstacle to recovery. *International Review of Psychoanalysis, 11,* 327–344.

Auerhahn, N., & Laub, D. (1987). Play and playfulness in Holocaust survivors. *Psychoanalytic Study of the Child, 42*, 45–58.

Auerhahn, N., & Laub, D. (1990). Holocaust testimony. *Holocaust and Genocide Studies, 5*, 447–462.

Auerhahn, N., Laub, D., & Peskin, H. (1993). Psychotherapy with Holocaust survivors. *Psychotherapy, 30*, 434–442.

Auerhahn, N., & Peskin, H. (1999, April). *Action knowledge and acknowledgment in work with Holocaust survivors.* Paper presented at the meeting of the Division of Psychoanalysis of the American Psychological Association, New York City.

Bergmann, S., & Jacovy, M. (Eds.). (1982). *Generations of the Holocaust.* New York: Basic Books.

Chasseguet-Smirgel, J. (1999, April). *In panel: Perspectives on therapeutic action.* Paper presented at the meeting of the Division of Psychoanalysis of the American Psychological Association, New York City.

Fonagy, P. (1999, February). *Attachment, the Holocaust and the outcome of child psychoanalysis: An attachment-based model of transgenerational transmission of trauma.* San Francisco: San Francisco Psychoanalytic Institute.

Fremont, H. (1999). *After long silence.* New York: Delacorte Press.

Karr, S. (1973). *Second generation effects of the Nazi Holocaust.* Unpublished doctoral dissertation, California School of Professional Psychology, Berkeley.

Kestenberg, J. (1982). A metapsychological assessment based on an analysis of a survivor's child. In M. Bergmann & M. Jacovy (Eds.), *Generations of the Holocaust* (pp. 137–158). New York: Basic Books.

Kogan, I. (1989). The search for the self. *International Journal of Psychoanalysis, 70*, 661–671.

Kundera, M. (1997). *Identity.* New York: HarperCollins.

Laub, D., & Auerhahn, N. (1993). Knowing and not knowing massive psychic trauma: Forms of traumatic memory. *International Journal of Psychoanalysis, 74*, 287–302.

Levi, P. (1978). *Survival in Auschwitz.* New York: Collier.

Peskin, H. (1981). Observations on the First International Conference of Children of Holocaust Survivors. *Family Process, 20*, 391–394.

Peskin, H. (1999, April 19). Holocaust denial: A sequel. *The Nation*, pp. 34–38.

Peskin, H., Auerhahn, N., & Laub, D. (1997). The Second Holocaust: Therapeutic rescue when life threatens. *Journal of Personal and Interpersonal Loss, 2*, 1–25.

Peskin, H., & Karr, S. (1982, June). *Consistency and change of parent-child relationships in survivor families: A ten-year followup of children of survivors.* Paper presented at the International Conference on the Holocaust and Genocide, Tel Aviv, Israel.

Valent, P. (1994). A child survivor's appraisal of his own interview. In J. Kestenberg & E. Fogelman (Eds.), *Children during the Nazi reign* (pp. 121–135). New York: Praeger.

Valent, P. (1998). Resilience in child survivors of the Holocaust: Toward the concept of resilience. *Psychoanalytic Review, 85*, 517–536.

Wilkomirski, B. (1996). *Fragments: Memories of a wartime childhood.* New York: Schocken.

CONCLUSIONS AND FUTURE DIRECTIONS

BRIAN G. PAUWELS

In the preface to this volume, we briefly considered some of the factors that have in recent years helped traumatic stress become a relatively unitary field of its own. We also noted that some circumstances, the nature of which are not completely clear to us, have to some extent impeded this progress. In this final section, we have two goals. First, we reflect upon the breadth and variety of trauma research in both its content and methods and discuss how this breadth relates to the progression of traumatic stress research as a distinct scholarly endeavor. Second, we review what we believe are some of the important future directions in traumatic stress research as the field continues to build upon its present foundations.

The contributors to this volume have demonstrated the diversity of post-traumatic stress research in terms of the range of phenomena it covers, as well as in the different methodologies used to conduct such work. Clearly, the contexts in which traumatic stress develops are numerous; it manifests itself in injuries due to accidents, sexual victimization, war, personal losses, repressive political or economic environments, as well as in other circumstances. Studying trauma in these vastly different arenas necessitates the use of a heterogeneous collection of methods and perspectives. Indeed, in the limited number of contributions presented here, we have seen a variety of methodological tools for collecting, interpreting, and explaining the information generated by instances of traumatic stress. Structured and semistructured interviews, questionnaires, archival records, written narratives, clinical assessment instruments, personal testimonies, and other techniques have all been used to gather the data that are the basis of our understanding of traumatic stress.

In our view, the actual complexity of trauma phenomena and the different environments in which trauma occurs has in some ways required the use of multiple methodologies. Clearly, a structured interview or questionnaire may provide valuable information in one setting while being less appropriate in another. Just as the source of trauma, its victims, and its long-term effects can vary widely within the field of trauma research, the "tools of the trade" have remained flexible. However, one potential implication of having a myriad of methodologies for trauma work is the possibility that such heterogeneity diminishes the notion that traumatic stress studies constitute a single field of scholarship. This issue has certainly been addressed before (e.g., Figley, 1993), and the great scope of trauma presented in the previous chapters causes us to consider it again.

From our perspective, it seems less appropriate to judge the cohesiveness of traumatic stress work on the specialization of its methodology than on the nature of the phenomena of interest. The field of traumatic stress studies, as the definition presented in our preface suggests, is a broad one indeed. Clinicians, social psychologists, sociologists, and scholars from other disciplines will of course use their own particular methods and strategies to better understand traumatic stress and its consequences. Depending on their own background and perspectives, they will approach traumatic stress with different levels of analysis in mind and therefore incorporate the methods they believe are most appropriate for such analysis. It is of course incumbent upon the researcher, theorist, or clinician to recognize the potential shortcomings of his or her present approach and consider ways for which they can be compensated. To do so requires communicating openly with other members of the field and drawing upon the resources offered in the journals, professional organizations, or published volumes that will update one's knowledge. Our point here is that a plethora of methodologies, although in some ways detrimental to the development of a single, cohesive field, is also reflective of the breadth of trauma itself. Multiple contexts and environments for trauma also require multiple levels of explanation and, consequently, multiple methodologies. As the field progresses, it is certainly our hope that a more standardized, widely acceptable set of methods eventually emerges. However, the pursuit of this goal should be done with full acknowledgment that the domain of interest, traumatic stress, is itself inherently complicated and that it will frequently be necessary to draw upon manifold techniques to measure and explain it.

In addition to illuminating the large domain of the traumatic stress field and its various methodologies, the chapters here pointed out several lines of research that we believe are particularly important for future consideration. Although theorists, researchers, and applied scholars have already pursued these areas in at least a preliminary manner, there are a few topics and questions that we would like to highlight to conclude this volume.

First, one aspect of reactions to a traumatic event that we find particularly intriguing is the scope of such reactions across people who are more or less directly affected by the initial event. For example, one type of trauma that has emerged all too often in the United States is the multiple killing of schoolchildren by their own classmates. Because of the recency of such events, it is difficult at this time to determine the exact nature of the traumatic stress that the individuals affected by these incidents will experience or the steps they will take to overcome that stress. However, a theme that has become apparent is that any analysis of such reactions can go beyond just those individuals who were directly involved in the incident and their families. Rather, responses to the trauma are also exhibited by the school administration, the local community, and society in general. Judgments of blame, causal attributions, suggestions for prevention, threatened legal action, and proposed changes in legislation constitute just some of the reactions that emerged from numerous individuals, some of whom were very close to the crime while others were less directly affected. An interesting question is, What determines when the response to a traumatic event is restricted mainly to those who are personally affected, and when do these events provoke a meaningful response from a wider range of observers? In addition, when widespread reactions do occur, which of them will be maintained over an extended period of time, and which will simply dissipate as news of the event fades from daily headlines? These are important questions to consider, since such events can potentially shape public policy regarding issues such as liability, prevention, and organizational responses to traumatic events.

A second direction for research that we would like to highlight is the need for more cross-cultural work on traumatic stress. As the contributions by Carlson et al. and Malkinson and Bar-Tur demonstrate, both the sources of and reactions to traumatic events can be linked to the specific cultural, economic, and political environment that exists at a particular time. The influence of these factors takes place on several different levels. At a societal level, the types of formal organizations available for helping individuals respond to trauma may depend in great part on whether the governing institutions of a country allocate resources for such organizations or take steps to formally recognize the seriousness of certain traumatic events. At a family level, the expectations and norms followed by members of the social network surrounding a trauma victim may facilitate the victim's recovery in one culture but potentially impede that recovery in another. At an individual level, a person's own beliefs about what is either an appropriate or inappropriate response to trauma may greatly affect how that individual expresses his or her grief and interacts with others affected by the same traumatic experience. Clearly, a comprehensive theory of traumatic stress must take into account the enormous influence of the social, political, and cultural factors that provide the background in which responses to trauma take place.

In closing, this collection represents some of the latest work on traumatic events and the reactions that follow them. The various contexts in which trauma may occur each present their own particular challenges to their victims. In addition, these contexts present both conceptual and practical obstacles to the scholars who attempt to document victims' reactions and the coping techniques they use to overcome these events. To fully explain the stress as well as the resilience that characterizes the victims of trauma, students of this field must often rely upon theoretical perspectives and methodologies as diverse as the domain of interest that they study. Strategies from disciplines such as clinical psychology, social psychology, sociology, and others have been incorporated in the attempt to expand and improve the work of traumatic stress theorists, researchers, and practitioners. As the field of post-traumatic stress continues to develop and change, we hope that the contributions offered here provide additional inspiration, tools, and directions for those seeking to describe, understand, and assist individuals dealing with the consequences of trauma.

References

Figley, C. R. (1993). Foreword. In J. P. Wilson, & B. Raphael (Eds.), *International handbook of traumatic stress syndromes*. New York: Plenum.

INDEX